Analyzing Leaders,
Presidents and Terrorists

Analyzing Leaders, Presidents and Terrorists

Diane Holloway, Ph.D. with Bob Cheney

Writers Club Press

San Jose New York Lincoln Shanghai

Analyzing Leaders, Presidents and Terrorists

Writers Club Press
an imprint of iUniverse, Inc.

For information address:
iUniverse, Inc.
5220 S. 16th St., Suite 200
Lincoln, NE 68512
www.iuniverse.com

ISBN: 0-595-23264-7

Printed in the United States of America

Contents

Preface

We should talk a bit before we proceed. This will not take long but you should know that the author's perspective comes from years of analyzing people in therapy. People are diagnosed and treated for problems that usually arise from deviations in stages through which most of us pass. Some people are sent to therapy because of problems with moral turpitude. Many come to therapy because of problems in their love life. Still others have problems in their careers, often including their leadership style. Finally, many people are looking for better ways to cope with stress.

The leaders in this study will be analyzed according to standards often used to evaluate patients. These standards, however, were developed in Europe and America, so they may not apply to people who grew up in other cultures. We cannot judge people by absolute standards because morals, upbringing, love life, leadership and stress management differ among individual families as well as among cultures.

Despite these limitations, the impulse to judge leaders is found in all of us. After all, leaders on the world stage affect the lives of millions of people. By what standards do we ordinarily judge these people? They differ for each of us.

One of the greatest problems in writing this book was making it understandable to the average person who has no psychological training. The terminology and reference standards to be used by the author are set out in the Introduction. They serve as a guide for the discussion of each leader. While it is not necessary to understand them well, a cursory glance will prepare the reader for what follows. Now let us begin.

Introduction

"From the moment of his birth the customs into which an individual is born shape his experience and behavior. By the time he can talk, he is the little creature of his culture." Ruth Benedict

Is It Hard to Analyze Leaders?

It must be very satisfying to judge others because we tend to do it all the time. We go to a restaurant and judge the service given by waiters. We judge the food prepared by the chef. We judge the performance of athletes, musicians and actors and applaud them or boo them. We judge television programs by watching them or turning the dial to another station. We judge our children and our mates constantly, whether they know it or not. We certainly judge our bosses and leaders. Often we can only show them our judgment by quitting a job or voting for another candidate. But that doesn't keep us from talking about them in judgmental ways.

Why do we sit in judgment so frequently? Does it make us feel superior to render judgment about others? Does noting their errors make us feel more perfect? Does a negative judgment yield a little revenge for what we feel someone might have done to us?

Judging is certainly not difficult to do because we don't feel that we need any special training for it. It requires no particular effort and is so simple that we can sit around the house or the bar or the bridge table doing it. It extends across all peoples in the world and we can be sure that people are judging us just as we judge them. Of course, just because we all do it doesn't make it right or accurate.

1

Some people get paid for judging. Wine and beer producers pay high wages for good tasters. Car manufacturers spend much to capture the criticisms of consumers to create products that they will buy. The government pays analysts to judge which way the market will move, how other governments will respond to our actions, and which employees can be placed in which positions.

People who get paid for judging usually make their judgments by using a set of criteria in common use by many. Physicians try to judge a patient's complaints and physical condition to offer a diagnosis and treatment plan. Psychologists try to judge patients objectively in order to offer them the best help in improving themselves in areas that they want to improve. They, like other professionals, go through a great deal of training to learn to refine their judgments so that they are more accurate and helpful.

Judgment can be subjective and use no particular criteria except our own limited experience about the subject being judged. That is probably the case as we sit around and discuss politics and politicians. Since the beginning of time, we have been tempted to criticize those who occupy our highest positions of influence. It doesn't end with just our own leaders, either. Although we may know little about other nations and their leaders, we readily offer opinions about them. Ask anyone what he thinks about Truman, Nixon, Castro, Khrushchev, Hitler, Osama bin Laden or Saddam Hussein and you will probably get an earful.

Many say it is impossible to be fair when analyzing people of other cultures. They say that cultures vary so much that you cannot compare people with each other any more than you can compare societies with each other. Third world countries differ from first world countries in fundamental ways that change childhood, love, morals, leadership, and stresses. All that being true, we will introduce some possible standards or frameworks that may be loosely used to analyze leaders.

Some years ago, psychologist Abraham Maslow presented a theoretical hierarchy of needs. He postulated that people came into the world needing to survive and that physiological needs were of the gravest concern. Once satisfied with adequate food, water and activity, needs to be safe came next. As a person felt secure and protected, Maslow postulated that he or she could begin to build trust in others. If a caretaker was trustworthy in providing basic needs, individuals next wanted to be accepted and cared about by others. Beyond acceptance by others, people might also strive to build confidence and self-esteem. This could come from achieving status, prestige and respect. Maslow thought the highest need was self-actualization. He believed that few people could reach that pinnacle of self-actualization or self-realization. He thought those who did would enjoy having produced and integrated their unique self.

This table summarizes Maslow's hierarchy of needs with the highest level need at the top and the earliest need at the bottom.

Table 1: Maslow's Hierarchy of Human Needs

Self-actualization

Self-esteem

Social

Safety

Physiological

Clare Graves, another psychologist, took Abraham Maslow's hierarchy and re-examined it. He believed that individuals, like countries, are constantly changing according to the conditions in which they live. Graves applied the hierarchy to groups of people in various cultures.

More recent psychologists Don Beck and Christopher Cowan have published a version of Graves' theory applying them to specific nation-states in their book, *Spiral Dynamics*. Their work demonstrated the complexity of comparing societies and leaders with each other.

They concluded that more people in third world countries are focused on staying alive, and they may operate more instinctively. They may eat when hungry, steal food and water from others to survive, procreate without restriction, and seek warmth and protection from the elements. They often operate as small clans or tribes using violence to assure their survival and eliminating threats to their existence. They have rules within in which superstition, ritual, kinship and folklore are valued for physical and social survival. Thus leaders in places such as Somalia will have different priorities than leaders of France.

Leaders of a second or third world country who seek conquest, glorification, and expansion may impose their will on others. They may use violence to eliminate resistance and achieve their goals. Their outlook could be called egocentric because they believe they have a right to do whatever they want whenever they want, without respect for the opposition. Their goals may often be masked in the name of gods or powers. They may be punitive or believe that "might makes right." They may operate as feudal empires such as the Taliban in Afghanistan.

A second world or first world country may live for the future instead of living just for today. Their leaders often value traditions, morals, rules, discipline, and meaning. Their society (which could include Singapore or Israel) might be described as a conformist or authoritarian democracy. However, democracies come in many forms including China and Russia more recently.

Some nations and some Islamic groups oppose capitalist countries. They may claim that capitalistic countries occupy, control or try to influence local beliefs and lifestyles. These non-capitalist countries often view themselves as more pure than capitalists. Some of them believe that only the purist of people will meet their reward in the afterlife. They may believe that outsiders come in and contaminate their way of life, and thus feel justified in attacking these impure intruders.

First world and capitalist countries such as the United States and the United Kingdom use strategies to enhance long-term advantages on the world stage. These may be economic strategies or image and status ploys. Capitalist countries, unlike fundamentalists, believe in a world based on consumers and providers trading with each other, and acting on their own behalf in order to prosper. These countries and leaders believe in scientific achievement, growth, materialism, coalitions, and subtle coercion rather than overt force. Some have called these systems multi-party democracies.

A few first world countries use sensitivity, human bonding and consensus to achieve long-term goals for the good of the largest number of people. Some Scandinavian countries and the Netherlands exemplify this holistic orientation. The community is valued above the individual. Their leaders foster sharing, caring and a system benefiting all equally. They may additionally employ ecological knowledge and social democracy to improve the health and life of the whole planet. These societies are opposed to those who selfishly exploit others or who ruin the natural "pristine" environment.

However, within each nation or people, there are pockets of other orientations. For example, in the United States, South Central Los Angeles may operate much like the West Bank of Israel with conflicts over human rights. The deliberations of the city council of Phoenix may resemble the debates of the Netherlands governing bodies over air quality.

Now that we see how impossible it is to use the same set of standards to judge people of different cultures, we should have stopped here. But we continue. We are but human and we judge people by our own set of standards, whether that is fair or not.

This study is simply an experiment to apply the same standards used in the field of Western psychology to leaders of interest. Not only is it unfair to use such standards, but also many of these standards are just theoretical. Even though these theories have been around for many years, none have been proven in the scientific sense. They provide only a slightly more organized framework in which to examine people whom we already examine without any particular framework.

For example, we will examine the stages of maturation to measure leaders according to their upbringing and emotional development. We will discuss the stages of love in order to estimate a leader's ability to give and receive in their love life. We will look at healthy and unhealthy ways to reduce stress, to see whether leaders handle stress any better than we do. We will describe the stages of moral development to analyze the integrity of leaders. We will look at whether leaders cared more about getting the job done or more about their employees to guess about their leadership style. But let us bear in mind that these are only theories and our findings will be only guesses.

Erickson's Stages of Maturation

The goals of child rearing vary according to the conditions in which a family lives. In about 1915, Austrian founder of psychoanalysis Sigmund Freud theorized stages of development through which most children pass. His daughter, Anna, who became a child psychoanalyst, extended his theories even further.

One of her students, Erik Erikson, linked developmental stages and social processes and extended these. He believed that people passed through a variety of stages throughout life from infancy to old age. He conceived of eight stages, which will be briefly described here. While this has considerable applicability to the Western world, it has limitations when applied to other cultures.

According to his theory, a child learns by age one and a half years whether he can trust a caretaker. If a mother, father, or others feed him, cuddle him and protect him from pain, he will begin to trust them and feel comfortable with them. If his caretaker fails to meet these basic needs, he will be left with a distrust of others. This may lead to paranoid disorders, with suspicions that others not only don't care about him but want to do him harm. Thus a caretaker's inadequacy could cause a child to fear that unless he takes extra precautions to protect himself, others may be cruel or negligent toward him.

The child from one and a half to three years learns how to control his body and his emotions. Typical skills learned include how to stand up and walk, how to eat and drink, and how to control the urge to go to the bathroom. If a caretaker is excessively strict, the child may fear that he must never lose control of himself in any way. For him, a mess is a bad thing and brings about much shame. Children who were unduly punished for lack of self-control may be hard on themselves and others, attempting to over-control everything and everyone.

As a child learns to control his body, walk and talk, he realizes that he is a separate person from his caretaker. However, prolonged separations from the caretaker at this age can cause an excessive fear of loneliness.

From three to five years, there is much curiosity about oneself and others. If this curiosity is constantly punished, a child may become shy, guilty or squelch their wish to learn. If curiosity is nourished, a child will learn about new things and master new skills. Children copy the behavior of those nearest them, just as animals do. A little girl may yearn to cook, sew, sweep, dress, and apply make-up by watching her mother. A boy may copy his father mowing the lawn, working on the car, shaving, and playing ball. By noticing their own body parts, boys realize that they are like father and brothers; and girls that they are like mother and sisters.

Children want to avoid pain and punishment, so they begin to obey their parents. As they realize what pleases or displeases parents and caretakers, they are beginning to identify with the morals of their caretaker. This is the first step toward developing morals. After some years, the child may develop a conscience that makes him feel uncomfortable when he does something that would displease his parents.

This identification with the parents may be disturbed if they have a very scary parent. A child may still copy a scary parent even though he may fear and dislike that parent. This may be to avoid punishment or rejection by the intimidating parent. He may also copy such a parent because he sees that parent win in family fights. The child does not want to be a victim, a fearful loser, who may even be physically hurt. So he may start doing the same distasteful thing that his parent does.

During the years from about six to eleven, children usually take pride in developing abilities. Skills create self-confidence. As a child sees what he can do, he tries to do more and wants to see what he can handle alone. Children who can't learn quickly begin to fear failure and competition, and may develop school problems. In sports, a boy's physical condition may impair his ability to learn skills and compete confidently. Girls who are not rewarded for skill mastery but are constantly rewarded for looking pretty will develop and act accordingly.

The teen years allow children to move back and forth from dependence on others to independence. As they part with their parents' protection, they become surer of themselves as adults. Impulsive self-destructive acts require more parental restraints. When parents fail to restrain children who act up, police and other authorities may have to take over the control or care of the child.

Children who have not learned to adequately control their emotions may be unsure of themselves. They may wonder if anyone can control them and act out to test whether others can stop them. These years involve sexual experimentation as hormones rage. Sexual experimentation invites possible disease, poor selection of early mates, pregnancy and unintended children. Such calamities are less likely to happen when good self-discipline has already been established.

Young adults need to feel that they can give and receive love. If they are reluctant to give love or feel guilty receiving love, they may find themselves alone. A lack of lovers can be especially unbearable when friends are falling in love around them. The challenge of controlling sexual urges to protect one's future can be formidable.

Older adults usually feel fulfilled by handling work, study, relationships and childbearing fairly adequately. Those who lag behind in these areas may feel stagnant. However, those who accept these responsibilities enjoy creating and generating rich, full lives for themselves and their children.

Adults in later years discover that choices constantly test one's honesty, loyalty, and frustration tolerance. Those who cope adequately with life's difficulties and temptations arrive at ego integrity, proud that they have avoided major pitfalls. They have self-respect and are respected by others. Those who have yielded to temptations or compromised morals may feel despair and failure. Those who overvalued the opinions of others may find it difficult to part with adulation when they retire from careers in later life.

Erikson's theory of maturational stages is summed up in this chart with the highest level of maturation at the top and the earliest stage of life at the bottom.

Table 2: Erikson's Stages of Maturation

Achievement	Deviation
Ego integrity	Despair
Generativity	Stagnation
Intimacy	Isolation
Ego identity	Role confusion
Industry	Inferiority
Initiative	Guilt
Autonomy	Shame, doubt
Trust	Distrust

Stages of Love

The earliest form of love that all humans seek is "unconditional love." Children need caretakers who will always be there when needed and who will forgive them for their many mistakes. Those who were not loved unconditionally may forever seek that form of love in relationships, only to be frustrated in their "urge to merge."

The next form of love is the subject of so many songs, poems, art and literature. It involves physical attraction and common bonds that draw each to the other. The beautiful girl or knight on a white horse makes the lover feel self-esteem. We believe that some special attribute attracted a lover, and we experience a sense of success that we are attractive. But romantic love is conditional. It is given only as long as we are seen as attractive. Attractions may last only a short time because young lovers often project their ideals onto their new lover. They ignore the flaws that appear as they get to know each other better. Young lovers are excited to see themselves in a whole new light as a giving, loving individual who can make others happy.

Romantic love often blossoms into passion. This carries a thrilling chemical high accompanied by many physical reactions. In fact, some enjoy the tension release and passion so much that they leave one partner to search for it with another. This selfish quest is to gain something for oneself despite whether the other partner has gained anything or not. Some youngsters hope that love will fix his or her life and remove problems. As their disappointment grows, they become hurt and forlorn.

Intimacy requires trust. We run a risk when we trust someone closely. We may fear intimacy because it requires us to be seen for what we are, warts and all. Everyone hates rejection and therefore fears exposing him or herself to hurt. Only when much confidence has developed can people take rejection in stride. Intimate relationships involve strong feelings: anger, loss of control, sexual ignorance, jealousy, reactions to the naked body. These are necessary if the transition from lust to love is to be made.

People who keep their emotions or their body hidden do not connect on the intimate level. They have not accepted their own imperfections and do not expect others to accept them either. Some want to possess their loved one like a trophy that one will not share with others. Soon they learn that loved ones must be shared and cannot be controlled. Eventually trust must be deep enough to expect that a lover will not stray when out of sight or with others. This level of trust or surrender moves passion beyond the search for pleasures and thrills.

Conflicts and power struggles are inevitable. Individuals must work out whether they can fulfill their goals while remaining in the relationship. Problems solved by talking rather than bullying lead to teamwork. Dreams of a different kind of mate, a different kind of life, and a different kind of love must be laid to rest. Compromises are required as love changes into an enduring relationship. Deep feelings such as devotion and compassion gradually replace shallow ones. This is achieved slowly. It requires giving up some individual freedom in return for mutual security.

The final stage of love is total commitment to one another. Each partner helps the other fulfill his or her potential. Besides inspiring each other, the relationship is a refuge from the world, a place to relax and to renew and reveal feelings. This stage includes a decision to remain true to one's mate no matter what happens. This table represents the stages of love with the highest level of love at the top and the earliest level of love at the bottom.

Table 3: Stages of Love

Achievement	Deviation
Commitment/calm	Disloyalty/anxiety
Compromise/surrender	Power struggles/conflict
Intimacy/trust	Fear of rejection/isolation
Lust/passion	Rigidity/tension
Romantic love/release	Identity confusion
Unconditional love/ acceptance	Undue urge to merge

Methods of Handling Stress

Stress comes in many forms. There can be a general hyperactivity and quickness to react to anxiety or any sign of danger. Such people are called hyperactive or Type A and may not have reliable methods of reducing stress. Some people hold in all anger, fearing rejection by others if they show anger. They may passively show their anger by continually being late or obstructing plans or even cutting their wrist to retaliate against someone.

Others may develop physical symptoms or imagined illnesses such as hypochondriasis, a condition that may bring sympathy from their imagined foe. Other people may become overly anxious when given more responsibility than they feel capable of handling. They may deliberately err to remove the mantle of responsibility from their shoulders. Some people feel anxious when others don't seem to accept them, which throws their self-esteem into doubt.

How do leaders handle problems, anxieties and stresses, which are inevitable in their chosen role? Stress upsets one's equilibrium. Anxiety rises in anticipation of danger. Sometimes, an unrealistic perception of events causes more fear than is appropriate to the situation. Unless a coping mechanism reduces anxiety and stress, it doesn't really calm the person. As stress and anxiety continue and frustration builds, some people retreat to coping methods used by children or psychotics, but which are inappropriate for normal adults. These methods don't remove the stress or help them regain their equilibrium. In fact, they often make things worse.

The methods used to handle stress become habitual. The patterns used most often are what we commonly call "character." Parents often reward children for mature coping habits that remove problems and improve functioning. They might reward good grades when a child substitutes scholarly achievement for lack of sports ability. They often punish children who use inadequate or childish coping mechanisms, which might include temper tantrums, making excuses, or risky sexual behavior or drug use.

Some people may use fantasies or dreams to create pleasing imaginary companions or situations. This may be seen in those who fear that intimacy will result in rejection and self-doubt. Some people project their own faults onto others, collect injustices, expect enemies, and become paranoid as they try to protect themselves from stress. Character or coping patterns are often visible for all to see.

Sigmund Freud first pointed out the common use of coping or defense mechanisms. George Vaillant categorized coping mechanisms according to how successful they were in removing stress, anxiety and problems. Those that resolve problems and return one's equilibrium were considered healthiest.

Table 4: Vaillant's Healthy and Unhealthy Coping Techniques

<u>Healthy/Reduces Stress</u>	<u>Unhealthy/Childish</u>
Altruism/serving others	Projection/distortion
Anticipation/planning for problems	Inhibition/regression
Asceticism/pride in avoiding temptation	Hypochondriasis/fantasy
Humor/making sport of problems	Intellectualization/rationalization
Sublimation/substituting safe acts	Risky acts/passive aggressivity
Suppression/postponing attention	Denial/ blocking

Stages of Moral Development

Many psychologists have studied the way we develop morals. They found that people learn to act morally according to what and how they are taught. An infant who wants a mother's love will be good because it brings a desired reward. Children begin to obey in order to avoid spankings, punishment and loss of love.

Teenagers desire the approval of their peer group and may risk parental disapproval to win the praise of friends. Respect for social order and a wish to avoid public embarrassment produces law-abiding behavior in adults. When individuals choose to act according to heart-felt individual ideas of justice they do the "right thing" whether or not others see them and whether or not others sit in judgment. People who handle money honestly even when there is no one to know differently fall in this category.

People may regress to lower levels of morality under stress. Nazi German officers may have hated to carry out executions and brutality. Soldiers being shot at by children and women may choose to retaliate and kill despite being personally offended by such behavior. Starving people may decide to survive through cannibalism despite their usual respect for human beings.

Religion does not necessarily determine morals because prisons are filled with Christians who broke commandments. Religious instruction, which threatens eternal damnation, is akin to the wish to avoid punishment by parental figures in the young child. Non-violence, however, may be a unifying principle, which minimizes pain and harm for everyone.

Self-protective mechanisms are at work in the young child. Children want to stay out of trouble. Children who lack trust in others may find themselves on guard at all times, expecting the worst. As time passes, to control their fears, they may begin to manipulate and exploit others. This may seem better than waiting for hurt, rejection or embarrassment. Such people begin to see the world as divided into those who rule and those who are ruled, those who control you and those you can control. This may result in amoral and lawbreaking activities.

Lawrence Kohlberg, a psychologist, has developed a theory about the stages of moral development. It is summarized here with the highest level of moral development at the top. The lowest or earliest stage of morals is at the bottom of the table.

Table 5: Kohlberg's Stages of Moral Development

Stage	Manifestations
Justice	Fairness and equity principles are used to determine actions
	People have equal worth with self
	Decisions made by the individual supercede conventions
	Discomfort is felt when integrity or principles are ignored

Social utility	Unbiased acts are favored because they benefit more people
	Individual reasoning replaces social conventions
Laws/ rules	Loyalty to the system replaces one's peer group
	Social conventions replace peer group acceptance
	Fear of being caught and humiliated determines actions
Peer approval	Actions are chosen to please one's friends
	Peer group acceptance is more important than morals
Hope for	Actions are chosen according to whether they bring rewards
reward	Actions bringing pleasure are chosen over painful ones
Fear of	Actions are chosen to avoid punishment and pain
punishment	Others (parents) decide whether acts are rewarded or punished

Leadership Styles

Leaders must balance concern for the task to be done with concern for the people carrying out the task. This is tricky and requires shifting gears rather than staying with a single management tactic. One method of measuring leadership style was a Managerial Grid developed by R. R. Blake and Jane S. Mouton of Scientific Methods, Inc. This grid shows whether a leader is more interested in production or people.

Leaders who are mainly concerned for people and lack concern for production use a good fellowship style to avoid conflict. These nice guys want to avoid criticism. If they give realistic appraisals of underlings, they may be called developers.

Leaders who mostly care about production consider workers a commodity, like machines. These tyrants keep decision-making to themselves and are quick to point out errors or remove employees from the job. Smart subordinates become frustrated with such leaders. New or less capable employees may see them as benevolent autocrats and their style may be acceptable.

Leaders with minimum concern for both task and people may be considered ineffective or deserters by their subordinates. They may also be called administrators if they give low-key instruction to their underlings. Leaders with maximum concern for both task and people are team managers. They use their people wisely to get the best job done. Some leaders are middle-of-the-road managers who use compromise, participation, and discussion. While not outstanding team leaders, they can be effective.

The managerial grid shown below demonstrates how a leader who is high in concern for people but low in concern for getting the job done is called a "nice guy". At the other end of the grid is the manager who has a low concern for people and a high concern for getting the job done, earning the label "tyrant". The leader who has a great deal of concern for people and for getting the job done is shown as "team manager."

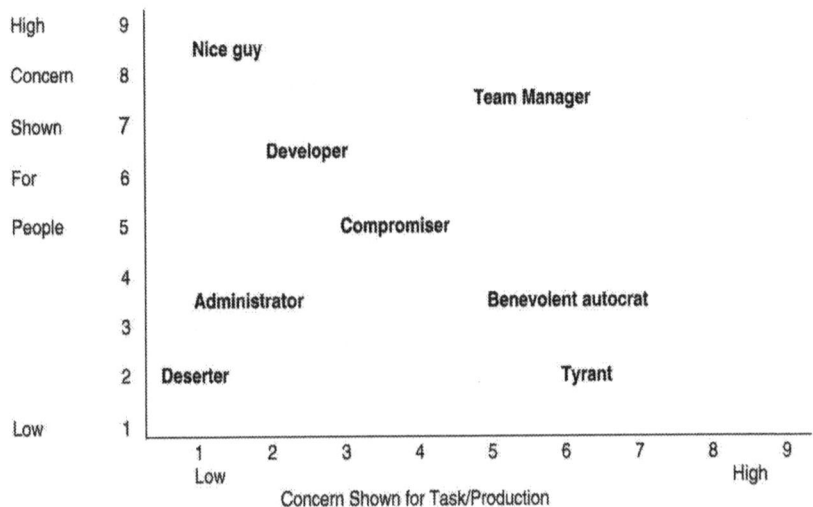

Table 6: Blake and Mouton's Managerial Grid

These theoretical standards have now been illustrated. We will now discuss the lives of each leader. Recent leaders have been chosen because they lived within our memory and we may be able to picture them and make our own analyses. These particular people were selected because they are all complex and fascinating. Each discussion will end with a summary in which the standards will be used. Let the analysis begin.

1

HARRY TRUMAN

o o o o o o o o o o o o o o o o o o o o o o o o o o o o o o o o o

"Childhood shows the man, as morning shows the day." John
Milton

1

Upbringing and Early Life

Harry Truman was born May 8, 1884 to John and Martha (Mattie)
Truman. His father was a hard-working, cheerful man with a rural
school education who aspired to be a stock trader. When he was 36,
John was asked to return to his birthplace to help his aging father's
farm. Since John hadn't made a go of livestock trading, he returned
without complaints. Several years later, John would ask Harry to
return to the farm to help when he was ailing, and Harry would do so
without complaining, just as his father had.

Harry's mother was born to a pioneering family. Mattie told her
children about the Red Legs who came to her farm when she was nine
years old. It was 1861 and they wore Union uniforms. They apparently
came because Mattie's family had a few slaves. They demanded food,
killed the hogs and hens, burned the barn and took off silver and a
featherbed. They threatened Mattie's 15-year-old brother with a noose
but when he refused to divulge information about family valuables,
they spared him.

When Mattie was little, guerrilla raiders representing the South massacred townspeople in nearby Lawrence, Kansas. In retaliation, 20,000 residents with Southern sympathies (such as Mattie's family) were moved away from their homes. They were sent to live in an outpost or detention camp. Mattie's family finally returned home at the end of the Civil War but they were very bitter toward the North. This sentiment lingered in Harry's mother. In fact, when visiting the White House, Mattie said that if her son made her sleep in Lincoln's bedroom, she would sleep on the floor.

These attitudes and bitterness affected young Harry. They had much to do with his eventual belief that the Marshall Plan was needed after WWII. He said, "Europe had suffered in the same way we had suffered after the War Between the States, and that made me think that Europe had to be rehabilitated by the people who had destroyed it."

Harry was the oldest of three children with a brother, Vivian, two years younger and Mary Jane, a sister five years younger.

Mattie had two years of college in the liberal arts, unusual for young women of the 1870s. She taught her children to read by using the Bible. She also played the piano and taught songs to her children. She soon noticed that Harry could not see well. She hitched up the wagon and took him to Kansas City where glasses were prescribed. Thereafter, Harry became a very avid reader. When he began school, his mother decided that the family should move 15 miles away to Independence, Missouri, so he could attend the better schools.

Mattie made sure that books of Shakespeare, Tennyson and Plutarch's *Lives* were available in the house for her children. When Harry was ten, she gave him a four-volume set of *Great Men and Famous Women*, which he devoured. Mattie was religious. After her son became President, she said, "I believe in true religion but I do not believe in making out that one is better than he is. I think Harry is that way."

Throughout his life, various family members and hired help lived in the household so that it numbered some 14 or 15 members at times. In this atmosphere, Harry learned how to get along with others. This contributed to his great gift of conviviality.

Harry loved his siblings. As Mary Jane grew, he would braid her hair, sing to her and rock her to sleep. He continued to help Mary Jane throughout his life. She once said that she probably never married because she couldn't find any man as good as Harry.

Harry helped tend cattle, thresh wheat, and shuck corn. When he performed these duties well, it pleased his parents. He wrote, "I used to watch my father and mother closely to learn what I could do to please them, just as I did with my school teachers and playmates." Harry had clearly identified with his parents and adopted their teachings and morals to avoid punishment and win their praise.

Harry's poor eyesight and glasses made him shy away from fights where they might break. He wrote, "To tell the truth, I was kind of a sissy." He became an avid reader, a pastime that served him well since he was the last American president without a college background. Using a very healthy method to cope with the lack of sports abilities, he substituted learning more than other boys for playing better ball than other boys.

At age 11, his parents moved into a larger house, and Harry began to take piano lessons. This gave him still another way to make up for the lack of athletic skill and stood him in good stead for the future. In 1900, his piano teacher took him to Kansas City to visit the famous pianist Ignace Paderewski. In a private backstage lesson, the great man showed Harry how to play his *Minuet in G.* Harry would later play this at the Potsdam Conference for Stalin and Churchill. He played it even later in the White House for President John Kennedy.

Harry worked in a drugstore from age 16, cleaning up in the morning before going to school. He traveled with his father to Kansas City to the Democratic National Convention. It was there William Jennings Bryan was re-nominated to run again against William McKinley. Harry and his father shared an interest in politics. This identification with his father turned out to be fortunate for all Americans when he became president.

Unfortunately, his father was financially wiped out in 1901. He had to move the family from Independence, Missouri to a smaller house in Kansas City.

Although Harry wanted to go to West Point, his application was turned down because of his eyesight. College costs were out of the question for the poor family but Harry did not complain. Unlike Lyndon Johnson, Harry never criticized his father for this financial downturn. In fact, he helped his father by taking a job as a construction timekeeper. He lived with rough talking labor gangs in tents and kept their hours for the payroll. It may have been this setting where Harry learned some of the salty language that he incorporated into his speech. Although he had called himself a "sissy," he tackled this job that might have scared other boys. This suggests a confidence in his ability to handle rough men without fear.

Next he worked as a bank clerk. He received excellent appraisals for his careful accounting. He stayed in Kansas City and lived with his aunt after his family moved to a small farm in Clinton, Missouri. Then he moved into a boarding house where a fellow boarder was the older brother of Dwight D. Eisenhower.

In 1905, Harry was summoned to return home. His father had become overwhelmed by his farm work after a flood. Harry had been living independently for some time. He gave up this independence to return to farm work to aid his family, so strong was his compassion for others and lack of selfishness. In addition to his farm work, Harry's father took a job for extra income as road overseer to aid the upkeep of roads. The improved quality of roadwork soon became evident according to newspaper articles. Harry saw that even though his father could not make a lot of money, he received the respect of others for serving and helping them.

Harry was accused of plowing the straightest furrows of any farm. He said of this, "They had to be straight or I'd hear about it from my father for the next year."

Harry spent his spare time after farm chores reading history and the latest agricultural methods. After several years, during which Harry assumed almost total responsibility for running the farm and homestead, his mother developed a medical problem. In March 1914, while she had a hernia operation, he held the kerosene lamp for the surgeon at her bedside.

This intimate event required that he help the surgeon while watching his mother's unclothed body bleed and writhe. She rewarded him with a car, thus contributing to his belief that good things come to those who help others. It was no ordinary car or cheap Ford, but a 1911 Stafford. He began to drive his young lady friend, Bess, and her girlfriends around the area.

When his father fell ill and died in 1914, Harry took over his father's roadwork position and also served as postmaster. He fell into this public service to continue his father's good efforts on behalf of citizens. More such opportunities awaited him.

2

Love Life

Harry fell for Bess Wallace when he met her in church but felt too shy to speak to her for five years. This shyness might have come about because he did not feel as confident in himself as a boy and young man, feeling like a "sissy." Finally he began to carry books for her and admired her skills in baseball, tennis, skating, dancing, and whistling through her teeth. She offered Harry the competence he lacked in sports. She was what he wanted to be.

In 1903, Bessie's father committed suicide. There was never any discussion about this event because it was so painful to the Wallace family. Bess and her mother suffered one of the most stressful events that can happen. Most women would cross-examine themselves and feel guilt for their husband's suicide, wondering whether they had caused it. Bess' mother chose to deny the tragedy by not discussing it. Bess and Harry accepted her method of coping with it.

Harry's brother married. Harry still dated no other girls. He continued to write Bessie and finally was invited to dinner with the family. Bessie's mother may have been inordinately critical of men and protective of her daughter. The connection between this and her husband's suicide is an interesting but unanswered question. There he dined and entertained everyone by playing the piano. This "sissified" substitution for sports had given him a little edge in courting.

On September 12, 1911, 27-year-old Harry wrote Bess, "I never was fool enough to think that a girl like you could ever care for a fellow like me but I couldn't help telling you how I felt…I have always been more idealist than practical anyway, so I really never expected any reward for loving you. I shall always hope though."

Although his letter implies a lack of self-confidence as a beau, he was willing to reveal his shortcomings in intimate relationships. His love for Bess was largely unrequited. He had a grass tennis court built for her on the farm but she never came to visit.

In one letter, he apologized for his "girl mouth," for his father's debts and for his fears and wishes. Harry could have tried to cover his faults and show only his good side. The fact that he bared his flaws to Bess suggests a great capacity to intimately give and receive love. At long last, Bess finally agreed to be his fiancée.

Madge, Bessie's mother, held tight to her after her father's suicide. At age 30, Harry yearned to be accepted by Madge, who felt bitter and abandoned by her husband. To become rich and possibly impress her, he tried to develop a zinc mine but it yielded nothing.

When World War I arrived, Harry signed up in 1917. Finally, Bess agreed to marry him before he went in. But now *he* waited to be sure she did not become a widow or the wife of a war cripple. After so many years of wanting to marry Bess, it must have been very hard for Harry to think of her best interests instead of his own.

When he returned home from France, he and Bess had an argument the second day of his arrival. It was about his resistance to living with Bess's mother. Bess won. Thirty years later, Harry called it their final argument. Their honeymoon was cut short for Bess to return to Madge's side for a real (or imagined) illness. Harry apparently realized Madge's great need for Bess after her husband's suicide, and he chose to sacrifice a home of their own for Madge's home.

As time passed, Bess had two miscarriages. Then she had Margaret, which made them both very happy. After the problems with conception and delivery, Harry never pressed the wish to have more children, wishing to spare Bess more discomfort. His love for these two women was legendary, and is recorded in the love letters displayed in the Harry Truman Presidential Library.

Typical of Harry's moral stance, during his business trips he never allowed himself to be in a hotel room with a woman for fear of entrapment. He told a reporter, "Three things ruin a man: power, money and women. I never wanted power, I never had any money and the only woman in my life is up at the house right now."

Bess' mother had no interest in Harry's career and stated that she knew ten men personally who would make a better President than Truman. Madge believed Bess could have married better. When Bess was away, Harry was lonely and had headaches and nausea. He passed the time playing poker with friends and having a little whiskey.

As President, Harry made $75,000 a year. Nearly half went to pay his taxes. The president had to pay for their food and for the food served to guests. Bess kept the books, went over bills and wrote checks herself. But they went into debt each year of his presidency. In concert with Truman's morals and his study of great men, he had no interest in profiting from the presidency or abusing the power of the office.

The White House staff liked Truman's familiar simplicity and warmth much better than Roosevelt's distant personal style. Truman knew everyone's name, introduced servants to guests, and kept up with their personal lives.

Bess enjoyed recognition in Washington, D.C. As a senator, Harry put her on the payroll for clerical work, but she did little in addition to the role of keeping the expense books. Despite this practice, he criticized others who hired spouses for do-nothing jobs.

Harry was totally devoted to his family. Even when Bess left him to "go home," or when she was cold on his whirlwind trips home, he loved her dearly and tried to please her just as he had tried to please his parents. Harry wanted to be with his family one Christmas. He flew home in a snowstorm that had closed airports, only to have Bess give him the cold shoulder. When he returned to the White House, he wrote a rather critical letter to her but never mailed it. It said, "You can never appreciate what it means to come home as I did the other evening after doing at least 100 things I didn't want to do and have the only person in the world whose approval and good opinion I value look at me like I'm something the cat dragged in and tell me I've come in at last because I couldn't find any reason to stay away." He ended, "Kiss my baby and I love you in season and out."

Writing was often almost as good as talking things over for Harry. Sometimes he and Bess didn't talk enough, though. It was some time later when he learned that Bess' cold shoulder was anger that he didn't share the A-bomb decision with her. She felt that he had always shared everything with her, usually over a drink at the end of the day, and this "secret" made her feel shut out from his life and thoughts.

3

Military Experience

At age 21, Harry had signed up with the National Guard. In 1917 at age 33, he was two years beyond the Selective Service Administration age limit and had been out of the National Guard for six years. He was the sole support of his mother and sister. Despite all these things, the turning point of his life came when he joined the military in response to President Wilson's declaration of war in April 1917.

Aware of his lack of education, he dug into math, surveying and astronomy by working night and day. He studied maps and knew where he was going. He enjoyed the chance to visit places in France that he had read about. He began to be seen as a leader, not on the basis of brawn but brain. His coping methods to spend time learning to make up for athletics had paid off and served him well.

Captain Truman told non-commissioned officers, "I didn't come over here to get along with you. You've got to get along with me. You soldier for me and I'll soldier for you." And he did. He was fair to his men and transformed one of the worst batteries in the regiment into one of the best. He reduced the ranks of those subordinates who didn't follow rules. This man who had learned to follow rules for parental reward and love, did the same with those under him. They were rewarded when they followed his orders.

Sometimes Harry violated orders. He was bawled out for letting a soldier with a twisted ankle ride a horse rather than walk. He waited to give the order to fire on the enemy until the enemy was exactly within range. He knew the range of his weaponry and knew better than to order men to fire upon sighting the enemy. In the moral sense, he had reached the level where he no longer just obeyed rules of parents, peer group or society. He realized that in some situations one had to evaluate, make an independent decision, and risk the consequences. This level of moral development was what could be called social utility. Further demonstration of this kind of moral level can be seen in a letter to his cousin Ethel.

"You know justice is an awful tyrant and if I give one man a nice muddy wagon to wash on Sunday because he went to Verdun without asking me if he could, why I've got to give another one the same duty if he does the same thing even if he has the most plausible excuse."

The war gave Harry confidence that he could lead. He liked that role better than anything he'd ever done. He saw a way to combine his wish to serve, to receive respect, and to use his intelligence.

4

Path to Power

During the war, Truman met two men who became life-long buddies. Jim Pendergast and his family helped Harry become judge and senator. But first he tried to be a businessman with war buddy Eddie Jacobson. In 1919, Eddie and Harry opened a men's clothing store in Kansas City. It became a gathering place for their old army buddies who came for advice, money and to talk politics. When Jim Pendergast came in, he brought his brother Mike. It was Mike who became Harry's political supporter, urging Harry to run for county judge.

Harry's fervent wish to help others such as penniless army buddies led him to give and loan more than he could recover. After three years, the store was so deep in debt that they closed it. With Pendergast's help, Harry became Judge Truman at age 37. He pushed through programs to build better roads and jobs for the poor. He was also successful in eliminating graft and corruption in getting roads repaired.

Harry and Bess were delighted with their only child, Margaret. However, their family life was nearly disrupted when she was six years old. A man came to school to pick up Judge Truman's daughter. The teacher was curious because nobody called her Mary Margaret. She had the man wait. She called police and when the sheriff and Harry arrived, the man had disappeared. Margaret was guarded throughout the rest of her childhood because of this incident.

Harry was defeated in his second term for judge by a Ku Klux Klan candidate. He didn't let that disturb him for long. He began selling automobile club memberships while driving throughout the region. Harry's confidence that he could be a success was not limited to one career. He had realized that he could improve his lot by taking a job that was not his favorite occupation.

Then Harry met the father of Jim and Mike Pendergast, Tom. Tom liked Harry and supported his run for presiding judge of Kansas City. Harry held that position for eight years and made good on promises to cut the budget, eliminate waste and build needed new government facilities. He got a bond issue through which put 224 miles of new concrete roads in Missouri. Due to legal limitations, he couldn't run for another term. He wanted to run for governor of Missouri but Tom Pendergast had another candidate that he wanted to support.

Harry didn't know what to do. He was lost in his new desire for public service until Pendergast helped him run for the Senate. He gave Harry enough money to start his campaign, set up speeches at colleges, and print flyers. The press predicted that Truman would lose but he won by the farmers' vote. It was said that people could tell that Harry liked them, talked their language and understood their needs. Harry's openness with people was a terribly appealing quality. Politicians usually said only what the public wanted to hear.

In Congress, he spent much time in the Library of Congress researching committee assignments. Reading had always been his forte, but not public speaking. He avoided public speeches because he realized that was not where his strength lay. He developed many friendships, and one was with the plainspoken Vice President John Nance Garner. Because Garner liked him, Harry presided over the Senate from time to time. Without the need to deliver speeches, he was an adequate speaker.

The Governor of Missouri announced in 1940 that he was going to run for the Senate to replace Harry. Truman drove the state with an army buddy and spoke in town squares to farmers and citizens. He won because he campaigned better than his rival, covering more ground and speaking in the language of the ordinary man.

Despite negative rumors about the Pendergasts, Harry remained beholden to them for the rest of his career. If Harry made a friend, he was a friend forever. Pendergast was blamed for vote manipulation in an election. J. Edgar Hoover of the Federal Bureau of Investigation came to Kansas City in 1928 to indict Pendergast for tax evasion. As a result Tom served 15 months at Leavenworth Penitentiary. Although some avoided Harry because of his "gangster connections" with Pendergast, many came to like him personally. Much as he wanted to be elected, Truman never chose to win popularity on the basis of what others wanted him to be.

In 1940-41, Roosevelt tried to rally the country to fight Hitler. Harry supported the first peacetime draft in 1940. Aware of the shortage of qualified officers, and now a colonel in the reserves, he went to see George Marshall. The Army Chief of Staff told him he was too old to enlist and was more valuable in other areas. This wish to serve, even if it meant personal harm, excessive toil, and loss of Senate position was typical of the man who wanted to serve others.

Harry began to hear about profiteering in the construction of Ft. Leonard Wood in Missouri. He set out to visit the camp and investigate. His committee to investigate unlawful practices soon grew important in the war effort. News commentator Drew Pearson wrote: "Slightly built, bespectacled, a lover of Chopin and a shunner of the limelight, Truman is one of the last men in Congress who would be considered a hard-boiled prober. In manner and appearance, he is anything but a crusader."

Pearson saw the outer Truman, the "sissy" with a "girl mouth." He recognized that Truman was a truth-seeker who cared less for popularity than for finding out what could help or harm his country.

On December 7, 1941, Japan bombed Pearl Harbor. Truman's committee was investigating how faulty airplanes were being made. Using the findings of his committee, immediate action was taken to supply more dependable military goods. Harry was on the cover of *Time Magazine* in 1943 for his work and its importance to the war effort. The Truman Committee ended up saving American taxpayers hundreds of millions of dollars. His Special Committee to Investigate the National Defense Program had a mandate to "investigate all activities involving national defense." Truman described his job as being "to dig this stuff up now and correct it."

In his investigations, Truman learned of the existence of a very powerful weapon (The Manhattan Project). He backed off when so advised by War Secretary Stimson. Unlike Nixon, Truman never used secrets such as this to hurt or attack others.

In 1943, he was asked by Bob Hannigan to consider nomination for Vice President. He turned it down because he didn't want to succeed the popular Roosevelt. On a speakerphone, he heard Roosevelt ask Hannigan, "Bob, have you got that fellow lined up yet?"

Hannigan responded, "No, he is the contrariest Goddamn mule from Missouri I ever dealt with."

Then Roosevelt said, "Well, you tell the Senator that if he wants to break up the Democratic Party in the middle of the war, that's his responsibility."

When Roosevelt slammed down the phone, Truman was stunned. He said, "Well, if that's the situation, I'll have to say yes. But why the hell didn't he tell me in the first place."

Truman's reaction seemed to indicate that he was not confident that he was Roosevelt's real choice. But when Roosevelt put it in such a way that he would harm the Party and the country, he accepted.

When he was nominated for Vice President, Margaret's aunt decided it was time to tell her that her grandfather had committed suicide before she read it in the newspaper. Aghast and unable to face her mother, Margaret ran to her father. He reacted with fury and told her, "Don't ever mention that to your mother!" And she didn't. Harry's reaction was probably not the best from his daughter's viewpoint, as she later wrote. But Harry was focused on his wife, Bess. He always tried to spare his wife from the consequences of her father's suicide.

Vice President Truman was criticized for attending Tom Pendergast's funeral. The press and Bess criticized him for playing piano at a Press Club meeting where Lauren Bacall sat on his piano dangling her legs while singing. Although Harry never apologized for attending the funeral of his friend, he promised Bess that he would never play the piano in such a compromising situation again.

Typical of Roosevelt's secretiveness, he met with Truman only twice before he died. When Harry was summoned upon FDR's death April 12, 1945, he asked Eleanor, "Is there anything I can do for you?"

She said, "Is there anything we can do for you? You are the one in trouble now."

An hour later, Justice Stone administered the Oath of Office. Truman fervently kissed the Bible at the end of the ceremony.

Truman was the oldest vice president to succeed to the presidency. He was 60. He told reporters such as Allen Drury who later wrote *Advise and Consent,* "Boys, if you ever pray, pray for me now." Truman's disarming frankness endeared him to the press.

The good thing about this time was that the war was coming to an end. There was an air of optimism.

5

Leadership Style

The first day after his assumption of the Presidency, Truman startled everyone when he went over to the "Hill" to dine. He lunched with 17 men, mostly Senators, from both parties and both houses. He explained, "I want to have lunch with my friends."

Secretary of the Treasury Henry Morgenthau arrived to size Harry up. Truman said he didn't want to take up his time but needed a comprehensive report on the nation's financial standing as soon as possible. This demonstrated that not he, but Morgenthau was the one on trial.

He called his two rivals for the Vice Presidency. He asked Jimmy Byrnes and Henry Wallace to go with him to receive Roosevelt's body, which was arriving by train from Warm Springs. Pro-Roosevelt sentiment was part of Truman's greatest problem. The feelings of loss were felt in the government, the hearts of citizens and in soldiers who were fighting for their President.

J. Edgar Hoover brought Truman some FBI phone taps made by Roosevelt, which had to do with sexual liaisons. Harry said he had no time for such foolishness and didn't authorize it. He wrote in his diary during the first month of the presidency, "We want no Gestapo or secret police. The FBI is tending in that direction. They are dabbling in sex-life scandals and plain blackmail. This must stop."

Britain's Anthony Eden was impressed by Truman's air of quiet confidence in himself after only one month. He told Eden, "I am here to make decisions and whether they prove right or wrong, I am going to make them."

Winston Churchill didn't think much of Truman when he first met him at Potsdam July 16, 1945. He had really liked Roosevelt but was kind to Truman anyway. Truman wrote Bess, "I'm sure we can get along if he doesn't give me too much soft soap."

Truman threw a party for Joseph Stalin and Churchill and invited Eugene List to play the piano. There was no one to turn the pages for List so Truman did. Harry also played Paderewski's *Minuet in G*. Stalin thought little of Truman but Churchill grew to like him.

At the end of the summit, Truman told both leaders that the U.S. would soon use nuclear weapons on Japan unless they surrendered, and both approved. Stalin was unimpressed because he knew of the atomic bomb through espionage activities. Truman liked Stalin and thought he was better prepared and more business-like than Churchill. But he was exasperated that he could not get Stalin to commit troops to the war against Japan as soon as he wanted.

Truman's decision to use the atomic bomb to end World War II has often come under criticism. He had been told that the war butchery was horrendous, and that 50,000 allied prisoners of war had already died in Japanese hands. He was warned that two million people would have to be killed in a land invasion of Japan. He learned that 40,000 to 100,000 Americans would be killed in a Japanese invasion as well as

Japanese deaths of like amounts. Additionally, nobody knew exactly how powerful the atomic bomb was. There was also the possibility that war-weary Americans would be critical if soldiers had to die when the U.S. had spent billions of dollars to develop bombs to end these losses.

Finally, the decision was made to use the bomb. They decided not to bomb towns with Japanese shrines of art and culture and chose Hiroshima. Nagasaki was bombed three days later when the Japanese had sent no word of surrender. Truman wrote of headaches for days, but verbally expressed no regret for these decisions.

After the power of the bomb was realized, J. Robert Oppenheimer, the father of the A-bomb, thought, along with Dean Acheson and David Lilienthal of the Atomic Energy Commission, that the nuclear power secrets should be shared. In that way, a nuclear one-upmanship war could be avoided. Although dying of throat cancer, Oppenheimer went to Truman to plead this case. Truman asked why he was so upset. He held out his hands and said, "Mr. President, I have blood on my hands." Truman paused, reached into his pocket and took out a handkerchief and said, "I'm the President. I dropped the bomb. Take my handkerchief and wipe the blood off your hands."

It seemed that the end of the war was going to solve everything. It didn't but at least it brought the soldiers back home. The emotions as boys returned to girls resulted in the baby boom.

It must have been difficult for Truman to know how to handle the widow of the fallen president, Eleanor Roosevelt, but he solved that problem with aplomb. At the end of 1945, Truman sent Eleanor to be the only U.S. woman delegate at the first meeting of the U.N. General Assembly in London. She was indebted that he gave her a role. She wrote a newspaper column called *My Day* from 1936-1962. She both extolled the virtues and criticized some policies of the Truman administration.

Truman liked to surround himself with honest people of high integrity, industrious habits and the ability to simplify complex matters. In

General George Marshall, he found all this as well as with Dean Acheson, Clark Clifford and George Kennan.

After he made Marshall Secretary of State, he sent him to meet with leaders in other countries. He felt he finally knew more about what was really happening than he had under Marshall's predecessor Jimmy Byrnes, Roosevelt's protégée. He trusted Marshall as no one else. He wanted to reward him by calling the plan to help Europe the Marshall Plan, but it was Truman's as much as anyone's. The Marshall Plan was the Truman administration's effort to prevent the Soviet Union from dominating war-torn Europe. He believed the real communist threat was the Soviet Union instead of the American communists that McCarthy and Nixon were trying to root out.

Truman won the presidency in a surprise victory against Thomas Dewey in 1948. John Connally, who would later be governor of Texas, said it was because people identified with his personal characteristics. Even so, Connally said that some Americans feared Truman because, "There is a lack of faith in his bigness or ability to do the job and a lack of faith in the people around him."

Truman expected another world war when the Soviet-backed North Koreans invaded South Korea. He worried about more use of atomic bombs. He didn't want to provoke the Chinese and Russians into war, so he told MacArthur not to go into Chinese territory. MacArthur persisted in his demands and on November 24, 1950, China entered the war.

Harry had worried about MacArthur since June of 1945. He wrote in his diary that a big question after the war would be what to do with "Mister Prima Donna, Brass Hat, Five Star MacArthur." He continued, "It is a very great pity we have to have stuffed shirts like that in key positions. I don't see why in hell Roosevelt didn't order Wainwright home and let MacArthur be a martyr (on Corregidor)."

The 70 year old MacArthur sent word that his army was about to be destroyed and wanted to wage all out war and bomb Manchuria. Truman also learned that MacArthur wrote the Chinese saying that they should deal with him rather than the President. Harry felt he had to quiet MacArthur and relieve him of command to avert war. He handled it poorly. MacArthur learned he had been fired from the press. Truman later explained that he realized this would be an unpopular action but he did it immediately to take back control of the war and spare the world further nuclear warfare.

Truman saw his role as one of making difficult and unpopular decisions. The Constitution stated that only the president was the commander in chief of the armed services. Another equally unpopular decision was to rule that segregation in the armed forces was illegal. He made such decisions out of a personal conviction that he wanted to steer the country in the right direction.

Tension between Truman and Eisenhower was painfully obvious during the 1953 inauguration. At least four things caused it. Senator Joe McCarthy had alleged that General George Marshall supported communism. At first, Eisenhower did not denounce this allegation publicly even though Marshall had chosen Ike to be the Supreme Allied Commander in Europe. Truman was disappointed that Eisenhower didn't censure McCarthy. Second, Eisenhower had rejected Truman's offer to be briefed by the CIA just before the election. Third, Eisenhower considered divorcing his wife after having had an affair with an English aide. And fourth, earlier in 1947, Truman had asked Eisenhower to run for president and offered to be his vice president. Ike declined and there may have been a lingering feeling of rebuff.

Truman had a nice opportunity to visit the White House after he was no longer president. In 1961 after John Kennedy had been elected president, Truman was asked to play at the White House. He played Paderewski's *Minuet in G* and this time Eugene List turned the pages for him, reversing the event in Potsdam. This modest and helpful man was receiving the same kind of help that he once gave the noted pianist.

6

Stresses

Truman had a wonderful ability to socialize and formed long-lasting and intimate relationships with colleagues. He was very candid with his friends and used humor as a way to relieve tension. An example was when he said, "I fired MacArthur because he couldn't respect the authority of the president. I didn't fire him because he was a dumb son of a bitch, although he was, but that's not against the law for generals."

After Truman attained political office through the support of Tom Pendergast, Tom asked him to award a contract to a man who had poured donations into Pendergast's campaigns. After agonizing a long time and suffering headaches and insomnia, Harry told Tom he couldn't do it because the man was dishonest. Truman's physical symptoms under stress could not be called hypochondriasis because he did not use them to elicit sympathy or gain something. As time passed, Truman was delighted to realize that Pendergast would never ask him to do anything against his principles thereafter. Although he worried about losing Pendergast's support, he learned from that incident that Pendergast and others would support him as a man of principle.

Later, however, Pendergast would not run Harry for governor because he favored another candidate who would do favors for him. This made Harry feel very depressed. He had to decide whether to change his career since he would not trade his ethics to climb the ladder of success. He went to spend a few nights alone at a hotel.

At the hotel, he wrote out his thoughts and intended for nobody to ever see them. Some notes were later found, and they showed the depth of his despair. They also showed his method of coping by writing, self-analysis, and taking pride in his moral integrity. Among these notes, he wrote, "Since childhood at my mother's knee, I have believed in honor, ethics and right living as its own reward. I find a very small minority who agree with me on that premise."

His decision to continue in politics was later aided by Pendergast who helped him run, not for governor, but for the Senate.

After World War II, suffering Americans were replaced by greedy Americans and a flurry of good and bad bills were proposed to help veterans. Soon it seemed to Truman that every bill he sent to Congress was rebuffed. By December, he told an audience that General Sherman was wrong. "He said 'war is hell' and I say 'peace is hell'." As Harry became surer of his public speaking ability, he used humor in his speeches and interviews with reporters. But as his friends and colleagues knew, Harry had used humor and the ability to laugh at himself throughout his entire life.

When a railroad strike stopped the nation, Truman tried to let others solve it. When their talks failed, he threatened to call out the army and to draft the strikers. That ended the strike and he was praised for his toughness.

After the war, Truman feared that the country was not taking the communist threat seriously enough. Stalin had said the two cultures were incompatible and that war between them was inevitable. The two cultures struggled over who might have the greatest influence over European countries. Harry urged Congress to support Greece and Turkey to make them less vulnerable to aid offered by the U.S.S.R. This was the beginning of the Truman Doctrine. Other steps in this direction were the Marshall Plan to help war-torn countries and establishment of NATO (North Atlantic Treaty Organization). The Point Four program sent advisors to war-impacted countries to help with irrigation, agriculture, malnutrition, illiteracy, and overpopulation. This program became the precursor of the Peace Corps.

Truman was told that another part of fighting communism was the establishment of the Federal Employee Loyalty Program. This caused the accidental acceleration of Senator Joseph McCarthy's excesses. This was also the era in which Richard Nixon began to be noticed for his anti-communist interrogations in the House Un-American Activities investigations.

Harry was faced with what was thought to be certain defeat in his 1948 race with Thomas Dewey. He vigorously pursued a cross-country train campaign with Bess and Margaret. He boldly and tirelessly spoke to groups everywhere explaining his policies. He never criticized his opponent personally, nor did Dewey criticize him personally. Interestingly, a liberal Democrat named Ronald Reagan endorsed Truman over Dewey.

One of the stresses that Harry faced was how to judge character in those who approached him or pandered to him. He appeared to be a fairly good judge of character in the case of Nixon. He wrote of Nixon in his memoirs: "How many people remember our history and realize how close Jefferson came to losing the election in 1800, and how close Aaron Burr came to being our third president, which would have been as bad as electing Richard Nixon today…He is a shifty-eyed goddamn liar…He's one of the few in the history of this country to run for high office talking out of both sides of his mouth at the same time and lying out of both sides."

Some presidents like Ronald Reagan did not like to fire people. Truman faced up to such personnel issues and the subsequent criticism rather than leaving the details to others. Firing MacArthur was not easy to do, especially when it was shortly followed by other problems. His firing of MacArthur for insubordination in 1951 inspired Samuel Huntington to write his famous *The Soldier and the State.* Huntington's penetrating analysis of the relationship between the military and society found Truman to be a liberal at home but conservative in foreign affairs.

Shortly after Truman ordered Gen. MacArthur to stop talking to the press, his lifelong friend, Press Secretary Charlie Ross, died. Also Margaret was to have her first recital, which received negative press reviews. Uncharacteristically, Truman publicly blew his stack at the reviews. He wrote the reporter who criticized Margaret saying, "Some day I hope to meet you. When that happens you'll need a new nose, a lot of beefsteak for black eyes, and perhaps a supporter below."

When this letter leaked out to the press, Truman received hundreds of critical letters. One contained a posthumous Medal of Honor from the parents of a boy who was killed in the Korean War. Truman kept the letter for several years because it stated that the parents regretted that Margaret was not in Korea to receive the same treatment as their son. Whenever Truman erred, he tried to remember and learn from it.

America had changed during World War II. Women picked up the slack when men left. Rosie the Riveter was a different sort than the girl boys left behind. Even Margaret Truman was one of the new types of women with a budding musical career that could only be stopped by bad critical reviews. Despite the fact the Truman was married to old-fashioned Bess, he tried to promote the new type of woman in his daughter. He was in the same quandary as so many American men of the times. Fortunately, Margaret went on to have an excellent career as an author.

7

Accomplishments

In 1947, he established the CIA and NATO to mobilize war-weary Americans against the communists in a "cold war." He also reorganized the armed services under the Department of Defense (DOD) and established the Air Force as a separate branch of service under the DOD. Up to then, the army and navy were rivals for projects and publicity.

In the same year, he established a loyalty program to get Americans to recognize the need to preserve freedom against totalitarianism. He encouraged George Kennan to publicize his policy of "containment." This policy avoided direct attack upon the Soviets by helping Europe and Japan rebuild, developing a hydrogen (H) bomb, and psychologically "containing" the USSR. This non-violent approach worked fairly well and is one reason that Truman is now rated highly.

As black GIs returned from WWII, despite a lifetime of personal prejudice, Harry supported civil rights. He said, "I'm the president of all the people." He was the first president to attack racism and did so by pushing an anti-lynching bill, voting rights act, and creating the Fair Employment Practices Commission. In 1948, he desegregated the armed forces and prohibited discrimination in housing and interstate transportation.

He recognized the new Jewish state of Israel on May 14, 1948, despite possible oil cuts by the Middle East. He had to go against his friend and esteemed colleague George Marshall in making this decision.

He ordered a Berlin airlift in 1949 after Stalin had blockaded the area around West Berlin. This was at a time when the Russians had exploded an A-bomb and the risk of retaliation existed. Britain and the U.S. supplied West Berlin by air for a year until Russia backed down.

Clark Clifford, an advisor to presidents from Truman to Carter, explained Truman's legacy thusly: "In the wake of the collapse of communism in Eastern Europe, the Reagan conservatives will claim that his defense budgets and muscular rhetoric turned the tide. But the policy that truly succeeded was born when within three years Truman unveiled the Truman Doctrine, the Marshall Plan, NATO, and Point Four. These were the accepted frameworks of foreign police from Eisenhower to Bush. He and his advisors believed that if we held the line against further Soviet expansion, communism would gradually become less dangerous and more open." It happened.

When John Kennedy was about to debate Richard Nixon for the presidential election of 1960, Truman said anyone who voted for Nixon could "go to hell." Kennedy was asked what he thought of that. Obviously pleased that Truman was more anti-Nixon than anti-Kennedy, Jack said, "Maybe Bess can control him but I can't."

In recognition of his work for national medical insurance, President Lyndon Johnson presented the first two Medicare cards to Harry and Bess Truman.

8

Summary

Truman's parents loved him openly so he learned to trust them and felt that he could trust others. This prepared him to share himself without fearing harm or disapproval by others. He learned to please his parents by doing what they asked and accepting their rules. He later tried to please others as he had pleased his parents. While this usually worked, he found that some few used him for their own purposes, unlike his parents. Also from his upbringing, he developed habits of self-educa-tion, hard work, perseverance, self-confidence in his worth, relaxed interactions with intimates and the trait of loyalty.

He passed through all the theoretical stages of maturation from trust to ego integrity without any deviation. He also developed the ability to love and totally commit to his wife and family by having first experi-enced the unconditional love of his own parents.

He mainly used healthy coping methods. These were altruism and service to others, anticipating problems by planning, and facing prob-lems with humor. He also sublimated wishes with acceptable substi-tutes, and suppressed or postponed attention to problems by writing unsent letters.

He developed the highest level of morality and experienced physical symptoms and discomfort when integrity or principles were ignored. He operated most of the time at the highest level of moral develop-ment. He let fairness and equity guide his actions, believed that all peo-ple had equal worth, and sometimes made decisions against the crowd, risking unpopularity.

His leadership was strong with almost as much concern for his sub-ordinates as for the task that must be accomplished. He was intimately involved in decision making with his team, and took responsibility for making the final decision. His leadership would probably be best cate-gorized as a team manager.

Harry died in 1972 and Bess in 1982. An example of his humor even in later life was his comment, "A statesman is a politician who has been dead 10 or 15 years."

2

ADOLF HITLER

"No man is fit to command another that cannot command him-self." William Penn

1

Upbringing and Early Life

Hitler's father was first named Alois Schicklgruber. He later became the ward of Johann Heidler, pronounced "Hitler." Hitler described his father in *Mein Kampf* as the son of a poor cottager. Alois ran away from home at 13. He left the northern border of Austria against the warnings of older villagers and went to Vienna. He apprenticed as a cobbler for four years. After experiencing hardship and poverty, he gave up his trade and became a civil servant at age 17.

He became a customs official for the Austrian Ministry of Finance for ten years. He then was promoted to provisional assistant in Linz. He was next promoted to assistant collector in 1870, and then to assistant inspector where he stayed from 1871 to 1891. He changed his name from Heidler to Alois Hitler in 1875.

An example of his views was contained in some advice he gave about a career in the customs service. He said one must show absolute obedience to superiors, work in every kind of weather and added that immoral people wouldn't last in that occupation.

Adolf's father wore a uniform with gilt buttons; a hat embroidered with gold lace; and sported a moustache. His colleagues called him rigid and pedantic. He was also kind, earthy, warm and even humorous. Interestingly, colleagues and friends of Adolf described him similarly to his father.

Alois' first wife, an invalid, divorced him because he had affairs with maids and waitresses. He had an illegitimate son with a waitress. She named the boy Alois after him. He married the waitress and adopted her son. They had another child but his waitress wife developed tuberculosis and was sent away for treatment. He took up with a maid, Klara Polzl, who may have been his niece. The neat, quiet, modest Klara called him "Uncle." She became his common-law wife when his second wife died.

Alois was 23 years older than Klara. Alois asked a priest for dispensation to marry. After the request was sent to Rome, the couple was granted permission to marry in 1885. Klara gave him six children, four boys and two girls. Adolf, born April 20, 1889, and Paula, born in 1896, were the only survivors of their union. Neither left descendants.

Adolf came along after Alois' first son (Alois) was seven. Alois' first daughter, Angela, was five when Adolf was born. Adolf had the two older siblings, and two younger ones would be born. When Adolf was five, a brother Edmund was born. He would die of measles when little Adolf was 11. His youngest sibling, Paula, was born when Adolf was seven and outlived him, as did Angela and Alois.

Adolf's young life was filled with moves from one place to another. Little Adi, as he was called, was three when they moved to Passau for his father's promotion to this little village west of Vienna on the Danube River. When Adolf was five, a week after Edmund's birth, his father left for Linz where he received yet another promotion. Because of the new infant, the family didn't join Alois for a year. Adolf became a mama's boy and was allowed to do what he wanted while Angela and young Alois were at school, and Edmund asleep.

Adolf carried his mother's picture until the day he died and probably put her on a pedestal. He had more fear mixed with awe for his elderly father who was 52 when he was born. The age difference made closeness with his father impossible, and he never gained the feeling that his father cared much for him. Thus he grew up with unconditional love from only his mother, and a fear of his older, awesome, distant father.

In 1895, when Adolf was six, his father retired at age 58. They moved again to the village of Hufeld. His father became a beekeeper. He was stung regularly because he used only the smoke of his cigar to protect himself. Their farm had a stable, orchard, horses, cows and a hayloft. After he started school, Adi mainly saw his father as an authoritarian old man, retired from business life. He was performing menial chores but still commanding the household and his young wife.

Adolf began school at age six, walking there with older sister Angela. He was proper and usually the best student. He was smaller than other boys but argued with them and became, he wrote, a "little ringleader." He continued, "I had scarcely any thoughts about my future career," and "I had no sympathy for the course my father's career had taken." It was clear that he did not want to identify with his father or his father's profession. In fact, he was probably a little afraid of his father.

His strict father was not only distant in age, but was a no-nonsense man. Their farm didn't do well because the land was poor, so they moved again in 1897 when Adi was eight. He had moved four times in eight years. In Lambach, he attended a school attached to an 11th century Benedictine monastery. The beauty of services, the ritual and music appealed to him. Adi took lessons to sing in the choir. For two years, he thought of becoming a monk and rising to the status of abbot, the superior of monks. Once a priest caught him smoking, like his father, and admonished him.

Adolf's older half-brother, Alois, left home in 1898 and became a ne'er-do-well. In 1900 he was imprisoned for theft and served five months. Two years later, he served another eight months in jail. He traveled about Europe, and eventually returned to run his own café in Berlin until World War II ended.

Adolf's family moved again in 1898 to Leonding near Linz. His father set up beehives and Adi attended elementary school. Alois drank with other old cronies, and went to church only on the birthday of Emperor Kaiser Wilhelm II.

Six-year-old Edmund died of measles when Adi was ten. Reports suggest that Adolf changed from an outgoing boy to a morose, self-absorbed, nervous child. He was said to sit out by the cemetery where Edmund was buried. He was obedient, quiet and meek with his father. He attended a practical school rather than a college preparatory school after elementary education.

He drew pictures and thought of himself as a potential artist. However, his works were not displayed like that of other children. Not a particularly sturdy boy, he probably tried to substitute art for more athletic activities. Unlike Harry's substitution of piano and reading for lack of sports ability, Adolf's way of coping with his lack of athletic prowess brought him little reward.

His family was in mourning for their lost three children. Adolf became a lonely boy who lived in a dream world. All his father's hopes had fallen upon him as the only surviving son except for his half-brother, Alois, the failure.

He had to repeat the ninth grade because of poor marks. When Adi learned he would have to repeat a grade, he told his father in a fearsome confrontation that he wanted to leave school and study painting. His father, a fiercely masculine sort, said, "Artist; no! Never as long as I live."

The stubborn boy decided to show his stubborn father that he should be allowed to quit school. He did this by lowering his school performance. This indirect method of getting back at his father could be called passive-aggressive. By this time, Adolf had begun to feel that his father was against him and that he must find ways to look out for his own interests. This distrust in his father's love for him would color his views of many men later on, and leave him with a deep-seated paranoia that people were against him.

He found his father's military magazines and saw pictures of the Franco-Prussian War that excited him. He played war games with other boys and enjoyed pretending he was a leader. He demanded absolute obedience from his pretend subordinates. In this, he was copying his father's advice about working for the customs service. He was also reproducing the same behavior that he had to show toward his father.

His old father's fearsome authoritarianism produced a rebellious young Adolf. Teachers described him as lacking in self-control, argumentative, willful, arrogant, bad-tempered and unwilling to submit to school discipline. He reacted with anger when teachers corrected him or advised him. However, he demanded subservience by schoolmates among whom he saw himself as a leader.

During this period, he read Karl May novels about Americans who killed evil red skinned Indians roaming Arizona, Texas and New Mexico. The hero, Old Shatterhand, shouted, "I am great, I am marvelous" after each raid and quoted the Bible to demonstrate his right to butcher the inferior race.

Some teachers remembered Adolf as being extremely pale and skinny, almost sickly, and he used to talk to himself. This was a symptom that he was moving into unhealthy methods of coping with loneliness and stress. His stress increased when his father died suddenly of a stroke. He died when Adolf was 13. Adi had already felt distant from his father and now had the added burden of feeling deserted just when he needed to form up his own male identity.

Klara received half of her husband's pension; death benefits and each child received a small financial bequest. Adolf could now afford to reside at the boys' school in Linz. There he impressed the housekeeper as a nervous and formal child who passed time by reading and drawing. Later in the year, his half-sister Angela married.

Adolf did poorly at school and became a sassy, indifferent student. He fell behind other boys in class who were industriously learning a variety of skills and pastimes. He gave one teacher, Father Franz Schwartz, a very hard time. He disobeyed the father and criticized religion. Without the presence of a father, young Adolf was testing the limits of other adults to hold him in check. Despite his poor grades, he passed at age 15 on the condition that he must drop out of school. But he didn't.

After a resentful attendance at his confirmation, he was sent to Linz for schooling where he roomed with another student. There he teased and humiliated the housekeeper's elderly husband treating him with total disrespect. The elderly husband may have reminded him of his own father. He was probably too intimidated to taunt his own father but he took his revenge out on this elderly man. He appeared to have no male with whom he could identify.

Sometimes his need for attention made Adolf play the school clown. He did so poorly in school that he was not eligible for higher education. After a respiratory illness, he finished his last required course and celebrated passing with a drunken spree. He used his graduation certificate to wipe himself after going to the bathroom. He then had to go back to the schoolmaster for a duplicate to show his mother. The schoolmaster humiliated him and Adolf promised himself never to get drunk again. Although he was free of regular schooling, he may have taken an art course at this time still hoping to develop some talent or skill.

In 1905, Klara sold the house at Leonding and moved to Linz. Adi slept late and if his mother wanted to waken him, she or sister Paula would kiss him. This was because he hated being kissed and would leap out of bed. He dressed well, carried a cane as an affectation, and a notebook to make observations and draw sketches. He was a night owl, attending opera, drinking little and did not date girls. He had a few friends and thought of himself as an expert because he read so much in his areas of interest. He sketched buildings adding changes to make them bigger or more grandiose. His behavior during this time suggests that he had not made a firm identification with his father and had an unclear sexual orientation.

He met another opera lover, a young man named August Kubizek who played viola and trumpet. Kubizek listened as Adolf talked with great intensity. When Kubizek finished work in his father's upholstery shop, he and Adolf strolled the city together at night. They would sometimes encounter Adi's old schoolmates who asked what he was doing with himself. His embarrassment at not doing more caused him to become irate. He turned his jealousy into anger and criticism of his ex-schoolmates.

Adi, who had little experience with close friendships, was possessive of his new friend and wanted Kubizek to have no other friends. In 1953, Kubizek wrote *Hitler, the Friend of My Youth* in which he described their relationship. Adolf drew up plans for a two-story dream house for them with a circular staircase, fancy doorways and a huge music room with servants. They discussed traveling Germany in summers and needed only a winning lottery ticket to afford it. Hitler calculated and picked a lucky number, and seemed stunned and furious that he didn't win. His possessiveness, the dream house and plans to make music and art together suggest that he perhaps saw Kubizek in an almost romantic way. His expectation of winning and rage at losing the lottery suggest that his fantasies were obscuring reality.

Young Adolf and Kubizek went to the Linz Opera House. Adolf loved Richard Wagner's opera *Rienzi*. Rienzi, a Roman, liberated the public from oppression by nobles. The people hailed him with phrases such as: "Heil, Rienzi! Heil, the tribune of the people!" Adolf told Kubizek after the opera that he would one day lead people. That night, wrote Kubizek, he changed his ambition from being a painter to a dictator.

Adolf's mother died when he was 18. He was distraught and shortly moved to Vienna. In 1908, he convinced Kubizek's father to support his son while he studied music in Vienna. There, Adolf took a small apartment for the two of them. Kubizek described how young Hitler paced the floor while speaking, making his poor companion dizzy. Ever the night owl, Adolf survived on a meager pension from his parents' will, did not work or attend school, and went to operas in the evenings.

Adolf wrote his own opera with Kubizek's help. He wrote of Wieland the Smith, a Norse hero about whom Wagner tried to write an opera. The king Wieland served made him lame. Wieland got revenge by raping the king's daughter and killing the king's sons. He drank a victory toast from their skulls before flying off in wings he had made in his blacksmith shop. After writing the first act, Hitler lost interest in the project. However, these aggressive and violent scenes probably stimulated Hitler's fantasies.

He read opera librettos, architecture, mythology, music and philosophy. He wandered the streets mentally tearing down and redesigning the city's architecture. He designed an idea for a strolling orchestra that might bring music to more people. However, when Kubizek criticized any plan, Adolf became enraged. He did not want reality to intrude into his inner world where he could create and destroy whatever he liked. He was not progressing in the area of industriousness, which usually gives young people their perseverance, tolerance, and sense of confidence in their new skills.

He lived like a young Werther, Goethe's character, with dramatic storm and stress in his daily life. He imagined that he was extraordinary. He took Kubizek to visit Parliament. They enjoyed watching the anti-Semitic Mayor of Vienna speak directly to the masses. He joined the Anti-Semitic League and wanted Kubizek to do likewise.

At this time before he had experienced sex, he began to think that war and prostitution should be outlawed. He walked down the street of a red light district denouncing the problems of society that fostered prostitution. Kubizek wrote that Adolf never masturbated nor accepted dates with prostitutes, and he hated homosexuality.

Kubizek spent the summer of 1908 with his family so Adolf moved to another apartment. He attended art classes but his work was too poor to take the art final exams. He was told to apply to the School of Architecture. However, he could not attend without a diploma from his high school.

He wrote in *Mein Kampf* that this rejection made him hard and took him out of the life of a "milksop." He wrote that he was forced to enter the "world of misery and poverty, where he became acquainted with the people on whose behalf he would afterward wage his struggle."

In actuality, his inheritance was running out. He couldn't afford to attend operas. He went to a homeless shelter for five days. There he met Reinhold Hanisch who showed him how beggars survived. They went to live in a house for poor men for some months. He painted postcards and posters that Hanisch sold for a pittance to support the two of them. When Adolf preferred to read newspapers and leave postcard orders unfulfilled, he lost clients. This forced him to move out of the poor house.

He stayed a few days with a Hungarian Jew who gave him a coat, as well as room and board. He made a police report accusing Hanisch of selling his works and absconding with the money but the report had various lies. After an aunt died, he received a small inheritance.

Basically unemployed, he had time to read. He had become interested in the writings of Georg Von Schoenerer who advocated an all-German Reich. Von Schoenerer wanted to incorporate Austria, some of Poland, Bohemia, Switzerland, and Italy into a Reich that would dominate Europe for generations. Adolf also read about graphology, parapsychology, physiognomy, phrenology, telepathy and the power of the will. He read Adolf Josef Lang who wrote about the threats to the Aryan race by apelike inferior races such as the Slavs and Jews. The beauty of the pure Aryan race in physiognomy captured Adolf's artistic sensibilities.

2

Military Career

Adolf went to visit his half-brother, Alois, in Liverpool, England. He expected Alois' family to wait on him as his mother had and he did not lift a hand to help. He created an unfavorable impression except that he played with their toddler. He discussed learning English and settling in England or America.

Alois was unaware at first that Adi had gone to England to avoid military service. He soon learned that Adolf had been using his dead younger brother's birth certificate so he could dodge the Austrian draft. The authorities had learned of his lies and were on the lookout for him so he decided to leave Austria. However, he left for Vienna after five months, having never learned English nor a trade.

In 1913, he was 24 and didn't know what he wanted to be or do. He left Vienna for Munich and took a small apartment. There he painted and read political books. He traded chores for breakfast with his landlords. He told them that there would soon be a war. He stated that his lack of a trade would make no difference in a war. He also confided to them that he thought the seed of athletic men could provide a seed bank of formidable potency. This revelation, described many years later by the landlords, suggests that Hitler could not distinguish between things that were too intimate to discuss with mere acquaintances. His frankness and radical ideas shocked many people.

On January 10, 1914, the Austrian police served a summons for him to report on January 20th in Linz for jail because he had evaded military service. On January 19, a lawyer helped him write a letter that described why he should not be imprisoned. He lied that he had only just received the summons the day before, that he didn't live in Linz, so didn't know they were trying to reach him.

He wrote, "I earn my living independently as a painter…With regard to my failure to report for military service in the autumn of

1909, I must say that this was for me an endlessly bitter time…For two long years I had no other mistress than sorrow and need…I nevertheless kept my name clean, had a blameless record with the law, and possessed a clear conscience except for that one constantly remembered fact that I failed to register for military service…It would seem that a moderate fine would be ample penance…I request that this affair may not be made unduly difficult for me."

They did not imprison him but sent him for a military physical in Salzburg on February 5, 1914. Physicians wrote, "Unfit for combatant and auxiliary duty, too weak, unable to bear arms." However, when Archduke Ferdinand was assassinated June 28th, 1914, Hitler was inspired to get involved. He requested permission to serve in a Bavarian regiment to fight for Germany. Fighting for Germany, he would not be serving his father's land or "fatherland" where he had suffered so much criticism and humiliation. His loneliness and aimlessness came to an end when he entered the military.

He continued to draw pictures while he served. He won medals in his rank as a corporal, where he was a dispatch runner. Later he said he was a front-line soldier but he only ran up to deliver messages. He began service in August 1914, and kept a notebook. He excitedly wrote his lawyer in 1915 about an attack by the English, a counter-attack by the Germans, and being one of four dispatchers awarded the Iron Cross second class. His superior was wounded. Hitler wrote, "This was the most terrible moment of my life. We worshiped Lt. Col. Engelhardt." Engelhardt wrote later saying that Hitler had used his own body to protect and shield his commanding officer from enemy fire.

Hitler won four more medals, one of which was the Iron Cross first class for carrying a message across heavily shelled ground. It was a Jew, Lt. Hugo Gutmann, who recommended him for the Iron Cross.

The war was giving Hitler's life purpose. He began to criticize the German high command, feeling that they didn't know how to win. He believed an iron will was the answer. This was partly because he was reading Schopenhauer's *The World As Will and Idea* during the war.

In the battle of the Somme, Germans were resting when an English shell hit their dugout in October 1916. Some were killed and Hitler received a shell splinter in the face. Shortly, a shell fragment hit his thigh while he was running a dispatch route. Litter bearers got him and he returned to Germany by train. He recovered after two months. He wanted to return to action and despised soldiers who maimed themselves to avoid duty. He loved war and finally had solidified his identification as a man rather than a dilettante.

In fall 1917, his troop learned that the Russian front had collapsed. Lenin had brought about a revolution in Russia. When he heard of a German munitions workers strike, he told others he thought Jews, Marxists and the Kaiser were behind it.

Nobody sent Hitler letters or presents and he declined offers from soldiers to share their gifts. He kept himself apart from their conversations. He did not salute Gutmann, the Jew who got him the Iron Cross, saying Jews got the cushy jobs. He criticized women, officers, soldiers, Jews, Masons and creature comforts. He now believed he was tougher than others, could endure more and needed less pampering. He continued his art and painted a sunken road, a farmhouse, buildings shattered by the war, churches, and soldiers, including him, marching.

President Wilson asked Congress to declare war on Germany on April 2, 1917.

That same day, George M. Cohan wrote the memorable *Over There*. The Americans entered World War I in 1917.

On October 13, 1918, chlorine gas flowed into the trenches and blinded Hitler. The Germans surrendered a month later on November 11. The Kaiser left Germany. In December, Hitler was one of the soldiers who volunteered to guard a prisoner of war camp at Traunstein.

He began to attend councils for soldiers, workers and peasants. He worried that Jews planned to seize power all over the world. He had read of some Jews leading movements in Germany and other countries. He wrote in *Mein Kampf* that he tried to persuade soldiers not to fight for Jews and was arrested for this on April 26, 1919. He informed on soldiers that sympathized with the Soviet Army. This generated his release from jail and he became an undercover agent. He began to spy on the German Army and report on fellow soldiers.

He took a course at the University of Munich, which taught that the German race was the master race. One day in class, a student protested the anti-Semitic view proposed by the professor. Hitler defended the professor's view and the audience was enthralled at this, his first public speech.

He was invited to indoctrinate soldiers about Jews and "the insanity of the bloody Soviet dictatorship." Hitler gradually came to be seen as an expert on the "Jewish problem."

He wrote on September 16, 1919, about the proper attitude to be cultivated toward Jews. "We are faced with the fact that there lives among us a non-German alien race which does not want...to renounce the emotions, ideas and aspirations peculiar to it, yet nevertheless possesses the same political privileges that we do. The emotions of the Jews remain purely materialist...Their power is the power of money, which in the form of interest endlessly and effortlessly increases...Rational anti-Semitism must be directed toward a methodological legal struggle against them and elimination of the privileges they possess...The final aim must be the deliberate removal of the Jews."

German military authorities got wind of the German Workers Party, a small political party started by Anton Drexler. It was later known as the National Soziealistiche Deutsche Arbeiter Partei (NSDAP). Some 40 railway men joined for nationalism, anti-Semitism, and support for the war. The enemies were Jews, strikers, war profiteers, Bolsheviks and malingerers. Adolf was asked to investigate the party by his superiors in 1919 and became a card-carrying member after one month. This was the beginning of his path to power.

3

Love Life

If Adolf had any confusion about his sexual orientation, it began to be resolved when he had a platonic love affair at age 17. He gazed at a beautiful young girl who used to stroll with her mother. He never dared to speak to her for fear of rejection. He asked his friend Kubizek to investigate and learned that her name was Stephanie. He wrote her many poems and became jealous when he saw her flirting or walking with another man.

He told Kubizek that he was sharing glances with her, and that she could read his mind and knew he was in love with her. This fantasy suggested a regression to his childhood. He probably felt that his mother, like all good mothers, could read his mind because she cared for his needs before he could express himself well.

He was inhibited and thought he could not introduce himself to Stephanie because he had no occupational credentials. According to Kubizek, he thought of kidnapping her or killing himself by jumping off a bridge into the Danube, or going to college and then claiming her. He was desperate to learn how to participate in romantic love.

Nothing came of that relationship. Following that, Hitler apparently had occasional short flings with women amounting to little until 1929.

At age 40, he was receiving donations from his political work. He maintained a simple life in a two-room apartment but had a Mercedes-Benz and a chauffeur. On income tax reports, he called himself a writer and listed only income from *Mein Kampf* (to be discussed later) and omitted his donations.

On September 15, 1929, he took a nine-room apartment and hung his own watercolors on the walls. His half-sister, Angela, then a 46-year-old widow, became the house supervisor of employees. Angela's daughter, known as Geli, had the bedroom next to Hitler. She was 21 and her spontaneity and seeming lack of guile attracted Hitler. Distrustful people are often attracted to those who are trusting, guileless, and adoring.

Hitler loved her and threatened other men who showed interest in her. Despite this, he kept her at arm's length. He feared intimacy too much to share himself with her deeply. His love was limited mainly to lust and passion but he did try to help her make more of herself. He encouraged her to take singing lessons, but this met with little success. He drew her in the nude and even made obscene drawings. Some said he whipped her with his bullwhip. She was a self-indulgent, ambition-less, hotheaded young woman by all accounts.

On September 18, 1931, she and Hitler quarreled long and loudly just before he drove off to give a speech. After he left, she shot herself in the heart with Hitler's revolver. Servants discovered the body. Rudolf Hess and a doctor helped Hitler avoid a detailed investigation. Authorities concluded that suicide was the cause of death.

It was said that Geli and Adolf argued because she wanted to go to Vienna and Uncle Adolf didn't want her to go. Others said that she argued with Uncle Adolf about a young man she wanted to date.

After her death, he kept to himself for two weeks, and got permission to enter Austria to visit her grave. He visited again seven years later when he entered Austria in triumph. He carried her picture and kept her room just as it was. He had her portrait painted from a photograph and her bust sculpted. When he no longer had to risk intimacy, he could idealize her and their relationship.

Eva Braun became his mistress in 1932, five months after Geli's suicide. Eva resembled Geli in movement. Few people knew of Adolf's relationship with Eva because he required such discretion. Eva was jealous of his adoration of Geli and had heard of her suicide. She tried to shoot herself after a few frustrating months with the ever-absent Hitler. Three years later, she tried to overdose on sleeping pills because she believed Hitler was unfaithful to her. In 1936, he gave her a villa and a Mercedes-Benz, and she lived in the villa with her sister.

In 1939, "Hitler maidens" were created to exemplify Hitler's myth about the Aryan race and their purity. He was always gracious with them, smiled, kissed their hands and bowed deeply.

In Hitler's will, Eva was listed as the first beneficiary after the bulk of estate was left to the party. He left annuities to Eva, his sister, his half sister and a monetary gift to his half brother.

4

Path to Power

A member of Adolf's new party won favor with Hitler by writing about him. He described Hitler as a German savior, a common soldier, and a bachelor who needed no women because of his mission. He told how Hitler quoted the Bible, Cicero, Strato, and yet used gutter language. Shortly, Adolf addressed a crowd of 2,000 at the Hofbrauhaus on February 24, 1920, on behalf of the NSDAP.

In 1921, some of the NSDAP party founders wanted Hitler to listen to them instead of dictating to the party. He left for six weeks, during which attendance fell. When he came back and threatened to resign, they begged him to stay. Behind the scenes, he agreed to return if he was given dictatorial powers. He wanted to purge the party of foreign elements and those opposed to him. However, when he gave speeches, he said that he had no ambition to run the party but just wanted to serve Germany.

On July 29, 1921, he invented a new title for himself. First he was "Unser Fuehrer" (our leader). Later he became "Fuehrer" and then "Der Fuehrer."

Julius Streicher and Hermann Goring joined his party, which now had 4,500 members. In 1922, Hitler asked for "storm troopers" to break up political meetings, beat up Jews and communists, kill enemies, and destroy Berlin's government. By the end of 1922, he had approximately 400 storm troopers. They were the progenitors of the armies of SA and SS troops.

On August 16, 1922, he was invited to speak to 40,000 people in the Munich town square. His storm troopers marched in with two bands. When he spoke to the crowd, he rationalized the overthrow of the Berlin government. When he planned a march on Berlin, he was threatened with arrest. So he ceased and went to Berchtesgarten to make plans. He promised authorities that he would not attempt a coup, but he lied. Lies and rationalizations became habits as he dealt with obstacles or planned his coups.

On September 18, 1922, Hitler referred to World War I in a speech. He challenged Germany saying, "It cannot be that two million Germans should have fallen in vain...No, we do not pardon, we demand vengeance."

Hitler and his storm troopers went into a beer hall rally. He announced that he was taking over the government. The following morning his men marched on the center of Munich. As shots were fired in the melee, his shoulder became dislocated and the coup was thwarted.

He was arrested two days later and imprisoned for high treason on November 11, 1923. At his trial, he testified that he was a destined leader meant to destroy Marxism. He said, "You may judge us guilty a thousand times over, but the Goddess of Eternal Justice will smile and tear to tatters the brief of the state's attorney and the verdict of this court. For She acquits us!" Castro would later use similar words at his trial in Cuba. Hitler and three others were given five-year sentences and the rest were given lesser terms.

Prison life was not difficult for Hitler. He received gifts, food and wine to bribe guards, and exemptions such as having visitors at any time. His chauffeur and his secretary Rudolf Hess were allowed to live with him, and he was allowed to read his writings to other prisoners.

He wrote *Mein Kampf* (my struggle or my battle) while in prison. It described him, what he planned to do, and outlined his desire to conquer the world. He expressed his hatred of Jews, extolled the purity of the German race, and proposed the need for living space to the East.

He wrote that these tasks required a supreme authority (himself) and propaganda to set up the proper atmosphere in the country.

The warden at Landsberg Prison commuted Hitler's sentence saying, "Hitler has shown himself to be an orderly, disciplined prisoner. He is taken up with the writing of his book to defray expenses incurred at the time of his trial. He proposes to refound and reanimate his movement, but in the future proposes not to run counter to authorities." Hitler was released December 20, 1924, having been detained approximately 1½ years.

He held his first public meeting of the National Socialist German Workers Party on February 27, 1925. He spoke on his usual topic to return fallen Germany to her state of grace from the evils of enemies such as Jews and Bolsheviks. He offered himself as the savior of a purified and avenged Germany. He added a new theme of the lost sheep returning to the fold. This suggested that he would forgive people who submitted themselves to a greater power, namely his power. The man who was so overlooked as a child was finally arranging for his own glorification.

Hitler's party got only 12 seats in 1928 out of the 491 seats in the Reichstag. His strange appearance and repetitious speeches made him a laughable figure by comedians. But unemployment rose because of many unsecured loans and business bankruptcies. The more misery, the more his promises appealed to people. Germany became unable to continue paying reparations from World War I. That helped start the stock market crash that shook New York in 1929. The 1930 election brought Hitler's party 107 seats. Symbols of his party included a swastika flag, an arm's-length salute, brown shirts imitating Mussolini's black shirts and the "Heil Hitler" greeting.

In 1930, Hitler ran against Hindenburg for the presidency and got only 30% of the vote. Hindenburg got 50% and other candidates got the rest. The president needed an absolute majority so a re-run gave Hitler 36.8% and Hindenburg got 53%. Hitler asked Hindenburg to appoint him Chancellor of the Reich and Prime Minister of Prussia.

Hindenburg declined but offered him Vice Chancellor. Hitler refused the position.

Hitler was interviewed by three foreign correspondents including American H. V. Kaltenborn. When Kaltenborn asked why he was so antagonistic to Jews, he became furious. "You have a Monroe Doctrine...You exclude any would-be immigrants you do not care to admit...We demand the same right." He added, "Dictatorship is justified if the people declare their confidence in one man and ask him to lead."

Kaltenborn wrote, "No one who preaches autocracy can lead the German people to anything but ruin."

In March 1933, the election gave Hitler 43.9% of the vote with 288 seats in the Reichstag. He did not have a clear mandate but called it a "colossal victory." Hitler wanted a law that put him above the law. It was called "Law for the Relief of the Distress of the People and the Reich."

On July 25, 1934, Hitler sent 150 men to kill the Austrian chancellor in Vienna while he attended an opera. They were quickly arrested.

On June 29, 1935, Hitler and his henchmen began to arrest SA (storm troopers) and replaced them with the SS (elite troops) in an action called "The Night of the Long Knives." The next day he gave orders for 150 SA soldiers to be executed by eight SS sharpshooters.

Hitler told the president of the Danzig Senate, "And behind my back they laughed at me and said I had no power...I've given them a cuff on the ear that they'll long remember." Hitler had finally found a lethal way to repay anyone who was opposed to him. Violent retaliation became one of his unhealthy methods to deal with problems.

When Hindenburg died a few days later, Hitler wanted no more elections. So he abolished the title of president and remained Fuehrer and Reich Chancellor. Soon after he became Chancellor, Nazi writers used to refer to him as the "unknown corporal" and "unknown soldier" since Germany never established an "unknown soldier" tomb like other countries. Soon Hitler referred to himself as the "unknown soldier." As he gradually referred to himself in the third person, he began to see himself as a divine person, godlike, and lost track of his human imperfections. He believed his own hype.

In the spring of 1936, German troops marched into the Rhineland and met no opposition. The Rhineland had promised not to remilitarize according to the Treaty of Versailles in World War I. Hitler lied again and said, "Germany has no further territorial claims of any sort in Europe." He continued lying because it had turned out to be such a successful ploy for him politically. People actually believed him and nobody lifted a finger to stop him.

German born Henry Kissinger wrote about Hitler's rise to power. He said, "When Hitler took over in Germany, he had a relatively easy task. He had only to rearm and reoccupy the Rhineland, and Eastern Europe lay defenseless before him. When France did not move following the occupation of the Rhineland, it was all over…By 1941 everyone knew that Hitler was a maniac bent on world domination—but the world paid for its insistence on psychological certainty with millions of lives."

Hitler attended the 1936 Olympic games in Berlin and claimed to be at peace with the world. Goebbels arranged a Party Day in Nuremberg with a drama like a Wagnerian opera. The hero, Hitler, was acting like Siegfried and waged war against the world. By this time, Hitler commonly wore a bulletproof vest and a pistol and had a bulletproof lectern. His appearances were like religious ceremonies as he sternly and stiffly exhorted the crowd with his speeches.

In 1937, he told his top six commanders that Germany deserved more living space. He proposed to act against Austria and Czechoslovakia before France and Britain could gain strength to prevent him. He decided to create a civil disturbance in Austria and send in German troops to restore order. In actuality, he had become consumed by a desire to prove his greatness by taking over the world, and simply rationalized to give his staff reasons to expand their conquest.

He met the Austrian Chancellor Schuschnigg on February 12, 1938. Hitler had learned intimidation at the hands of his own father. Thus he shouted at this calm, self-assured professional man. Hitler noted the Chancellor's fear and made a list of demands. The Chancellor said he hadn't the power to sign for Austria, and signed only an instrument of surrender. Schuschnigg returned to Austria and ordered a plebiscite to see if the public wanted to join Germany or remain independent. Hitler was furious and ordered the German army to march on Austria the day before the plebiscite. He reacted to having his wishes blocked with violent retaliation.

On March 12, 1938, troops and bombers descended upon Vienna. German soldiers arrested the Chancellor, and Hitler spent the night in Linz, his former home. He addressed the Linz public saying that providence had called him to restore his homeland to the German Reich. *Deutschland Uber Alles* was sung. Hitler visited with his old friend, Kubizek, and promised to build a new bridge, opera house, theater, and concert hall and make Linz one of the great cities in Greater Germany. Then Hitler entered Vienna, a city he told the Hitler Youth leader he loved, but told Goebbels that he wished they had resisted so he could have "shot the whole place to hell." He seemed to want to destroy Austria, the land of his earlier hurts.

5

Leadership Style

Sometimes, people wonder how Hitler managed to convince his associates to follow him. Hitler apparently imbued his male relationships with an almost romantic element. Goebbels was attracted to Hitler's decisive and emotional speeches in 1926. He switched over to Hitler's side at that time, and addressed the party on Hitler's birthday. Goebbels said, "He is 37…Adolf Hitler, I love you because you are both great and simple."

Goebbels, an unattractive man with a clubfoot, was delighted when Hitler suggested they vacation together. He wrote of Hitler on July 24, 1926, "He is like a child, kind, good, merciful. Like a cat, cunning, clever, agile. Like a lion, roaring and great and gigantic." Hitler followed this with giving Goebbels red roses (a romantic type of gift) and leadership of the Berlin branch of the party.

Hitler impressed the poor and the ignorant. He often invoked providence and spoke as if he were in direct communication with God. He said, "I believe that it was God's will to send a boy from here into the Reich, to let him grow up, to raise him to be the leader of the nation so as to enable him to lead back his homeland into the Reich." He was allowing his fantasies of greatness to devour him.

A communist in a private vendetta over a homosexual lover killed one of Hitler's storm troopers named Horst Wessel. His killing was depicted by Nazi propaganda as a political assassination and Wessel became a Nazi hero. The *Horst Wessel Lied* was Wessel's poem set to a sailor's marching song and became the most rousing Nazi party song.

"Banner up! With ranks tightly closed,
The SA (storm troopers) marches with calm, firm step.
Comrades shot by the Red Front
And reactionaries march with us in spirit.
Clear the streets for the brown battalions,
Clear the streets for the storm troopers.
Filled with hope, millions already look toward the swastika.
The day of freedom and bread dawns.
Blow the roll call for the last time,
We all stand ready for the fight.
Soon Hitler flags will flutter over all streets,
Servitude will only last a short time longer."

Hitler often described those whom he opposed as evil. "I see in Herr Schuschnigg one of those forces who wish to create evil...and on me the grace was given on the day of the betrayal (Schuschnigg's call for a plebiscite) to unite my homeland with the Reich." It was Hitler who was evil, but he projected this onto his enemy in Austria. Did Hitler believe he was good and others were evil in a sort of deluded state of mind? Or did he realize that he was lying and just hoped everyone would believe him? Either way, his strategy worked because stunned leaders could not use logic against a seemingly illogical man.

Hitler's weapons were surprise, cunning and terror. In May 1938, he was preparing a fall invasion to take the Sudetenland of Czechoslovakia. Two million people, many of whom had German ancestry, inhabited the Sudetenland. That little democracy was an obstacle in Hitler's long term plan to take over the Soviet Union. When his intended victims decided to mobilize, Hitler acted humiliated. He used propaganda to pretend that the Czechoslovaks were arresting Germans. In this instance, he was simply being dishonest to get his way.

Alarmed at Hitler's intentions toward the Sudetenland, English Prime Minister Neville Chamberlain visited him to discuss this. After listening to hours of Hitler's emotional monologues, Chamberlain decided to leave, realizing that Hitler was set on invading Czechoslovakia. But Chamberlain appeared to believe that this was the extent of Hitler's goals. The chances are that he personally feared Hitler's wrath and hoped Hitler would set no further goals.

Czechoslovakia could find no allies to come to her aid and conceded at Chamberlain's recommendation. On September 22, 1938, Chamberlain agreed to a slow takeover of the Sudetenland. Then Hitler began screaming irrationally that it must take place immediately. Hitler seemed terribly impatient and like a child who wants what he wants when he wants it.

Chamberlain could not discuss things with the emotional Hitler. So he went to his hotel and offered the next day to mediate between Germany and Czechoslovakia. Hitler issued a memorandum of takeover within 48 hours. Chamberlain was offended and called it an ultimatum. Hitler said he would permit the takeover to be delayed three more days. Chamberlain left for England as if he had won an argument.

By this time, Hitler was convinced that if he sounded loud, crazy, irrational and scary, others could not reason with him and would let him have his way. He often used this same tactic with his staff when they tried to advise him to re-think some plan.

When Hitler heard that Czechoslovakia had not agreed to be taken over immediately, he ranted and raved about their leader, scholar Dr. Benes. In some sort of envy of the well-educated man, he accused Benes of wandering around the world while Hitler had fought at the front lines in WWI. In an emotional speech in which he seemed to have lost control of himself, he screamed on September 27, "This is the last territorial claim I have to make in Europe, but it is the claim from which I will not recede and which, God willing, I will make good."

Hitler, Daladier, Mussolini and Chamberlain signed the Munich Pact on September 29, 1938. Terms of the Pact included evacuation beginning October 1st and completion by October 10th. Hitler held a banquet to celebrate the Pact. He was proud that this victory cost Germany no soldiers since it was won by blackmail, terror and intimidation. Only Mussolini dined with him. The French and British representatives did not join him.

Five weeks later, Hitler began his battle against the Jews on Kristallnacht. It was so named because of the broken glass of Jewish shop windows on the night of the pogrom. Over $23 million worth of damage was done that night throughout the whole of Germany. Not only SS soldiers but also German citizens everywhere participated. The world was stunned.

Hitler stated that his three political goals were the unification of the German people, the destruction of Jews in Germany and the destruction of Bolshevism. In 1939, he was 50 years old and probably felt the need to hurry along. He felt that Poland would fall easily because weak noblemen ruled it. He thought Russia would crumble readily because Stalin's purges of Russian generals left the army leaderless. But his next objective was Czechoslovakia. He was bolstered by his success in the Sudetenland.

He invaded while the Czech president and foreign minister were visiting with him, on March 15, 1939. He told them to order no resistance if they wanted to avoid bloodshed. He carried on emotionally about the mistreatment of Germans and the disregard for the German minority in the Sudetenland. Goring threatened to bomb Prague.

The Czech president, Dr. Emil Hacha, fainted, and was revived by a physician. He was ordered to call his Army and order no resistance to the invasion. He then signed an agreement to "lay the fate of the Czech people and country in the hands of the Fuehrer of the German Reich." Germany took control of Czechoslovakia without a shot being fired. Hitler's emotionality won over men who had been trained to be logical.

Hitler went by train to Prague and in the Hradcany castle, beat his chest like a gorilla as his generals watched. He sailed to the Baltic six days later to watch the surrender of Memel, a fortress city given to Lithuania in the Versailles Treaty. He promised that no power on earth would ever separate Germans again.

World War II grew out of World War I. Germans were still angry that they had to give up Alsace/Lorraine to France after WWI, which they acquired in 1870-71. They were still upset that they had to surrender Silesia and West Prussia after the war to the newly reconstituted Poland. They were also humiliated when their army was reduced to a small contingent, and their fleets and air force were abolished, and they lost all their colonies in Africa and the Pacific. The occupation by the French and British and the reparation policies following WWI eroded German pride. Hitler used these insults as he rallied Germans to his point of view.

On April 28, 1939, Hitler gave a speech avoiding Franklin Roosevelt's invitation to sign a ten-year non-aggression pact in return for improved trading terms. He said, "Mr. Roosevelt, I have endeavored to attain all this (reunification of Germans) without spilling blood…I, who 21 years ago was an unknown worker and soldier of my people, have attained this." He was cleverly saying that non-aggression was part of his strategy because he had shed no blood, but he was really dodging the pact because he intended to use aggression against more countries.

When Hitler established the policy to remove Jews, he used the powerful emotion of envy to turn Germans against them. The German worker under Hitler resented the wealthier, educated, cultured Jew. Poor German soldiers might have little education or money, but now they could belong to a new aristocracy, the Aryan race.

Hitler's favorite composer was Richard Wagner and he often had Wagner's music performed at party rallies and functions. It was not only Wagner's music that appealed to Hitler but his anti-Semitic views. Wagner wrote a book called *Judaism in Music* in which he insisted that Jews poisoned public taste in arts. Wagner founded the Bayreuth festival, which was used as a Nazi propaganda tool against the Jews during the 1930s and 1940s.

Hitler did not stop at purging his society of Jews, however. As many as 220,000 homosexuals and 173,500 handicapped people may have finally been exterminated, not including East Europeans, Slavs and Gypsies.

In 1939, Hitler issued an order to kill the incurables in hospitals to make room for his soldiers. He had the sick and insane sent to prisons and allowed to starve. Gas chambers of exhaust fumes sped up the deaths somewhat and the following spring, they were disguised as shower rooms. Hitler had come to a point in life where he lied to anyone to get his own wishes fulfilled. He had lost all sense of morals and had not even the most basic need to be good for fear of being caught or punished. Nobody could stop him or punish him.

Hitler used secret agreements with world leaders to keep them from becoming enemies. On August 23, 1939, he signed a non-aggression pact with the Soviets to keep from facing war on two fronts. He secretly promised to give them Eastern Poland, Finland, Estonia,

Latvia, Rumanian Bessarabia and soon added Lithuania. This was a more beneficial arrangement for the Soviet Union than pacts with Britain or France that yielded no territories. It was not until 1989 that *Pravda* acknowledged for the first time that Hitler and Stalin had secretly and illegally divided Eastern Europe into these spheres of influence.

After Hitler obtained the German-Soviet Pact, he ordered a few prisoners to be drugged and shot near the German border, attired in Polish uniforms on August 31st. The next morning, he spoke about Polish attacks on German territory to justify attacking Poland. September 1, 1939, Germany began to bomb Polish cities, took Lithuania and gave Estonia and Latvia to Russia. Two days later, England delivered an ultimatum to Germany.

Within a month, Hitler told his generals that he would attack Britain, France, Russia, Holland and Belgium. He said, "I want to destroy the enemy...In all modesty I must say that I am irreplaceable. I am convinced of the power of my intellect and decision...The fate of the Reich depends only on me."

In view of his success thus far, his associates were awed, intimidated, and believed him. He led, they followed, and there was no discussion or sharing of goals to be done. Hitler was a tyrant, but only because his subordinates feared losing position if they engaged him in debate.

Mussolini thought that Hitler would become closer to Stalin than he was. He wrote, warning Hitler of the consequences if this were to happen. Hitler did not answer for two months, allowing Mussolini to remain anxious. When they met on March 18, 1940, Hitler raved about his victories. Mussolini just listened to the monologue. He then agreed to finish off France if Germany had sufficiently weakened French forces.

Hitler and his generals planned a surprise attack on Norway and Denmark using ships flying British flags. The attack began April 9, 1940 in Copenhagen harbor. With little resistance, the German Empire now extended to the Arctic Circle.

In May, Germany attacked Belgium and Holland. The French and British, who had replaced Chamberlain with Churchill, were unable to protect Belgium and Holland. Hitler gloated at the signing of the armistice document when Paris fell in June of 1940. He bragged that he would redesign Berlin with the grandeur of Paris in the future.

Curiously, Hitler had held back his forces proclaiming respect for the British and French. He said that he wanted to seek peace with them because the British Empire should survive as a stabilizing influence in the world. Perhaps his wish to spare Britain was connected with his enjoyable visit there.

He spoke of wanting to use English men as slave labor. He discussed bringing in English women to mate with SS officers to produce a new race of Anglo-Germans. These sexual offerings were part of Hitler's erotic appeal to his men. He promised that the intelligentsia and Jews would be liquidated, and this appealed on an even baser level of human envy and retaliation.

When Hitler's soldiers disliked him, it was not because of his terrible policies but because he interfered in military operations. Sometimes his orders resulted in needless deaths. Additionally, they disliked Hitler's lies about the reasons for a course of action. They also feared disagreement with him and feared countermanding his orders. Many of his generals were filled with ideals of honor, and were horrified at the massacre of Jews, priests, intellectuals and aristocrats in Poland, and later in the Soviet Union.

In December 1940, Hitler instructed the Luftwaffe Air Corps to move to Italy to help extricate Mussolini from his military quagmires in North Africa and Greece. The following month, he met Franco and asked Spain to enter the war in return for Gibraltar and colonial territories in Africa. In their nine-hour meeting, Hitler talked seven hours and was exasperated when he felt he had achieved nothing. Describing the meeting to Mussolini, he said, "Rather than go through that again, I would prefer to have two or three teeth pulled out."

Hitler also had trouble with finesse and silence. Marshal Petain, the 84-year-old French hero of WWI, was silent and evasive, saying that France had suffered too much to mount an offensive against England. Hitler was perplexed when he could not rattle the old man. In the end, he thought he had persuaded Petain and promised Mussolini that Petain and southern French (Vichy) troops would help conquer General de Gaulle and the Free French underground.

When Hitler finally did attack the Soviet Union, he wanted an easy win. He met with Molotov in Berlin on November 12, 1940. They were to discuss how the world would be divided between Germany, Italy, Japan and the Soviet Union. Molotov asked hard questions like why German troops were in Finland only a few miles from the Soviet border. Hitler was claiming to have beaten England just as they had to go to a bomb shelter. Molotov said, "If England is beaten, why are we sitting in this shelter?" But when Molotov left for Moscow, Hitler knew Russia only wanted peace.

Stalin liked Hitler's invitation to the spoils of the British Empire. He was willing to agree if Germany withdrew from Finland. Behind Stalin's back, Hitler called him "a cold-blooded blackmailer." But as many said, "It takes one to know one."

On December 18, 1940, Hitler dictated, "The German Armed Forces must be prepared, even before the conclusion of the war against England, to crush Soviet Russia in a rapid campaign." His men thought he was too impatient, once again.

On March 30, 1941, Hitler lied to his generals. He said that he had evidence of a secret agreement between Russia and England in order to justify his plans to invade the Soviet Union. The war against England was for him a necessary evil. The war against Britain was never one of Hitler's original aims. So finally, in April 1941, he started the eastward campaign he had always desired. German night raids on England faded out in favor of Operation Barbarossa, the campaign against the Soviet Union and Bolshevism.

Meanwhile, Germany had conquered Yugoslavia and Greece by the end of April 1941. Every place the Germans advanced, they had to round up and murder Jews, then leave troops to occupy and administer the area. As they spread thin, resistance groups took hold in many countries. Hitler was obviously biting off more than he could chew.

The British learned the date of the secret invasion of Russia, June 22, 1941, and sent word to Stalin. Stalin could not believe that Hitler would betray him. He dismissed the warnings of a German attack and did not make preparations. As a result, the Soviets endured immense losses but had enough time to defend Leningrad. It did not fall as Kiev had. This was the beginning of a long hard campaign against the Russians and many stresses for Hitler.

6

Stresses

Hitler eventually realized the projected eight-week war on Russia would be much longer than he expected. Additionally, the Japanese attack on Pearl Harbor caused the entrance of the U.S. in the war. Then on December 11, 1941, Hitler declared war on the United States. He was finally realizing that he had to fight on too many fronts. But world events in Japan and the United States were taking away his control.

On December 12, 1941, he issued an order called Nacht und Nebel (Night and Fog). This was a psychological ploy to deter his enemies. He understood the tremendous fear of the unknown so told his subordinates to reveal little information about those taken prisoner. He said, "A more effective and lasting deterrent can be achieved only by the death penalty or by taking measures that will leave the family and the population uncertain as to the fate of the offender. Deportations to Germany will serve this purpose."

On April 26, 1942, he lied in a speech to the German public saying that Russia was defeated. This statement fulfilled his wish. Perhaps he expected a quick victory over Russia. But he was losing track of reality because he risked terrible embarrassment if the public found out that Russia had not been defeated. It was probably by 1942 that Hitler could no longer be considered of sound mind.

He gave himself a new title, Supreme Law Lord, and placed himself above the law. Earlier in December 1941, he had dismissed his commander in chief and took his place. When Hitler took command of the army from von Brauchitsch, he overestimated his own reputation as commander of the army. He was not attuned to the public sentiments. He erroneously believed that replacing von Brauchitsch with himself would steady the dwindling trust in German strength. Instead it hastened the loss of the Luftwaffe, which now occupied second place to the army. The war on two fronts, east (Russia) and west (Europe and America) was hard to sustain.

He met with Mussolini in the spring of 1942 and continued his lengthy monologues. Mussolini correctly realized that Hitler's monologues were his way of keeping anyone else from criticizing his ideas. Mussolini's aide and son-in-law, Ciano, wrote of the meeting: "Hitler talks, talks, talks, talks. Mussolini suffers—he, who is in the habit of talking himself, and who, instead, practically has to keep quiet."

Hitler, believing differently than his generals who knew the facts, thought that the Russians were in flight. By this time, his subordinates knew that he was in psychotic denial of German losses. Hitler came up with another supposedly clever psychological ploy, which he delighted in springing on his men as if he were more profound than they. He ordered attacks intended to embarrass Stalin on his namesake town of Stalingrad and oil fields at Grozny in the Caucasus.

Khrushchev was in charge of the defense of Stalingrad. The Germans had to fight in Stalingrad for five months against formidable Russian troops. When German generals asked Hitler's permission to withdraw, he told them to stand firm and await supplies for the 300,000 soldiers trapped in Stalingrad. Goring's Luftwaffe could not deliver the supplies. Other troops were ordered to move toward the trapped soldiers, despite Russian fortifications. The generals recorded Hitler's comments when they warned him that such a tactic would fail. He said, "It all would be interpreted as weakness." The one-time "milk-sop" did not want weakness to show, so great was the hatred for his former self.

The Soviets offered Germany an ultimatum to surrender in return for rations, medical treatment, keeping their rank and medals, and returning to Germany after the war. Hitler responded, "Surrender is impossible." Hitler's troops were furious but dared not confront him directly.

Finally, Col. General Friedrich Paulus lied to Hitler just as Hitler had lied to him about reinforcements that were supposed to arrive. Paulus said his men died for the Fuehrer. In actuality, the Russians captured them. Some 24 generals and 180,000 men were marched to Siberian prison camps where most did die. Hitler finally heard about the surrender and capture. He proclaimed that he wished that Paulus and the men had killed themselves.

Hitler ranted about how his soldiers should "have closed ranks, formed a hedgehog, and shot themselves to death with their last bullets. When you consider that a woman who has her pride goes out, shuts herself in her room, and immediately shoots herself just because someone has made a few insulting remarks, then I can have no respect for a soldier who is too frightened to do the same thing."

Hitler was, of course, referring to the suicide of his niece, Geli, after he argued with her. In his stress at losing so many men because of their "weakness," he was regressing. He inappropriately compared an angry woman who killed herself to get back at Hitler with soldiers facing certain death unless they surrendered. He had seen Geli's suicide as a sort of noble gesture of courage and believed that outnumbered soldiers should kill themselves in a similar fashion.

At this time, Hitler told Himmler that Jews should die in agony. He wanted to achieve revenge for military losses by making someone suffer as he himself was suffering emotionally. He studied death methods and decided freight cars with quicklime coating would inflict burns and excruciating agony before death over a lengthy four day period.

In October 1942, Hitler sent Goring to reassure Mussolini that the Germans would continue fighting. Mussolini harped on Rommel's oil crisis and the troublesome British base on Malta. The following month, Hitler sent a reluctant Rommel with Goring to see Il Duce. He wanted Rommel to explain himself. Mussolini advised the two that they should call off their pointless war against Russia. Rommel felt similarly but did not tell that to Mussolini.

In January 1943, Hitler decided to break up the capital navy ships because he felt they were outmoded and unsuitable for a fast-moving war. The Commander-in-Chief of the Navy resigned and U-boat specialist Admiral Donitz became his successor. However, by the end of April, the majority of U-boats had not returned from their missions. In this, as in so many of Hitler's decisions, he ignored the advice of his men and made his decisions alone and against their wishes.

On July 10, the allies landed in Sicily. Allied fighter planes from Malta and North Africa attacked German bases in the south of Italy and Sicily. Hitler ordered, "Not one German soldier must leave the island...Europe and Germany are being defended in Sicily." He insisted that no soldier flee, surrender or show any weakness, on behalf of him. He had come to feel that the world judged him by the behavior of his troops.

On July 19, 1943, Hitler flew to Mussolini and lectured him for two hours about defending everything to the last man and the last bullet. He admonished Mussolini saying that the Italians were not disciplined. He stated that he would give them no more tanks unless Germans occupied Italy and took over. Mussolini wanted to surrender and end the war.

A few days later, Hitler called Goring to tell him that Mussolini had resigned and that Badoglio had replaced him. Hitler sent SS troops to pluck Mussolini out but soon realized that without an army, Mussolini was nothing. Uncertainty about Italy lay heavy on the Hitler administration. The new Italian administration was even harder for Hitler to handle when Badoglio requested six times the tons of grain that Mussolini had requested.

Hitler still hoped to win the war in Europe by use of new submarines and rocket bombs that would fall on London. On June 6, 1944, the allies sped toward Normandy but information about the landing leaked. The German command had come to a point where they kept things from Hitler so that they could make their own decisions. Nobody woke Hitler and no resistance plans were made. Thus the Normandy invasion gave Hitler real problems.

He met with Rommel who asked to withdraw behind the Seine to develop a trap for the allies. Hitler would not allow retreat. Rommel noted that Hitler had tasters try his food before eating at mealtime. Hitler had realized that he could no longer trust his own staff after five attempts on his life.

On July 20, 1944, some generals made the sixth attempt to kill Hitler using a time bomb. Other attempts failed because Hitler continually kept his timetable a secret. Of the 24 men in the room, after the bomb went off, four were dead or dying. Hitler's legs and right arm were burned, and his eardrums were cracked. But he walked out.

Within hours, Hitler met with Mussolini who had been flown in from Italy. Adolf showed Mussolini the room where the bomb exploded. He assured him that German fighter production and new jets would soon mop up the enemy in Normandy.

Conspiratorial suspects of the July 20th bombing were given the choice to be shot or kill themselves. Hitler addressed the nation by radio and assured them that he was alive and that the usurpers were to be ignored or arrested. Some 7,000 were arrested and 2,000 death sentences were issued. Hitler wanted the main conspirators to be hung on piano wires from meat hooks and filmed. He wanted an execution that yielded the most pain. With little else to gloat about, he watched their agony with sadistic pleasure. Despite executions and arrests, he continued to suspect his generals and had become extremely paranoid, with good reason.

He lost confidence in the Luftwaffe and had taken over control of turbojet production, in search of a "blitz bomber." By August 1944, production figures had to be brought to him each week. He checked them with distrust and made the allocations personally. He shared decisions with nobody. In fact, when he found that SS generals like Himmler were meddling in the production of jet planes and V-weapons, he was enraged.

In November, 1944, having run out of able-bodied men, Hitler had formed a plan for the Hitler Youth. Boys 16 through 18 were to pilot the new Volksfighter, to defend the Reich without any training in power flying or any fighter pilot schooling. Fortunately, the crash of the first commander of a jet-fighter unit put an end to this plan.

The plan to use untrained children suggested that Hitler was ready to take down his entire nation with him in defeat. He no longer saw the war as separate from himself. He believed that if he could not survive as a winner, he and all Germans should perish. The degree of his embarrassment for being weak was of monumental proportions. This sensitive rigid man who had been raised so sternly by an aging authoritarian father was now paying back an entire people for his own early discomfort at not fitting into normal society.

He told his generals in desperation on December 12, 1944, that the allies had diverse aims and would crumble under pressure. His men no longer believed his delusions and rampant lies. He exploded in rages, cursed them, twitched, drooled, limped, shook, and ordered them to continue to fight. He didn't want to lose any land that Germans had taken even though the allies had now re-taken many areas.

In February, 1945, he said, "I have been Europe's last hope. To take her I had to use violence." On March 19, he said, "If the war is to be lost, the nation will also perish...It is better to destroy that and to destroy it ourselves."

He ordered that factories and supply armories, railroads, bridges, water and electrical plants and communications be blown up rather than fall into enemy hands. His people began to take over more of his duties, listening to his orders without carrying them out. He now muttered to himself incomprehensibly. On April 20, he was 56. Roosevelt had died eight days earlier. Eva Braun came to "share his fate," she said.

On April 25, Goring wrote that he was going to General Eisenhower with an offer of surrender and would assume "the total leadership of the Reich with complete freedom of action at home and abroad."

He was carrying out a decree of 1941, which appointed him as Hitler's successor. Martin Bormann said Goring should be stripped of titles and tried. Hitler agreed and said he'd always known Goring was lazy, corrupt, incompetent, and a lifelong drug addict. Hitler wrote a letter forbidding Goring to act for him.

On April 27, Hitler told Goebbels why he stayed in Berlin. "I remain for the reason that I thereby have a greater moral right to act against weakness…The captain goes down with his ship."

He asked his valet to burn his body and personal possessions after he killed himself. When it no longer mattered, he decided to fulfill a promise to Eva Braun. He granted her wish to die married. About midnight, a justice of the peace married Adolf and Eva. After champagne and food, he said, "Death will be a relief for me. I have been betrayed and deceived by everyone."

He dictated his testament, left his paintings for an art gallery in Linz, and made Bormann the executor of his mementos. He left money and belongings to his half-brother and sisters, Eva's mother, his co-workers and his secretaries. He also stipulated that what he possessed belonged to the Party, or if the Party no longer existed, to the State.

He left a "political testament" as well. He wrote, "In these three decades only love for my people and loyalty to my people have guided me in all my thoughts, actions and life. War was desired and instigated exclusively by those international statesmen who are either of Jewish origin or working for Jewish interests." He expelled Goring and Himmler in his political testament for "their secret negotiations with the enemy, without my knowledge or approval, and by their illegal attempts to seize power."

He added, "I ask the commanders of the army, navy and air force to strengthen by all possible means the spirit of resistance of our soldiers in the spirit of National Socialism, emphasizing especially that I too, as founder and creator of this movement, have preferred death to cowardly flight or even capitulation."

Potassium cyanide poison was tested on Hitler's dog, and after her death, her newborn pups were shot. The radio news broadcast Mussolini's death by partisans along with his mistress. Then Hitler shook hands with some twenty people assembled for a leave taking. Down the hall, the SS officers were having an orgy with naked girls, as they often did, and made too much noise. Hitler ordered them to stop.

Hitler and Eva were alone in their room. Hitler had a bullet hole in his temple. Eva had bitten the vial of potassium cyanide. Someone took a picture of Hitler with a picture of his mother on his chest. The bodies were taken upstairs to be burned using gasoline. Hitler died on April 30, 1945, wanting to outwit his enemies and avoid agony and humiliation. Many have said that in the end, he resorted to his early cowardly ways of avoiding pain and loss of self-esteem by his suicide.

7

Accomplishments

Hitler ended unemployment in Germany by creating World War II, just as Roosevelt ended the Depression with World War II. Hitler therefore also ended unemployment in other countries. In 1939, the year war came to Europe, nine and a half million Americans were unemployed. That was 17% of the labor force. Almost as many

(14.6%) were still unemployed the following year. The war then doubled and redoubled expenditures, and before the end of 1942, unemployment was minimal. In fact, in many places, labor was scarce. There is, of course, a moral difference between spending for welfare and spending for war.

Another positive result from Hitler's regime was the German autobahn. Seen by General Eisenhower, it became the model for the United States interstate highway system.

8

Summary

Adolf's father was an old authoritarian civil servant who seemed scary and critical of Adi's art interest before he died in Adolf's 13th year. The family moved so many times in Adolf's first eight years that he couldn't form close friendships. This plus his distant and fearsome father left the boy unable to trust others. He feared rejection for not being manly or talented. His mother, a young woman who died when Adolf was 18, apparently loved him dearly but could not control the defiant young teen.

The undisciplined boy, a dilettante without a job, was left to drift about without a clear sexual or occupational identity. Finding himself capable of running errands and informing on fellow soldiers in the war, he began to see himself in a more manly way. Early on, he placed women and his mother on a pedestal and only later in life began to have sexual relations with them. He never reached intimacy in his sexual relations, unable to share himself for fear of rejection. His fear of being seen as weak by enemies made him require that his troops kill themselves rather than surrender.

In his maturation, he experienced deviations at every stage including distrust, shame and doubt, inferiority, role confusion, isolation, and despair.

He coped with stress by distorting or denying reality, regressing to earlier beliefs and behaviors, and violent fantasies to get even for perceived humiliations. He dreamed up horrible pain and retaliations for enemies, and tried to make others suffer as much as he felt he had suffered early in life. His leadership was tyrannical with almost no concern for his subordinates. He offered them promotions, medals, titles, roses, lovers, orgies, wealth, revenge, sadistic pleasures, participation in creating a "perfect" race, and death with honor. He never included others in decision-making and lied to them to get them to carry out his wishes. They began to act behind his back and finally tried to kill him.

His moral development faltered early, because of the distant and lacking relationship with his father. By the stage of peer approval, he simply stopped trying to please others. He lied whenever possible to avoid punishment such as when he was arrested as a draft-dodger. By the end of his life, he lost all moral sense. He then decided to remove himself from punishment as the allies neared his bunker in Berlin. Hitler's death was announced over the radio and Wagner's *Gotterdammerung* was played as if he had ascended to the heavens with the Valkyrie.

3

MAO TSE-TUNG

o o o o o o o o o o o o o o o o o o o o o o o o o o o o o o o o
"Morality knows nothing of geographical boundaries or distinctions of race." Herbert Spencer

1

Upbringing and Early Life

Mao Tse-tung (sometimes spelled Zedong) was born December 26, 1893, in the farm village of Shaoshan, about 30 miles southwest of Changsha. He began to work on his parents' farm at the age of six, and enrolled in the primary school at the age of eight. He worked mornings and evenings and attended school by day. Their three-acre farm was considered modest but adequate to support a family. Mao began to help his father with his accounts on the abacus since his father had only two years of schooling. This might have made it easy for him to think he was smarter than his father at an early age.

Mao's mother spoke a different dialect and bore seven children. Out of their two girls and five boys, only three survived. Mao was the eldest of the three boys, born when his mother was 27. He often lived with his mother's parents.

His father had been a soldier and had a quick temper and firm views, many of which conflicted with young Mao. He learned about tyranny from his father because Chinese fathers were the ruling power in the family. Mao's father often used the cane to wrench obedience from his son. Mao wrote later that his father would give the farmhand eggs with his rice every month, but no meat. But Mao said, "To me, he gave neither eggs nor meat."

His mother was a devout Buddhist but his father had no particular religious affiliation. His pacifist mother was upset when 10-year-old Mao fought with a classmate. But she rewarded him when he shared his lunch with another student who was poor. After she died in 1919, Mao said that she had loved him and others impartially, never lied or cheated, was neat and clear in her thinking and her home.

He said, "My mother, a kind and generous woman, criticized my attempts at open rebellion against the ruling power. She said it was not the Chinese way." But Mao soon dismissed his mother's advice just as he dismissed her habits of neatness and became sloppy and disorganized in his person and living quarters.

It appeared that Mao believed his parents loved him and he developed normally through the stages of trust and autonomy. He had some trouble in identifying with his father, a man whom he both feared and rebelled against. This threw his sexual identity into a slight confusion as was attested to by people who believed him to be too lacking in masculine identification. To some extent, he had the same problems in his male identification as did Hitler. Initiative was not encouraged in any Chinese children, all of whom were raised in very rigid ways to close their eyes to new learning and not explore their world.

As a youth, Mao studied Confucian texts. He disliked the obedience required of students who were taught maxims by rote memory, while swaying in rhythm. He also disliked the deference required by those in authority. He refused to stand up while reciting, saying that he could be heard just as well while sitting. He began to cut classes believing that he could teach himself from books. When his principal reprimanded him, Mao said he would attend classes only if he were permitted to ask a teacher questions. If the teacher could not answer, Mao asked the principal to fire him. The principal could not agree to this child's terms.

When Mao was 13, his father told some houseguests that he was lazy and useless. This loss of face hurt Mao so badly that he ran outside. His father chased him to a pond where the little fellow threatened to kill himself by jumping in and drowning. His father tried to stop him by insisting that he apologize on bended knee. He agreed to bend on one knee if his father would not beat him. He later said that he learned from that to use open rebellion against authority figures rather than to be totally meek and submissive.

In that year, he left school and began to work full time for his father, who had purchased another acre of land. His father hired a laborer and expanded the farm, eventually growing tons of grain. Soon he wanted to apprentice little Mao to a rice shop but the boy rebelled.

When Mao was 17, a famine led to a revolt. This resulted in the execution of some rebels whom Mao considered very much like himself. He resented the way they were treated unjustly and executed. He and many fellow students sympathized with the rebels. This, he wrote later, was the awakening point in sharing complaints with others about the governing powers.

During that same famine, Mao's father exported grain and was furious when some hungry villagers seized a shipment. Mao didn't sympathize with his father's anger, but he also didn't approve of the villagers stealing from grain producers.

Mao was a voracious reader and read many historical novels about China. He soon came upon a book warning what might happen to China unless foreign influence was stopped. The author suggested developing new communications systems such as railways and telegraph, industrializing, creating libraries, and introducing parliamentary government into China. Mao read about how China had lost Korea, Taiwan, Indochina and Burma. He also learned of the defeat of China by Japan in 1895 and about the repression of the Boxer Rebellion in 1900. His studies opened his eyes to the lowly position China occupied in the worldview.

His father gave him no money for formal studies so he left the farm at age 17 in 1910 and found tutors in a nearby town. He went to study in Changsha where he hoped to find answers and leaders whom he could respect better than his own father. When he read yet another book predicting the subjugation and dismemberment of China, his political consciousness was aroused.

He learned that Sun Yat-sen and his collaborators believed in using western ideas to save China by making it into a state of socialism. Mao had read about and admired Napoleon, Rousseau, Lincoln and Washington. He thought China needed such men and he particularly admired warriors and nation builders.

At age 17, he was six years older than other students in Changsha and much taller. He blamed his father for the ridicule he endured because his father had not paid for his education earlier. He disliked the wealthy class with whom he was attending school. In his immaturity, he continued to blame others for whatever situations he disliked.

In 1911, he read a paper supporting a wish for a republic led by Sun Yat-sen. He and his friends cut off their pigtails, a custom which had been imposed upon the Chinese by alien rulers, the Manchus. He also forcibly removed the pigtails of fellow students, against their will in some cases. Being so much larger, he could manhandle the smaller students.

He joined the revolutionary army during the 1911 revolt led by Sun Yat-sen. After this revolt, Yat-sen built an army with help from Soviet advisers and Chinese Communist organizers. Mao later wrote that he wanted to "help complete the revolution." But he never got to fight because the leaders came to an agreement within a short time and Mao returned to his books.

He read a great deal about and discussed socialism and social reform. At this point in his life, he was uncertain about what to do with his life and had not solidified his identification. He considered such careers as soap making, police officer, law, commerce, and other things. He withdrew from school but continued to read Charles Darwin, J. S. Mill, history and geography. His parents still refused to support him. He finally decided to be a teacher for which he attended school from 1913-1918.

Mao, from Hunan where they ate red peppers and were noted for their vigorous personalities, wrote about the possible relationship between red peppers and revolution. He was beginning to desire a more masculine and virile identification from the ingestion of red peppers. In 1917, he wrote an article about using exercises to strengthen the body and character. "Our nation is wanting in strength...If our bodies are not strong, we will be afraid as soon as we see enemy soldiers."

The same year he joined a radical group, which eventually joined the communists. They believed the evils were religion, capitalism, autocracy and repression of the individual. The goals of this group suited rebellious Mao because it rejected the bonds of father and son, prince and subject, and husband and wife. This strengthening of the body appeared to make him feel that finally he was a man and could compete with other men in any arena of life.

Around 1919, Mao became a library assistant at Peking University, while attending classes part-time. He added work as a laundryman to supplement his income. He developed some friends at this time who followed his leadership for years and years until their final victory in 1949. But his two closest friends did not. One died in the revolutionary struggle and the other, Hsiao Hsu-tung, became his enemy. The three had called themselves the three heroes or three worthies and thought that they were the most brilliant of the school. They also developed physical endurance through long walks and exposure to the elements. Mao even ran an ad to meet young men interested in the future of their country and met Li Li-san with whom he would clash later on.

On May 4, 1919, Mao was involved in a student demonstration. Students were against the Paris Peace Conference decision to give Japan the province of Shantung, instead of returning it to China. They burned the house of a minister who was associated with the decision that favored Tokyo over China. Many Peking students were arrested for this. In Changsha, Mao organized a group to boycott Japanese goods. In his first very serious act, he created a demonstration calling for the beheading of the aforementioned pro-Japanese minister. This began Mao's career as a professional revolutionary.

He studied the October 1918 Bolshevik Revolution. He accompanied some students, including Chou En-lai (sometimes spelled Zhou Enlai), on a work-study program to France. By the summer of 1920, he wrote, "I considered myself a Marxist."

Mao returned to Changsha in 1920 and organized a branch of the Socialist Youth Corps, and founded the Society for the Study of Marxism. He set up a Cultural Book Society. He began to learn how to combine his wish to get work done with the assets of his people. He asked the area governor to make a storefront sign, knowing that the man was proud of his talent in calligraphy. Meanwhile, Mao remained head of the primary school, drawing income while becoming a labor organizer.

In 1921, Mao was involved with covert communist meetings. His communist cell discussed whether to collaborate with Sun Yat-sen. In August 1921, he created a "mass education" movement to hear lectures on modern ideas, backed with money and facilities by Americans and the Chinese YMCA. Mao ingeniously involved village gentry to obtain backing for programs while organizing worker strikes among miners, stonemasons and printers. He was sometimes at his wits end trying to convince leaders from Moscow about how communism could be used in China. Moscow denounced Chinese communists for their lack of influence among workers and their Confucian mentality.

Mao wanted to prove to communist leaders that he was an exceptional person. His real feelings were expressed in some 1923 writings. He had learned that 35 men died while striking against railway worker dues they were forced to pay to capitalists. He wrote, "Don't they know that the aggression of the English imperialists against China is even more atrocious than that of the Japanese imperialists?" As for America, he wrote, she was "the most murderous of hangmen."

By this time, the 400 members of the Chinese Communist Party were funded and set up by the U.S.S.R. They provided Sun Yat-sen with a modern army trained by the Soviets. Chiang Kai-shek headed it and Chou En-lai ran the political department. However, Sun was thoroughly opposed to being a mere puppet of Moscow.

Now 30 years old, Mao moved to Shanghai to serve on the Central Committee of the Chinese Communist Party. He had no overly righteous objections to being backed by Moscow. Party members criticized him saying he was too partial to Russian influence.

In the first of several uses of hypochondriasis as a defense against pressures, he reacted to the criticism by retreating to his native village claiming illness. Meanwhile, the Russians forced the Chinese Communist Party to accept Dr. Sun Yat-sen, a strange and volatile character who died in 1925.

After this, Mao found the peasants were angry at foreign-owned businesses that inflicted harsh working conditions on them. When Chinese workers struck, British and French owners had them shot in strikes during 1925. Mao wrote, "Formerly, I had not fully realized the degree of class struggle among the peasantry."

From 1925, Mao organized peasant associations with slogans like "Down with the militarists," "Down with the imperialists," and "Down with the rich foreigners." Mao was faithful to Stalin as he worked with Russian-backed Chiang Kai-shek and gave lectures to the Peasant Movement Institute. Mao placed his brother in charge of the Propaganda Department of the Institute, and Mao soon became the editor of the weekly organ.

2

Love Life

When Mao was 14, his father arranged a marriage with a distant relative who was 18. They did marry but she died three years later and they had no children.

Later, he was strongly influenced by his ethics teacher at Peking University who believed that China could be stimulated with western ideas. This man soon died but had been a liberal about sex, was for women's rights and thought that China should not meddle with the sexual activities of widows. This man was the father of a young woman that Mao began seeing. In the process, Mao absorbed many of his future father-in-law's ideals. Before he died, this professor recommended that Mao be appointed director of a primary school.

With sufficient status and salary, Mao felt respectable enough to marry his deceased teacher's daughter. The two shared radical ideas and both were involved in plots against the current repressive government. His wife had joined the Chinese Communist Party in 1927, led a women's regiment during the Nanchang uprising, and was a forceful character.

The young woman, Mao's wife from 1920 to 1930 (Yang K'ai-hui) was executed along with Mao's younger sister (Tse-hung) in 1930. The assassins were the Chinese Nationalist forces (Koumintang, led by Chiang Kai-shek) who occupied Changsha briefly in the midst of this power struggle. Her activities and her marriage to an enemy, Mao, made her a prime target.

He was not with her at the time she was killed, and sorely regretted her death. He also anguished over what happened to their children. Of their three children sent to Shanghai, one died, and the Communist Party sent two to Moscow. One of those two died in Korea from American bombs. The other returned to China but was not in good health.

Within months after the assassination of his wife, Mao began to live with a girl half his age named Ho Tzu-chen. She bore him five children over the next nine years, one during the "Long March" on which she had accompanied him.

In a newspaper interview shortly before he met his fourth wife he made an interesting comment. He closely questioned the female interviewer about love and what it had meant to her. Then he recited a poem to the reporter about his wife who had been assassinated in 1930.

He had given that poem to his wife's friend. Her husband died in 1933 fighting the same forces that executed Mao's wife. Mao's wife's name meant "poplar" and the woman's dead husband's name meant "willow." Mao's poem was called *The Immortals*.

"I lost my proud poplar and you your willow,
Poplar and willow soar lightly to the heaven of heavens.
Wu Kang, asked what he has to offer,
Presents them respectfully with cassia wine
The lonely goddess in the moon spreads her ample sleeves
To dance for these faithful souls in the endless sky
Of a sudden comes word of a tiger's defeat on earth,
And they break into tears of torrential rain."

Legends said that Wu Kang, a Faust-like figure who sought immortality, lived forever in heaven cutting down cassia trees, which sprang back to life. The tiger represented Chiang Kai-shek's army, which executed his wife, and when Chiang was defeated, Mao and many others joined in emotionally triumphant tears.

The female interviewer, Agnes Smedley, thought Mao was effeminate and vaguely repelling at first. Then she found him to be warm, dignified, isolated, ruthless, and a man with intellectual depth. He cared little for his appearance and habitually sucked in his cigarette smoke with an unpleasant noise.

In 1937, Ho Tzu-chen, his wife and the mother of his children, became ill and was sent to the Soviet Union for treatment. While she was away, he fell in love with a well-known film actress with the stage name of Lan-p'ing from Shanghai. In 1939, Mao married his fourth wife, Jiang Qing (Lan-p'ing). The Party leadership objected to the marriage but Jiang promised to restrict herself to being a housewife and having no role in politics. His followers were disappointed that he abandoned his "Long March" companion for the seductive actress.

In the 1960s, contrary to her agreement to have no role in politics, she made a bid for power. She tried to reform the Beijing Opera during the years of the Cultural Revolution (1966-1976). She took part in all important government activities and was supported by a coterie that Mao called the "Gang of Four."

During the Cultural Revolution, Mao used songs to stir the people. *The East Is Red* became the Red Chinese anthem and told the history of China's revolution. Some words, which were played over loud speakers throughout workplaces, are these:

"The East is red, the sun has risen.
China has produced Mao Tse-tung!
He works for the people's happiness,
He is the people's savior."

When President Richard Nixon visited Mao in China in 1972, he said this of Jiang. "I have never met a more cold graceless person. As we sat together at a propaganda cultural program she had arranged for my visit, she showed none of Mao's warmth or Chou's grace." He continued that she had "allowed her communist ideology to destroy her femininity."

When Mao died in 1976, Jiang lost the support for her political activities. She and the "Gang of Four" were arrested. In January 1981, Jiang was sentenced to death. She enjoyed a two-year reprieve. Authorities also ruled that there would be a permanent deprivation of her political rights. The sentence was changed to life imprisonment in January 1983. Suffering from throat cancer, she was released on bail for medical treatment in early May 1991. Ten days after her release, she allegedly committed suicide.

3

Military Experience

Chiang Kai-shek decided to carry out Sun Yat-sen's goal to lead an army to overthrow Peking warlords. He expected Soviet help but it did not appear because Leon Trotsky's committee was involved in dealings with supporting Japan at China's expense. Stalin seemed unclear about whether to support Japanese or Chinese communists. He said, "The Canton government should in the present period decisively reject the thought of military expeditions of an offensive character." But Chiang Kai-shek led a coup in 1926 and provoked the Soviets into accepting Chinese offensives against the Japanese.

Mao and Chiang saw themselves as enemies representing two sides of the Chinese struggle against subjugation by outside forces. Mao trained young guerrilla fighters as rural agitators after Chiang's surprising coup. Mao held six months of training for his agitators in military and political issues. Meanwhile, Chiang Kai-shek declared himself part of the "world revolution" to overthrow imperialism. Mao prepared his men to overthrow the feudal landlord class. Stalin feared a clash between Mao's peasants and Chiang's army and decided to support Chiang.

Mao reported to Moscow on the groundswell of the peasant initiative at a meeting in 1927. He said, "There is already a high tide of the peasant movement in Hunan and Hupei, and on their own initiative the peasants have refused to pay rent, and have seized political power." He continued to demonstrate to Moscow that peasants could be motivated to overthrow capitalists and that the communist revolutionaries didn't have to be urban workers. This was a theme that Fidel Castro would illustrate later in Cuba.

During the same year, Chiang Kai-shek broke with the communists. The Soviets could see that it made no sense to support his troops any longer. In fact, an attack on the Soviet Embassy in Peking was punished with arrests and executions of many communists.

Mao saw his opportunity to convince Moscow of his belief in communism. He told his peasant forces to confiscate the land of anyone who owned 4 ½ acres or more. His father had owned three acres originally. Pressures mounted as others in his party opposed his views, arguing to take the land of only big landlords. For at least the second time, he retreated from his post pleading illness again, reacting to criticism from within his own party.

Shortly, he was asked by the opposition to the government and to Chiang's forces to lead an armed uprising. Although his uprising was defeated, his soldiers became the guerrilla army that he would eventually lead on the road to Peking. It was finally decided that only the land of really big landlords (72 acres) would be confiscated, rather than the smaller properties of 4 ½ acres. The Central Committee of the Communist Party in China now looked to Mao as the leader of their troops. They advised Mao to kill off the capitalistic large landlords, bullies, and bad gentry to establish the "common people's political power."

Mao's men, numbering several hundred, sabotaged railroad lines to disrupt trains, confiscated land, and carried red flags. He used terror and assassinations in the countryside to rout out foreigners. He was criticized for advocating that his peasant troops have delegate meetings. Word of this objection did not reach him until he had enlarged his troops by merging with two bandit chiefs.

Since childhood, he had admired the bandit heroes of popular Chinese novels who, like Robin Hood, stole from the rich to aid the poor. Before long, he acquired forces of nearly 10,000, armed with long spears and rifles. He faced a constant desertion problem as the men became homesick and left. These problems weighed heavily on him.

Despite the growing size of his Red Army, he wrote in 1928, "The vast forces of the oppressed classes have not yet been set in motion."

He began building up a base area. He was told to correct the "peasant mentality" by attracting the proletarian working class leadership of the city, using the Russian model of communism. He responded that the Chinese revolution would not suffer just because "the peasants become more powerful than the workers." In actuality, Russian peasants were less educated and less capable than Russian workers but in China, Chinese peasants were often as well educated and as capable as Chinese workers.

Then came the 1929 American stock market crash. Moscow erroneously thought that this signaled the collapse of capitalism. They hastily informed the Chinese communists to overthrow the landlord-bourgeois regime and set up a dictatorship of peasants and workers.

Mao's army of 20,000-30,000 men of varying classes was having much success but this was partly because they allowed rich peasants to keep all or part of their good land. He began to struggle for power with wealthier Chinese communists who had been trained in Moscow. He arrested opposition leaders and conducted revolts that cost 2,000-3,000 lives. Although he ruthlessly got rid of rivals, he appeared to take no particular pleasure in killing or torturing enemies, unlike Hitler.

The Soviets, believing that peasant communism was not their goal, tried to dilute Mao's power by giving Chou En-lai authority over the Red Army. Mao had studied military tactics by reading from Sun Tzu (500 B.C.). He concentrated his few troops in a surprise attack on one small part of the enemy troops and called it "pitting ten against one." By maintaining secrecy on the movements of his troops and acting swiftly, his attacks were successful. By the time Mao's army of 30,000 faced Chiang Kai-shek's 100,000-man army, he had perfected his surprise attacks using focused small groups.

In 1933, Mao began his "land verification" program to assure that land was taken from the rich and given to the poor properly. He wrote, "In the course of the verification more than 300 families of landlords and rich peasants were discovered, 12 counter-revolutionary elements called 'bit tigers' by the peasants were shot, and counter-revolutionary activities were repressed."

Mao suffered from malaria in 1934 but when he recovered, was told to take his 100,000 troops and march them 6,000 miles to fight Japan. The army was under the command of Chu Te and Chou En-lai who were aided by a German military expert trained in Moscow. On the "Long March," Mao used a strategy of having some men dress like Chiang Kai-shek's soldiers, infiltrate them, and take over a city, often without firing a shot.

His innovative strategies and military successes caused him to be placed in control of the Chinese Communist Party in 1935 and he was soon named Chairman of the Politburo. His army left behind some men to fight delaying actions, and one of those casualties was his brother, Mao Tse-t'an who was killed in action in March 1935.

His new power or his victories inspired him to write poems on the "Long March". He wrote:

"They say that the strong pass is iron-hard;
And yet this very day with a mighty step
We shall cross its summit,
We shall cross its summit!
The hills are blue like the sea,
And the dying sun like blood."

As they neared Chiang Kai-shek's forces, Mao ordered a few men who were disguised as enemy scouts and locals to cross a river and obtain ferries. It was a successful operation and they brought Mao's army across the river undetected on ferries for nine days. Mao also had his men call out as if they were wounded and needed water and supplies until they drew fire. This allowed the main force to cross nearby unobstructed.

After one such clash with the enemy, after Mao's men broke through the last barriers near the Great Wall of China, he wrote this poem:

"The sky is high, the clouds are pale,
We watch the wild geese flying south till they vanish;
If we reach not the Great Wall, we are not true men.
Already we have come two thousand leagues."

4

Path to Power

Yasser Arafat was once asked whose career he most admired and he answered Mao's. The reason was, he told a reporter, that Mao took a basically illiterate people who were addicted to drugs and made them into a world power to be contended with.

Mao's final path to power had begun with his ingenious military strategies. Moscow and the local Communist Party were now valuing Mao's political foresight, earlier ignored. In 1936, Mao could see the advantages of unifying China to fight foreign invaders like the Japanese. He abandoned anti-Chiang Kai-shek slogans. He merged his forces with Chiang's declaring that they had a common enemy. They offered principles of national independence, freedom and democracy. Mao's greatest appeal was to the peasants with the promise of a unified China in the face of Japanese invasion.

Chou En-lai, who earlier fought with Chiang Kai-shek, was convinced of Mao's superiority during the Long March. They formed a legendary partnership that endured until their deaths. Mao, Chou En-lai and others opened a "university" in Yenan in 1936. They began to train troops for the "anti-Japanese national revolutionary war" to save China from annihilation by Japanese imperialists. They trained officers, guerrilla leaders, political workers and others for periods of six months to one year.

Mao's writings from 1938 to 1940 were about military strategies or politics. He described guerrilla warfare in his book *Basic Tactics*. He preached "fearlessness." He wrote, "If we do not fear death, then what is there to fear about the enemy?"

Politically, he began to shape communism to suit China's needs and the needs of the country's rural peasants. The new democracy would be led by "several revolutionary classes" he wrote. This insistence upon including rural peasants flew in the face of Soviet advisers who believed that urban workers were the only revolutionary class. He carefully avoided open criticism of the Soviets. He wrote that the Chinese communists should not recite phrases from other countries but should learn their own history and be proud of it.

In response to pre-World War II Japanese aggression, Mao sent 400,000 troops to attack the Japanese in five provinces of northern China. Unfortunately, friction and violence had ended his collaboration with Chiang Kai-shek or the anti-Japanese invasion would have been larger. Because he was then unassisted by other troops, the Japanese opposition reduced his forces to 300,000.

As WWII drew near, in 1941 his party organ denounced President Roosevelt for enlarging the imperialist war by dragging America into war with Germany.

Mao's only remaining sibling, brother Mao Tse-min, moved to Sinkiang to work for a communist warlord in finance. When the warlord shifted his allegiance away from Moscow in 1942, Mao Tse-min was arrested and executed the following year.

Just after Hitler's invasion of the Soviet Union, Mao had urged American military and economic aid for the Soviet Union and China. He wrote, "The work which we Communists are carrying out today is the very same work which was carried on earlier in America by Washington, Jefferson, and Lincoln; it will certainly obtain, and indeed has already obtained, the sympathy of democratic America."

In 1944, Roosevelt's vice president (Henry Wallace) had pressed upon Chiang Kai-shek the importance of a united front with communist China to fight Japan. In fact, Roosevelt proposed to Chiang that General Stillwell lead the Nationalist and Communist Chinese troops. When Chiang declined, Mao criticized him. FDR withdrew the proposal. On April 13, 1945, Mao sent a telegram to President Truman offering his sympathy upon the death of Roosevelt.

As the Japanese surrender drew near, Mao's mood was more anti-American, perhaps because he had been largely ignored when he tried to communicate with U.S. representatives. In 1945, American reports carried stories that Chinese communists were hostile to U.S. Ambassador Patrick Hurley. Hurley met with Chiang and Mao with little success. Negative news reports of the meetings added to Mao's unhappiness with Hurley. He wrote, "Since I have been able to fight Japan with these few rusty rifles, I can fight the Americans too. The first step is to get rid of Hurley, then we'll see."

5

Leadership Style

The cult of Mao began seriously in 1945. He was being praised as the greatest revolutionary leader and statesman in China. China was called the prime mover and mentor of anti-imperialistic revolutions throughout Asia and Africa. In 1945, both Mao and Stalin proclaimed the same goal—a coalition government in China with communist participation. Stalin didn't want to disrupt agreements with Roosevelt at Yalta, however. Russia was in the process of creating a naval base at Port Arthur in agreement with Chiang Kai-shek. On the day of Japanese surrender after the atom bombs, Stalin and Chiang agreed that the Soviets could use Manchuria as a base of military operations.

Mao ordered his troops to occupy towns held by the Japanese. Chiang countermanded the order. Mao accused him of cooperating with the enemy instead of his own countrymen. Mao and Chiang met in 1945 for the first time since 1925. After 43 days of negotiations between the uncoifed Mao and the well-groomed Chiang, they agreed to reduce the size of their armies. But Chiang didn't keep his promise.

Only a week after the atom bombs in 1945, Mao wrote, "Can atom bombs decide wars? No, they can't. Atom bombs could not make Japan surrender…If atom bombs could decide the war, then why was it necessary to ask the Soviet Union to send its troops? Why didn't Japan surrender when the two bombs were dropped on her, and why did she surrender as soon as the Soviet Union sent troops?"

Most Americans were simply ecstatic that the war was over and the boys were coming home. The horror of the atomic bombs seemed to have stunned the world into peace. Mao was, of course, delighted that the Japanese were beaten so badly. His next task was to create a positive image for his soldiers. He won support as he distinguished the Red Army from other armies familiar to Chinese peasants. He did this by respecting the population and prohibiting his men from plundering.

However, despite America's assistance in eliminating the Japanese menace, in 1946 Mao wrote that the U.S. was the greatest enemy of the world's people and the most viciously reactionary of all the imperialist powers. The same year, Mao's Red Army in China was making steady gains against the Nationalist government forces of Generalissimo Chiang Kai-shek.

Truman told a group of editors from the McGraw-Hill Publishing Company that the difficulties with China were "very, very bad."

Mao moved into a vacuum in China, much as Lenin had done in Russia. At first he was thought to be a Soviet instrument but that was not the case.

By 1947 Mao's forces equaled Chiang's Kai-shek's in size, and 1948 brought communist victories over Chiang's troops. By December 1948, virtually all of Manchuria and Northern China had fallen to the communists. On January 1, 1949, Chiang handed over his presidency, declared his desire for peace, and established himself in Taiwan.

On April 20, 1949, the capture of Nanking near Mount Chung inspired this poem by Mao.

"Around Mount Chung, a sudden storm has arisen,
A million courageous warriors cross the great river.
The crouching tiger (Nanking)
And the coiled dragon (Mt. Chung)
Are more majestic than ever in the past.
The universe is in turmoil.
We are all exalted and resolute.
Let us gather up our courage and pursue the broken foe,
It is not fit to seek praise by imitating the tyrant of Ch'u
If heaven had feelings, heaven too would grow old,
The true way that governs the world of men
Is that of radical change."

Mao referred to the tyrant of Ch'u. This tyrant spared a foe's life only to be killed by him. Mao was insisting that he should eliminate all of his enemies in radical change.

In May 1948, the communists had taken over Czechoslovakia and consolidated the Soviet position in Eastern Europe. Toward the end of 1948, the Berlin Airlift was proceeding with great effect. Truman worried more and more about Maoist forces as they won one smashing victory after another. From Tokyo, General MacArthur was warning that the "fall" of China imperiled America. At home, the Red scare grew worse.

Throughout 1949, the Chinese Nationalist regime of Chiang Kai-shek had been crumbling fast before the onrush of the communists. In April, a communist army of a million men crossed the Yangtze River to the last provinces still loyal to Chiang. As Chiang's army was defeated, MacArthur wrote an article for *Time* magazine saying that the Red tide rising in Asia threatened to engulf half the peoples of the world.

In August 1949, the State Department released a massive report on *United States Relations with China: With Special Reference to the Period 1944-1949*. It stated that the U.S. had poured more than $2 billion into support for Chiang Kai-shek since the end of World War II, money and arms in a futile attempt to destroy communism in China. This had failed because of the internal decay of Chiang's regime, its corruption, lack of leadership and indifference to the wishes of the Chinese people.

This was particularly galling to Americans who had sent their children to church with money to support Chinese missionaries. Pearl Buck's books about Chinese peasants were widely read in America. Furthermore, Chiang and his Wellesley-educated wife were photogenic and regarded as American allies throughout WWII.

In 1949, Mao wanted to proclaim the People's Republic of China and elect a democratic coalition government to represent it. He invited countries to establish diplomatic relations if they would sever relations with the Chinese reactionaries led by Chiang Kai-shek. He said, "All Chinese without exception must lean either to the side of imperialism or to the side of socialism."

On September 21, 1949, a conference elected Mao to preside and change the name of Peiping to Peking, the northern capital. The conference was closed with "Long Live Chairman Mao."

On October 1, 1949, Mao formally proclaimed the establishment of the Chinese People's Republic. The most populous communist nation in the world with more than one fifth of the world population was officially inaugurated. Just as Truman began his presidency by joining forces with former opponents to receive Roosevelt's body, Mao did likewise. Among six vice-chairmen under Mao were Sun Yat-sen's widow, and a representative from Chiang Kai-shek's party.

In December, Mao and Chou En-Lai traveled to Moscow to negotiate formal ties to the Soviet Union. They went to Moscow on Stalin's 70th birthday. Mao stayed nine weeks securing an agreement of aid from Russia in the event of an attack by Japan. He also negotiated $60 million in return for allowing Russia to keep bases in Port Arthur and Dairen until 1952. Stalin, however, did not relinquish them and they were turned over to China after his death.

The communist bloc now governed one quarter of the world and the invasion of South Korea by North Korean communists seemed to Americans like communist expansionism. The American Communist Party cheered on the Chinese communists. By the end of 1949, the communist victory was complete in China.

On June 25, 1950, the Russian-supported North Korean communists invaded South Korea. This war resulted in 150,000 deaths of the Chinese in Korea.

Mao had to consolidate communist political control and repair the war-damaged economy. In December 1950, Mao urged peasants to kill a number of landlords. The number of victims was in the tens of thousands. The real wave of terror was, however, in the future during the "Great Leap Forward."

In 1950, Mao changed marriage laws so that women had equal rights. Free choice was the basis of marriage. This fit the current wishes of the time in China.

The invasion of South Korea by North Korea appears to have been provoked mainly by Stalin who supposed the U.S. would not get involved. At the same time, Truman promised that the U.S. would intervene if Mao's Chinese communists attacked Chiang Kai-shek's forces in Taiwan.

Mao's son, Mao An-ying, was killed in combat in Korea. He had studied in Moscow during WWII. Mao didn't want to be at war with the U.S. but MacArthur was about to cross the Yalu River. Mao tried to eliminate pro-American sentiment and authorized executions of counter-revolutionaries. This could have amounted to executions of more than a million people around 1951 but statistics were not kept.

The thought reform campaign of Mao truly revealed his leadership style. It was a consequence of the rectification campaign of 1942-1944. His attempt was to harmonize social discipline and conscious action. The destruction of Chinese identity and their respect for tradition and authority was being replaced by a new identity construction.

A son's respect for his father, long a part of Chinese tradition, was being replaced by piety toward Mao and his regime. He knew the importance of the father figure to the Chinese. He thought his ideas were correct and thought everyone would be better off if they thought as he did. This was his "brainwashing" of the public.

On October 23, 1951, Mao said, "Thought reform, and especially thought reform of all categories of intellectuals, is one of the most important conditions for the democratic transformation and the progressive industrialization of our country."

Thought reform was combined with the campaign of the "Three Antis" of 1951 (anti-corruption, anti-waste, anti-bureaucracy). It resulted in the purging of some people for other offenses as well. This was followed in 1952 by the "Five Antis" campaign. These involved anti-bribery, anti-tax evasion, anti-fraud, anti-theft of government property, and anti-theft of state economic secrets.

The latter campaign was linked to the previous campaign because bribery by businessmen meant corruption of civil servants. Peasants did not require landlords to till soil. Landlords were needed to direct their enterprises but their thinking was remolded to prepare them for their future role as merely salaried managers. Programs destroyed their independent power position. The threat of professional ruin drove some to prison, others to suicide, or anything rather than to "confess their sins" before their employees as thought reform required.

In February 1953, Mao looked like Stalin's faithful disciple when Stalin died. But Mao's warlike temperament made him different. Chou En-lai, an astute diplomat, helped end the Korean War with the exchange of sick and wounded prisoners in 1953, of which the Soviets approved.

Khrushchev visited Peking in 1954. He increased economic aid and returned Port Arthur and Dairen to China. The first step in the transition to a socialist economy in 1954 was announced. Mao said several five-year plans would turn China into a highly industrialized country. The income of cooperatives was distributed among members based on the amount of land, capital and labor they contributed. By 1955, only 15% of peasant families belonged to cooperatives. This accelerated rapidly.

In his speech on July 31, 1955, Mao said, "As this is being written, more than 60 million peasant households in various parts of the country have already joined cooperatives...By the end of this year the victory of socialism will be practically assured. We must continue to fight hard."

This combativeness and imagination, and faith in "conscious action" encouraged people to voluntarily make changes that other countries had to force upon citizens. But Khrushchev did not consult with Mao before the denunciation of Stalin in his 1956 speech. Mao had already suffered the resistance of peasants to collectivization, and poor harvest. Now anxiety was caused by Khrushchev's secret speech denouncing Stalin, followed by the Hungarian uprising.

Mao believed Khrushchev was deserting communism as he moved toward "peaceful coexistence." Mao said, "In what position does Khrushchev, who participated in the leadership of the Party and the State during Stalin's period, place himself when he beats his breast, pounds the table and shouts abuse of Stalin at the top of his voice? In the position of an accomplice to a 'murderer' or a 'bandit'? Or in the position of a 'fool' or an 'idiot'?"

Khrushchev's attacks on Stalin cast discredit on the world communist movement as a whole and indirectly on Chinese communists who came to power with Stalin's support. To counteract this, Mao developed a new slogan "let a hundred flowers bloom."

Mao's one hundred flowers campaign imposed hard physical labor on men who were not accustomed to it (intellectuals), or humiliating tasks such as cleaning the lavatories in the university where they formerly were professors. There was to be no victory for capitalists or upper class citizens. He wanted to stop the Chinese Communist Party members who were behaving like a privileged class.

In Moscow in 1957, Mao warned of annihilation if an atomic war were fought. But the Soviets had just secretly agreed to give China a sample nuclear weapon and directions for making them. Sputnik had just been launched.

In April 1958, Mao said that China's six hundred million people were "poor" and "blank." He went on to say, "Poor people want change, want to do things, want revolution. A clean sheet of paper has no blotches and so the newest and most beautiful words can be written on it." He wanted to write his own words onto the minds of his "blank" people so they would think as he thought. (His wide reading had probably included British philosopher John Locke who wrote that at birth a child's mind is like a blank slate or *tabla rasa*. It must be filled by his life experiences.)

So Mao began his "Great Leap Forward" or "permanent revolution." He wanted to fill the minds of his people with the right ideas, his ideas. He wanted to eliminate the last vestiges of private property and accelerate industrial growth. His suddenness met with resistance on top of bad weather conditions and poor crop totals. Some 20 million people died in this terrible experiment as Mao tried to find a short cut to communism by taking away all private property.

Mao's praise to those who followed him was not often openly voiced. But an example of his true loyalty to his closest colleagues was seen during the Cultural Revolution. Chou En-lai was being criticized by the Red Guards and they asked Mao to put him on trial. Mao defended him by saying that he would agree to a trial if he also were tried.

Khrushchev and Mao collided in the summer of 1958. On July 28, 1958, Khrushchev proposed a summit of the United States, United Kingdom, France, Russia, and India to settle the Mideast crisis. But three days later he made a secret visit to Peking because China and Mao had not been consulted. Then he withdrew the offer of the summit because of Mao's pressure.

Mao was hostile to "American imperialists" who maintained an alternative Chinese government in Taiwan, originally under Chiang Kai-shek. Then Mao started shelling offshore islands in August 1958. Mao's "millet plus rifles" triumphed over Chiang Kai-shek's "airplanes and tanks." Mao could not accept the modern world and modern warfare because he saw the world through his Chinese experience.

But Khrushchev didn't understand Chinese psychology. He also didn't understand how his actions provoked Mao. Khrushchev said of The Chairman, "Mao has always been a master at concealing his true thoughts and intentions." Khrushchev ridiculed communes to Senator Hubert Humphrey, as well as publicly suggesting that he didn't really believe in communism. Then he pressed Mao economically. Mao didn't run as a candidate for the Chinese Communist Party in 1958. Possibly this was because he didn't want to carry out Khrushchev's policies. Possibly it was because there was too much criticism of how poorly he had organized the communes. But his prevalence in the minds of the poor people was at monumental levels.

6

Stresses

Mao worried that people might criticize him. Early on he responded to the fear of criticism by getting sick and leaving for a while. Later when he had the power to do so, he had writers and propagandists revise the story of his life and his rule. He wanted to reshape history so that his words and actions looked consistent and benevolent. In this way he was able to fool his own people into believing what he wanted.

Mao was very practical and tried not to bite off more than he could chew, unlike Hitler. In this way, he minimized the stress he would have to deal with. Stalin asked Mao why he did not take Shanghai since he had taken so much other territory. Mao said, "There's a population of six million there. If we take the city, we have to feed all those people and where do we find food to do it?"

Mao retreated on the "Great Leap Forward" in August 1959 because the grain harvest had only been 250 million tons, not 375 as was needed. It was not the Paradise he had envisioned as a "short cut" to communism. It must have been humiliating for him to realize that his leadership brought the country close to ruin. As he did so many times, he retreated briefly from the political scene. Then he re-emerged with a new wave of militancy, a program he had devised to make his country strong and vigorous by using the rebellious energy of youth.

He revolutionized young people to join the military. He first tried to create a Youth League and moved eventually toward the more militant Red Guards by 1964. He created the slogan, "Learn from the Army." The Red Guard's bible was *Quotations from Chairman Mao.* He wrote that it took 15 sharp soldiers to take on one well-armed guerrilla.

An example from this book is the following: "Therefore, if a person at any time whatever, in any place whatever, regarding any question whatever, manifests wavering in his attitude toward Mao's thought, then, no matter if this wavering is only momentary and slight, it means in reality that the waverer departs from Marxist-Leninist truth and will lose his bearings and commit political errors. So we must follow Chairman Mao steadfastly and eternally!"

On September 9, 1959, Tass issued a statement that a border conflict between India and China caused Khrushchev to advise both governments to resolve this misunderstanding. Mao was insulted that Khrushchev put a fellow socialist state and a "bourgeois" power on the same plane.

Then Khrushchev visited President Eisenhower and saw Mao a few days later. At Mao's party for him, Khrushchev said that China was forcibly testing the capitalist system in Taiwan and Sino-Indian border clashes. He added that Mao should accept that there are two Chinas and accept losing Taiwan, which meant losing Chinese territory. Mao was incensed that Khrushchev would tell him to accept the loss of his own territory when the Soviets were so averse to accepting any loss of their territory and people.

Whereas Khrushchev was the kind of man who said what was on his mind, Mao did not. He would speak in cryptic sentences or using poetry to make his point obliquely. He would store up his reactions and let his feelings be understood by his actions. This was puzzling to many who spoke more directly.

In 1960, Khrushchev spoke at the Rumanian Communist Party Congress and called the Chinese "madmen" who wanted to unleash nuclear war. Soviet intellectuals talked of the Chinese as the new barbarians; peasants brainwashed by the loudspeakers in the fields with militaristic lives. They had the same view of China that Americans had of Russia during the Stalin era.

Mao had Chou En-lai lay a wreath at Stalin's tomb to create even more dissension with Khrushchev after the speech in which Nikita denounced Stalin. His technique of handling the insults from Khrushchev lay in clever non-violent retaliations.

The 1962 Cuban Missile Crisis convinced Mao that Khrushchev was unfit for communist leadership and he said so publicly. Following the crisis, Pravda attacked Mao in an article on January 7, 1963. Two days later, Mao wrote a poem that ended, "We must sweep away all the harmful insects (the Soviets) until not a single enemy remains." His methods of criticizing people were often indirect and veiled in a manner that could be called passive aggressive behavior.

Mao thought that he was the leader of the communist world revolution in 1963 because he had the larger population. He came out more directly and renounced Khrushchev's nuclear test ban treaty with the U.S. Some American communists picked up on Mao's sense of trying to be a true communist. People like Beatrice Webb, Lincoln Steffens and Paul Robeson pinned their hopes first on the Soviet Union's brand of communism. When that failed after Khrushchev's denunciation of Stalin's crimes, they looked to Mao's China. Later they would turn to Castro's Cuba.

In Mao's effort to prove that he was the leader of the world revolution, he wrote a letter to the Central Committee of the Communist Party of China on July 14, 1964. It was called *On Khrushchev's Phony Communism and Its Historical Lessons for the World*. He said that Khrushchev's revision of communism was paving the way for restoration of capitalism. "The socialist system is incomparably superior to the capitalist system," he wrote, in which "public ownership of the means of production replaces private ownership." He warned that imperialism would "do its utmost to destroy the socialist countries or to make them degenerate into capitalist countries."

When Mao ran into trouble with his party, he had a comeback by attacking the party leadership and the new chief of state. His Cultural Revolution, largely orchestrated by his actress wife, showed that Mao could get his ideas across indirectly by using the Shanghai press to attack Peking leadership.

He mobilized young adolescent students called the "Red Guards." But it was hard to keep the Chinese people happy once the intelligentsia and property owners had been displaced, humiliated, tortured and killed by peasants and Red Guards. As tension mounted, Mao had to rely on a leader of his military Red Guards (Lin Piao) to keep order. Thankful to Lin Paio, he named him as his successor. However, Lin Paio died in a plane crash after plotting to assassinate Mao.

In 1966, Mao's five-year effort to recover from the Great Leap Forward had vindicated him. However he decided to portray himself as healthy and vigorous in the Chinese Press. In a clever propaganda ploy, he had them cover a swim in the Yangtze River in July 1966, to demonstrate that he was capable of directing the country. Also during that year, his wife became a member of the Central Committee and was seen publicly trying to resolve conflicts with the Peking University over the "cultural revolution."

Posters placed in universities and areas to recruit the young "Red Guards" declared, "To rebel is justified…We will stage a great rebellion against whoever is revisionist and opposed to Mao Tse-tung's thought...We will reel as long as there are classes and class struggle."

Stalin's way was to rule through the party and when that didn't work, he purged it with the secret police. Mao insisted on acting through the masses rooting out those who "take the capitalist road."

During the Cultural Revolution, the masses were taught through Mao's little red book and buttons that it was right to revolt. He stated that the world was divided into three groups: the underdeveloped nations (including China), the developed nations and the two super-powers (U.S. and U.S.S.R.). As leader of the underdeveloped nations, he wanted to lessen the influence of the U.S.S.R. by receiving President Richard Nixon.

Nixon depicted Mao's room as "book-strewn." He described Mao's failing health, notable in his shambling stride and difficulty speaking. Mao stated, "I like rightists" because he knew that the Republicans were "rightists." After Henry Kissinger had complimented Mao's writings, he responded self-deprecatingly, "These writings of mine aren't anything. There is nothing instructive in what I wrote." Nixon wrote that Mao valued struggle above all else, and being a revolutionary, sought ideals worth fighting and dying for.

Nixon's historic trip to China opened relations with the Chinese communist regime. Relations had been distant since Mao's "Long March" drove American ally Chiang Kai-shek to his island retreat on Formosa, now called Taiwan. China was just emerging from the so-called Cultural Revolution during which fanatical Red Guards, in their zeal to enforce Mao's version of ideological purity, reduced thousands of intellectuals to menial work. Over a million deaths occurred during the era of the Cultural Revolution. The regime did not promote Nixon's visit. Mao and his aide Chou En-Lai wanted to see how things developed first. Secret visits of Henry Kissinger had paved the way.

In line with Nixon's comment that Mao valued struggle above all else, Mao replaced harmony with destruction of superstition. He removed submissive attitudes to superiors, fathers, elders and bureaucrats. His peasant Red Guards unleashed terror in 1966 when they beat several tens of thousands of people who disagreed with Mao's thought or were living in some capitalistic way. The Red Guards enforced a puritan morality as regards dress and behavior similar to the Afghanistan Taliban in 2001. Mao's greatest support in the end was from the Red Guards born after 1949 who were taught to regard Mao as their savior. Like Hitler youth and the Taliban, they smashed statues, burned books, defaced pictures, suppressed the intelligentsia and provoked suicides.

After Mao's death in 1976, and his wife's death in 1991, sons and daughters ("princelings") of the communist party officials continued to occupy important positions. The Tiananmen Square protesters in 1989 claimed that nepotism was a major problem with the princelings. Some say that Mao should not be judged harshly if his reign brought many deaths because he did not directly order them. Also many say people are not angry with Mao because the communist propaganda system has not allowed citizens to know the extent of losses during his reign.

7

Accomplishments

Mao's greatest achievement was the unification of China. He was aware of the needs and dreams of the Chinese in the 1920s and 1930s. But as time passed, he was no longer in harmony with China's needs. Mao tried to find a new way for China to enter the modern world that avoided Stalinization and democracy, but he failed. The goal to make China great by having its citizens learn rote Maoist sayings was not acceptable to scientists, technicians, skilled workers or the modern world. Mao used the Chinese way to do so many things that it seems hard to take him seriously as a pure Marxist, but he was. He made Chinese economic development grow by using people instead of machines, and combined handcrafts with industrialization.

His greatest shortcoming was in the agricultural area. He stressed the importance of land re-distribution to benefit peasants. His collectivism was achieved with less suffering and loss of life, however, than the Soviet efforts. In the late 1950s, the caloric intake probably fell below daily requirements and only extreme rationing prevented mass starvation. Agriculture recovered somewhat in 1962 with decentralization of production and resumption of private garden plots.

He was more successful in mobilizing peasants than the Soviet Union, which had always focused on workers rather than peasants. Chinese steel production far exceeded that of more modern countries like India. China even produced trucks, trains, scientific instruments, heavy machinery and the atomic bomb without imports from other countries. Mao always stressed that the Chinese should do things their own way rather than copying the West.

Mao's calligraphy was used to simplify the Chinese characters to increase literacy. People had to be able to read his words if he was to influence them. His calligraphy has often been displayed but consists of no more than his poems written in large artistic calligraphic style. The titles reflect the realities of his own life, such as *Struggle, The Long March* and *Being Lucid in Worldly Knowledge Is a Form of Scholarship: Being Worldly Wise in Human Affairs Is a Kind of Literature.* He continued the tradition of Chinese emperors who established their presence within their vast empires by inscribing the fronts of temples with calligraphy bearing their decrees.

During Mao's regime, he improved women's rights and reduced the sex industry. Prostitution was nearly eliminated by Mao. Since his death, the last twenty years have seen a relaxation in social controls that have introduced massive AIDS and HIV infections affecting perhaps 50% of some village populations.

On July 1, 2001, the Chinese Communist Party celebrated the 80th anniversary of its creation by unexpectedly declaring that private businessmen could be party members. Many Chinese were horrified that the party Mao founded to protect peasants and the working-class from capitalist exploiters would now accept them. The average yearly income per person is about $1,000 with 120 million Chinese living in poverty. So it is remarkable how rapidly millionaires emerged in the last few years. Many pundits believe that as long as the Chinese millionaires make their fortunes by skill and hard work rather than political connections or corruption, they are unlikely to have another proletarian revolution.

One on one, Mao was extremely well liked by the Chinese because he was so approachable, so friendly, so caring, and so personal. Many prize their little red book, copying out instructions in their daily diary. They recite his poems, sing his songs, keep his buttons including the ones that glow in the dark, and pass them on. His death meant the end of destructive political campaigns but also the end of a sense of purpose and belonging. That is the reason for the nostalgia for Mao within China to this day.

In 1993, Samuel Huntington published an article called "The Clash of Civilizations" in *Foreign Affairs*. He said that the fact that the U.S. and China could communicate more easily did not mean they were any more likely to agree with each other. He explained that religion was now a more menacing force than political ideology internationally. He wrote, "The dangerous clashes of the future are likely to arise from the interaction of Western arrogance, Islamic intolerance, and Sinic (Chinese) assertiveness."

8

Summary:

As Mao grew up, he did at times distrust his father and others. He became particularly rebellious in his early teens. He resisted identifying with his father and other authority figures. This left him with role confusion and doubts about himself and his virility. He made a point of strengthening his own and Chinese bodies and minds to resist authorities and foreigners.

Mao particularly disliked the humiliation inflicted by the Europeans on the Chinese, which was similar to authority figures imposing their will on children. He chose to overturn this traditionally authoritarian society using revolution and terror. His goal was to make each man an authority figure or a god. Although he passed through the stages of intimacy and generativity as he raised his children, he was not content with himself toward the end of his life. He was still trying to demonstrate his virility when he swam the Yangtze River in his 70s.

He was able to enjoy the various stages of love, enjoying first the unconditional love of his mother; romantic love with at least his second and possibly his fourth wives, and reached a level of emotional intimacy with those two wives according to all accounts.

Mao never lost his hostility and animosity toward imperialists. This stemmed from hostility toward his father. He even displayed this hostility toward the Soviet Union in his 1963 paper called *On Khrushchev's Phony Communism and Its Historical Lessons for the World.* His focus on anger showed that he tended to cope with stress by imagining that others were against him when they may only have differed from him.

He additionally coped with stress by hypochondriasis at times but this never kept him away from dealing with problems for long. Direct challenges were hard for all people steeped in the Chinese culture. Thus his retreat to illness was not unusual but was usually brief until he felt capable of finding new ways to challenge critics.

He also was able to sublimate using poetry, calligraphy, anticipation, humor, and patience in positive ways. These sublimations made him feel intellectually superior, replacing his earlier fear that he was educationally deprived compared to others. In fact, he felt extraordinarily superior to some "peasants" like Khrushchev.

Unfortunately, Mao taught that anyone who wavered in accepting his "teachings" was committing political errors. His replacement of China's traditional "harmony" with "destruction of superstition and the influence of the clan elders" was a monumental achievement. But he did it at some cost to his people. He insisted that Chinese youth be trained, like Hitler youth, to view him as the savior of China and to carry on his fight against authority figures. He left the next generation of rulers able to survive only by denouncing the terror and bloodshed of Mao's cultural revolution. If they had not, they would have been overthrown. He had criticized Khrushchev for denouncing the terror of Stalin's reign but Mao's successors had to do likewise.

His level of moral development ran into trouble when he was forced to follow social conventions that he didn't believe were fair. He favored individual reasoning. In some instances he believed in justice and fairness, the highest moral level, but in other ways he became so convinced that he was correct, that he stopped listening to the views of others. He felt that he and other communists were "better" than capitalists and had no trouble condemning them to death or hardship.

In terms of his leadership, early on he governed in association with others. In those years, he shared decision-making with others whom he felt were at least as progressive as he. He increasingly made decisions with a smaller coterie and surrounded himself with "yes" men. His leadership could be designated as a "benevolent autocrat." Some could call him a "tyrant," especially in his later years.

4

NIKITA KHRUSHCHEV

"Luck is a mighty queer thing. All you know about it for certain is that it's bound to change." Bret Harte

1

Upbringing and Early Life

Nikita Khrushchev was born April 7, 1894 in Kalinovka, near the Ukrainian border. His grandfather had been a farm laborer and his illiterate father was both a farmhand and worked in coalmines. At times, Nikita lived with his father's brother, Martin, who took him from the mines to the village. There he was "close to the soil" as his parents desired. He also spent some time with his grandfather in Kursk, who had served in the tsarist army.

His father was an alcoholic and told young Nikita that he once sold his belt for alcohol. Although Nikita despised his father's drunken behavior, he drank extremely heavily himself, especially in the company of Josef Stalin and his cronies. However, in his later life, he drank with more control when he began to mingle with other world leaders.

His mother took in washing. He wrote, "My mother dreamed of a day when we could return to the village with a little house, a horse and a piece of land of our own."

Nikita began attending a Russian orthodox parochial school at age six. He walked barefoot in the summers because shoes were hard to obtain. He said, "Every villager dreamed of owning a pair of boots." He held up his pants with a string and wiped his nose with his sleeve, he said of his youth.

As a child he was horrified when he witnessed a pogrom. He saw Cossack soldiers shooting at Jews and heard the villagers saying they would soon have boots. They set Jewish stores and homes on fire and told villagers they could do what they wanted to Jews on three specified days. He saw beaten and dead bodies being scavenged by the villagers.

He cleaned boilers after school and on weekends. When he left school after a few years, he began work as a pipe fitter in coalmines. When he was 15, his family moved to Yuzovka (later called Stalino, now called Donetsk) in the Donbass region of the Ukraine. There his father worked in a coalmine. At this time, he lived with his father "at the pit" while learning to be a metal fitter and pipe fitter at Bosse factory.

From 1912 to 1918, although his father wanted him to be a shoemaker, he worked as a metal fitter in French-owned coalmines. He worked with the father of his future wife, whom he married when he was 20. He began to read *Pravda*, the communist newspaper, in 1915. He was fired briefly for taking part in a strike against his employers. He began to represent miners at political meetings and rallies in 1917. The following year he met Lazar Kaganovich, a communist who became his mentor and promoter.

2

Military Experience

Nikita's occupation exempted him from serving in World War I. When he was 24, he joined the Bolshevik Party, only months before the October Revolution. After Vladimir Lenin overthrew the tsarist regime, he established Soviet rule with Leon Trotsky in October 1918. Trotsky formed the Red Army.

Nikita joined the Red Army in January 1919, serving in the Ninth Rifle Division. He was next attached to Budyonny's First Mounted Army. They fought against retreating White Russians, driving them to the Black Sea where they arrived in April 1920. He described how they drove through a hail of bullets to victory. There they celebrated the "proletarian" May Day holiday in the Taman Peninsula.

Khrushchev was Stalin's only associate who was directly involved in the Civil War of communists against capitalists.

In World War II, Khrushchev worked his way up through the communist party and was given increasingly important military assignments. He had considerable responsibility for the defense of Stalingrad. Once his troops regained control there, he governed the beleaguered city from a hidden command post. The Soviet military suffered greatly during the Nazi onslaught of World War II. This was partly because Stalin frequently purged military officers whom he considered to be rivals.

3

Love Life

After his marriage to Evfrosinia Ivanovana Pisareva whom he called Galina, they had two children, Leonid and Julia. After seven years of marriage, Galina died of typhus in 1921. Nikita was gone at the time because he was fighting in the civil war for the Bolsheviks.

Not long after that, he met Nina Petrovna Kukharchuk where he worked in the mines. She became a schoolteacher, and they began to live together in 1924. At that time, he was active at an Industrial Training School for the Communist Party. They had three children, Sergei, Yelena and Rada. They did not marry officially until 1965.

Although little is known about his wife, he described an incident in which a female physician in Moscow treated Sergei for tuberculosis. Nina informed Nikita that this physician was later fired because she was a Jew.

Many of Nikita's nights were spent away from Nina in all-night sessions with Stalin and his henchmen. They would drink, eat and watch movies away from their wives. Apparently Nina took this in stride and did not complain. They lived modestly and dressed in plain clothes. In fact, it was a point of honor with many high communist officials to dress no differently than common people.

Nina was seen in many pictures by Nikita's side at meetings with visiting foreign dignitaries. In a charming photograph, she is walking arm in arm with Tito's wife during a visit with the Yugoslav dictator.

Shortly after Stalin's death, Beria was trying to take over the reins of the communist party. He promised to build dachas (summer houses) on the Black Sea for all the top leaders. When Nina saw the plans, she told Nikita, "That's a disgraceful idea." She, like her husband, believed that this was a very non-communistic, even capitalistic, proposal.

However, Nikita and Nina entertained in a dacha in the woods near Moscow. Before the 1917 revolution, their dacha had been a summer home of the czars. It was a luxurious mansion larger than the White House, according to Richard Nixon. It had a marble staircase, beautifully kept grounds and gardens. Boat rides on the Moscow River were available for guests. In addition, Nikita and Nina had a limousine at their disposal.

When Richard Nixon visited Russia as Vice President under Eisenhower, he described Nina. "She had all her husband's energy but none of his boorishness. Her outgoing warmth was a welcome contrast to Khrushchev's often harsh demeanor. And unlike her more rough-hewn husband, she had refined interests: classical music, the ballet, French and Russian literature, and spoke of them knowledgeably."

Little is known about Khrushchev's love life but there is no suggestion of infidelity.

4

Path to Power

When Khrushchev returned from serving in the Red Army in the Russian Civil War, he was assigned by the Communist Party to be the Deputy Director of the mines where he had been a pipe fitter. He was appointed to be Party Secretary of the local Communist Party after Lenin died in 1924. He attended the Ninth Ukrainian Party Congress with his mentor, L M. Kaganovich.

In 1925, he was allowed to go to Moscow as a non-voting delegate to the Fourteenth All-Union Party Congress where he first saw Stalin. He stayed with other delegates in deplorable quarters. He described sleeping on mats next to married couples that had no privacy for sexual activity.

Nikita made his first recorded public speech at the Ukrainian Party Congress in Kharkov. He was again a delegate to the Fifteenth All-Union Party Congress in Moscow in 1927. In 1928, Kaganovich promoted him to Deputy Chief. Later he moved up to Chief of the Ukrainian and Kiev Communist Party Committees.

In 1929, at the age of 35, he asked permission to study at the Stalin Industrial Academy in Moscow to become a metallurgist. However, when he began to attend the Academy, his friendship with another student, Stalin's wife, would change his life. Nikita, who had never been blessed with much, finally had the luckiest break of his life. He had the good fortune to become a close friend of Stalin's wife and this would enable him to enter Stalin's circle of associates, which led ultimately to his ascension to the most important post in the Soviet Union.

Even before he served in the Civil War of the Reds (communists) against the White Russians, he was reading widely. He was greatly influenced by Emile Zola's *Germinal*. He wrote, "It seemed like they were describing my father's mine." This story of workers who risked their lives in strikes against their oppressors focused on the dangers of mine work. The hero, who lost his girl in a flood, lived to carry on revolutionary work.

Khrushchev did not remain loyal to Kaganovich. His ambition and greater involvement in the Communist Party was mainly fueled by good words to Stalin by his wife, Nadya. She studied, unbeknownst to most students, at the Academy and Nikita often worked with her on projects.

Impressed by comments his wife made, Stalin sent Khrushchev to a collective farm to study conditions. Stalin also helped him to be elected as the secretary of the Communist District Party under Kaganovich in Moscow. Khrushchev now gave up his goal of metallurgy in favor of making a career within the communist party.

In 1932, Stalin's wife died (suicide or homicide were rumored) but it did not affect Khrushchev's rise to power. He was next made overseer for the Moscow subway system, one of the most ambitious projects in Russia. He also participated in purges to rid Stalin of opposing influences, and gradually worked his way toward Stalin's inner circle.

In his effort to please his superiors, despite his agrarian roots, he tried to get rid of the last vestiges of private enterprise. He did this by reducing the size of farmers' private plots to one half acre. This move would earn him the everlasting enmity of peasants. When Mao had tried to do this in China, the results similarly earned him the enmity of farmers.

His big moment came in 1952 when he gave a one-hour speech at the 19th Communist Party Congress. Stalin, old and sick, also spoke at the 19th Party Congress for only seven minutes. He described the creation of a 25-man presidium to replace him but this never materialized.

When Stalin died, Khrushchev enjoyed being on the same level as others among Stalin's intimates. He teamed up with others to defeat and arrest Beria who tried to replace Stalin. Khrushchev then gave the famous "Secret Speech" in 1956 denouncing Stalin and citing his crimes. When Khrushchev's speech cast doubt on the deeds and sacrifices that many had made in Stalin's name, they were made to look foolish or guilty.

Although these revelations alienated many, Khrushchev became the Premier. He interacted with world leaders until after the Cuban Missile Crisis, the Kennedy assassination and the disastrous Russian harvest of 1963. Despite his short stature, he had a large impact on those he met. Richard Nixon described him thusly. "Of all the leaders I have met, none had a more devastating sense of humor, agile intelligence, tenacious sense of purpose, and brutal will to power than Nikita Khrushchev." But when he was deemed of no more value, he was replaced with Brezhnev and Kosygin.

5

Leadership Style

After Khrushchev denounced Stalin at the 22nd Congress of the Soviet Communist Party, Stalin's body was removed from its marble mausoleum in Red Square. Khrushchev extended the distance between himself and Stalin by moving farther away from Red China and Mao.

Khrushchev and President Eisenhower met in 1959 at Camp David. The wily Eisenhower told him of the pressure from his generals for weapons increases. He said that he often found himself giving in. He asked if Khrushchev had had similar experiences. Nikita replied that he had but bluntly emphasized that he talked back firmly to his generals.

In 1959, American reporters in Moscow were allowed to have their first press conference with Khrushchev. He had picked up the press conference technique from President Eisenhower. However, when the conference concluded, reporters had to write their stories, submit them to censors, and then, if they passed, send their stories to their editors. These delays made American editors despair of timeliness.

Russian newspaper editors enjoyed printing news about Khrushchev during these exciting times. One editor wrote, "Think of it, here was a man who had been at the bottom of society. He had made his choice and joined the Revolution when it was not clear who would win. He took the risk. You felt he believed."

When Khrushchev and Vice-President Nixon met in 1959, Khrushchev surprised Nixon with some unanticipated profanities and ribald humor. He particularly disliked Nixon's denunciation of communists in the House Un-American Activities with cohort Joseph McCarthy. Nikita wanted to get the upper hand by thus shocking the stuffy Nixon.

Richard was no stranger to profanity, but lacked candor, humor and spontaneity because he was not as comfortable with himself as Khrushchev was. Nixon was left admiring Khrushchev.

Later, in *Six Crises* he described his supposition that Khrushchev was a typical Russian alcoholic. He wrote, "He hardly touched the array of vodka and wine bottles…His famed temper is always his servant and not his master, his drinking is strictly for pleasure and is never permitted to interfere with business."

When Khrushchev met with President Kennedy in the Geneva summit, it was shortly after the Bay of Pigs invasion of Cuba. Many had told Kennedy to delay the summit but in an effort to reduce Cold War tension, Kennedy proceeded. Despite the bolstering from amphetamines given by his traveling physician, Dr. Max Jacobson, Kennedy ended up with a verbal thrashing by the older fighter, Khrushchev.

Khrushchev joked with Kennedy explaining that he owed his presidential victory over Nixon to the Soviet Union. Nikita said that the U.S.S.R. had cast the deciding vote over the unlikable Nixon. Kennedy asked what he meant. He explained that the Soviets waited to release U-2 pilot Gary Powers until after the election to keep Nixon from claiming that he could deal better with the Russians. Khrushchev said that Nixon was McCarthy's puppet.

Despite this banter, Kennedy had found Khrushchev to be completely unreasonable, tough and harsh. In fact, he was shocked by Khrushchev's militancy and brusqueness, and sensed that the premier thought the U.S. could be pushed around.

Khrushchev announced that East Berlin was to be under the control of East Germany and West Berlin would be an international city. If America interfered, Khrushchev threatened that there would be war. Kennedy used the word "miscalculation" when he said in such a war more than seventy million would be killed within the first ten minutes. Khrushchev lost his temper at the word "miscalculation" as if it implied that he made errors. He angrily responded, "So be it."

Khrushchev probably underestimated Kennedy because of his poor handling of the Bay of Pigs invasion of Cuba. When Khrushchev told Kennedy that he was about to sign a treaty with East Germany that would endanger American rights in Berlin, Kennedy wryly said, "It will be a cold winter."

Khrushchev was intimidating, aggressive, uncompromising, and unnerving. When Kennedy tried to debate Marxist theory and colonialism, he was outclassed. Basking in the glory of his one-upmanship, Khrushchev sat close to Jackie. When she asked about the Russian dogs that were being sent into outer space, he promised to send her one and did. When photographers asked him to pose with Kennedy, Khrushchev said, "I would rather pose with his wife."

When Kennedy returned home, he tripled the draft and called for $3.25 billion more in defense appropriations. Khrushchev responded by building the Berlin Wall so the embarrassing flood of East Germans into capitalist West Berlin would stop. This adroit solution by Khrushchev ended the crisis and the Wall actually saved the two countries from war.

After the Berlin Crisis calmed down, Fidel Castro's brother told Khrushchev that the Kennedy administration was plotting to assassinate Fidel and overthrow his regime. Fidel wanted missiles and nuclear weapons. Khrushchev agreed to begin installing missiles in Cuba. However, when the missiles were discovered, Kennedy made a stand. Rather than start a thermonuclear war, Khrushchev ordered his Russian ships to stop at the American blockade on October 26, 1962.

6

Stresses

An impulsive man, when Khrushchev ran into people, instead of say-ing 'Good morning' he tended to punch them in the stomach. In the Geneva 1955 meeting, he met Nelson Rockefeller who had accompa-nied President Eisenhower and John Foster Dulles. Khrushchev poked him in the ribs as he said, "So this is Mr. Rockefeller himself."

Khrushchev was a keen observer and quick learner. He returned to Russia believing that the Americans were dressed "democratically" whereas the Russian delegation wore baggy pants. He became more fashion conscious thereafter. He was also embarrassed that the Russians arrived in a two-engine plane whereas the others flew in on four-engine planes. He did the same in future meetings.

Khrushchev lacked a psychological understanding of complex char-acters. He had a wonderful peasant's "horse sense" about how most people operated. But Stalin was complex and devious, as was Mao Tse-tung. Even though Stalin occasionally got irritated at Khrushchev, he usually forgave him because Nikita had kindly and loyal attitudes. However, once Stalin thought Nikita leaked ideas about economics to others who took credit away from Stalin. As Khrushchev came to understand Stalin's egomaniacal need to be the only one who came up with ideas, things between them improved.

In 1956, Khrushchev sailed to England and came by train to Lon-don to see the countryside. He met with the Queen on condition that he wear a business suit instead of Russian peasant clothes, the mainstay of Soviets at high and low ranks. He complied, and was impressed by her questions and information. She asked about the plane they flew in, a jet passenger plane, which he was quite proud to describe. They also discussed how obsolete ships and bombers were compared to subs and missiles.

In 1956, Hungary's Imre Nagy tried to denounce the communist government and bring capitalism back to his country. He ordered Russian troops out but Khrushchev tried to build a coalition of countries to support him as he sent troops back in. He lined up China, Poland, Rumania, Bulgaria and Yugoslavia to aid the fight against Nagy. His coalition building worked for a time. However, he clearly wanted to maintain control of Hungary because he feared that nearby Czechoslovakia, Romania, Yugoslavia and parts of the U.S.S.R. would also try to divorce themselves from Soviet control.

He was angered that Tito received him quite coolly in 1963. But he was reassured that the Yugoslavs did not want to be taken into the capitalist camp and wanted to be an independent communist country. When Tito told him that Yugoslavia gained $70 million from tourism, he was envious. They had good roads, decent hotels and restaurants, which Tito said were necessary for tourism. Khrushchev began to develop amenities for tourists and reduced obstacles for visitors at borders. He believed such changes were acceptable as long as the means of production and the banks belonged to the people and the state was run by a dictatorship of the proletariat.

He wrote off Yugoslavia's debt to Russia after visiting Tito and loaned them equipment to build a steel mill. He said that he wished the U.S.S.R. could have traded more with the U.S. like Yugoslavia did. But he didn't think he should take out that irritation on Yugoslavia.

When his Virgin Lands program failed, he abandoned it even though it had been successful in 1956 and 1958. He had moved 500,000 volunteers to Kazakhstan to plow much-needed grain. They were funded to live primitively and succeeded in producing excellent harvests early on but the climate created a dust bowl and the program ended.

Khrushchev dealt with many leaders by offering trades for what he wanted. It didn't seem to work with Mao Tse-tung. He offered to build Mao a radio station in return for a Russian submarine base in China for refueling, repairs and shore leave for sailors. Mao perplexed him by saying "No, we don't want foreigners on our territory."

The Soviets built China a road from Peking to Ulan Bator in Inner Mongolia. Mao and Chou En Lai had said they needed a road from Peking to Kazakhstan and kept pushing. So Khrushchev was angry when the Soviets completed their half of the road and the Chinese did not build their own half.

He never learned how to cope with Mao. He wrote, "We used to lie around a swimming pool in Peking, chatting like the best of friends about all kinds of things. But it was all too sickeningly sweet." Mao had boldly asked Khrushchev for atomic secrets and criticized the Russian goal of peaceful coexistence with the West. In the end, Khrushchev thought Mao would not tolerate any other Communist Party being superior to his. As their relations deteriorated, Khrushchev took his minister of defense to task for publishing Mao's war writings.

Because of Khrushchev's simple and straightforward perspective of life, he did not realize that Mao was incensed when Khrushchev decided to denounce Stalin's crimes. Mao wanted Khrushchev to discuss this de-Stalinization of the communist party with other communist party leaders before doing it.

Mao told Mikoyan, Deputy Premier of the Soviet Union, in 1956 that Stalin's merits outweighed his faults. Khrushchev displayed less understanding of Chinese psychology than Stalin because he tried to use economic pressure to bring the Chinese into alignment. This angered Mao who thought he was as bad as the arrogant European and American capitalist countries.

The final insult was when Mao held a party to honor Khrushchev. There, Nikita indicated that China should let go of the territory (Taiwan) that was controlled by the U.S.-backed Chinese Nationalists. Mao thought Khrushchev was very rude by saying that China should sacrifice territory, especially when he would not tolerate Russia sacrificing territory.

By 1960, Khrushchev was calling the Chinese "madmen" who wanted to unleash war. He stated that international relations would depend mainly on relations between the U.S. and the U.S.S.R., not including China.

When Egypt's Nasser came to visit Khrushchev, they immediately liked each other. During the visit there was a sudden military coup in Baghdad. Nasser had just helped form the United Arab Republic of Egypt, Iraq and Syria. Khrushchev helped Nasser fly home with protection by permission from Iran. Nasser later performed a similar favor by offering shelter for Saddam Hussein who fled after trying to overthrow the Iraqi government.

Nasser had asked Khrushchev for help in building the Aswan dam. He thought the dam would increase arable land and produce wealth for any country investing in its future. Although Khrushchev felt the Soviets couldn't afford it, they wanted to build Arab trust and invested. Nikita was invited to throw the switch with Nasser in May 1964, to divert the Nile River. Nasser then released communist prisoners and the two forged a good working relationship.

Nixon said that Khrushchev used his humor as "a bludgeon to clobber his adversaries." He said that Khrushchev "kept needling me about my background as a lawyer, implying that I was a slick and dishonest manipulator of words, while he was an honest miner and worker." He added that Nikita could indulge in self-deprecating humor at times. As an example, Nixon was walking with the President of the Soviet Union (the figurehead) in Russia and beckoned Khrushchev to join them. "No, you walk with the President," he told Nixon. "I know my place."

However, Nixon pointed out that when Khrushchev came to America; he seemed sensitive to any change in the schedule. It was as if he thought he was being slighted or displaced by something more important. His angry reactions suggested to Nixon that he was an insecure little man, unsure of how well he was coming across to American political VIPs.

Although Khrushchev didn't like Kennedy's build-up of forces in Berlin and the bulldozers by the Berlin Wall, at least it was better than war. However, when the Kennedy administration began the airlift to

West Berlin, Khrushchev retaliated by increasing the budget of armed forces. The macho posturing between the two leaders worried many. It continued when Khrushchev announced three hydrogen bomb tests. Then Kennedy announced that the U.S. would resume underground nuclear testing.

Khrushchev could be a reasonable man. After Kennedy delivered a U.N. speech pledging not to provoke aggression but not to flee it, Khrushchev initiated an exchange of letters with Kennedy that lasted until the assassination. Kennedy granted an interview with Khrushchev's son-in-law, editor of *Izvestia*.

In January 1962, someone tried to assassinate Khrushchev when he visited Minsk with the leader of the Polish Communist Party. A single shot was fired and it was unclear whether it was from his bodyguards or elsewhere. He did not appear in public for three weeks afterwards. There had been two unsuccessful assassination attempts in 1956.

When the Cuban Missile Crisis took place, many feared that Khrushchev had underestimated U.S. willingness to fight. They thought that there would be a showdown in Cuba. Khrushchev realized that when Kennedy said other countries were on the side of America, and smartly gave Nikita a way out through diplomatic concessions, he better withdraw the missiles.

Kennedy sent ABC TV correspondent John Scali to the Soviet Embassy with a secret proposal. He promised not to invade Cuba if the Soviets would dismantle and remove missiles. The UN could inspect missile sites to insure Soviet compliance. In addition, Khrushchev asked for removal of missiles in Turkey, England and Italy.

Kennedy also knew that Khrushchev had to be handled correctly and must not be put in a position where he risked discredit and humiliation at home. Publicly, Kennedy avoided gloating after the Cuban Missile Crisis was resolved and instead congratulated Khrushchev on his statesmanship.

However, the results cost Khrushchev heavily in his relationship with Castro in Cuba. Meanwhile, the American public did not learn of the deal between the leaders to remove missile bases. They assumed that Kennedy was more persuasive than he really was. In Russia, Khrushchev began portraying himself as the victor.

Khrushchev and Kennedy established a "hot line" between Washington and Moscow. Next the Soviet Union made crucial concessions about the international inspections of nuclear facilities. This was a sign that Khrushchev was at last serious about a test ban.

The first time the "hot line" was used occurred on November 22, 1963. Lyndon Johnson used it to assure Khrushchev that the U.S. would not launch a missile attack. This was of concern because it was quickly established that Kennedy's assassin had lived in Russia and was a communist sympathizer.

7

Accomplishments

Khrushchev was a technical rather than a political expert. His agricultural successes and his oversight in constructing the Moscow subway were great achievements. He had two excellent harvests in 1956 and 1958 from his Virgin Lands experiments. These enabled him to produce consumer goods and invite debate on economic reforms.

He relaxed censorship to some extent but his policy of openness soon provoked new opposition. In 1955, he reconciled with Tito of Yugoslavia and met with Western leaders in Geneva. He also supported several independence movements among Soviet satellite countries such as Egypt and other Arab nations.

The impact of Khrushchev's denunciation of Stalin's crimes in 1956 was devastating to communist parties everywhere. This was immediately followed in 1957 by the brutal suppression of the Hungarian Revolution. These events cost the American Communist Party 85% of their membership and reduced their members to some 3,000 by 1957-58. While this may not have pleased Khrushchev, it was a victory for anti-communism in America.

In 1957, the launching of two Sputniks shocked the world and created a new view of Soviet superiority in science. The U.S. and the world had assumed that America was ahead in science and the space race.

Time magazine selected Khrushchev as man of the year in 1957 because he denounced Stalin, handled the resulting unrest, put satellites into space and acquired partnerships in the Middle East with Nasser in particular.

He was the first Soviet leader to advocate "peaceful coexistence" with the West, and to negotiate with the U.S. on reducing Cold War tension.

Despite his boasting about women serving in figurehead positions in the Soviet Union, women have fared no better there than in America. Men run things. In six decades of Soviet power, only one woman made it to the Politburo and Khrushchev put her there. Yeketerina Furtseva served as the only woman in the Soviet Cabinet from 1960 to 1974.

From the standpoint of the West, Khrushchev's greatest accomplishments lay in his courage to denounce Stalin, to avoid thermonuclear war, and to make and break relations with countries and leaders when it benefited his people.

8

Summary

Khrushchev was raised in penury and his family had to worry about whether they could provide the basic requirements of life such as shelter, food, water, safety, clothing, and medicine.

He developed normally given the conditions of poverty. He focused on unions and communism to improve conditions of the poor people. He was raised in a strict religious atmosphere but became a true believer in Marxist communism in his teen years. Although he disliked his father's alcoholism, he identified with him and there is no evidence to suggest that he was opposed to authority figures in general. He felt loved by his mother and this allowed him to trust others and be trust-worthy.

He was an industrious child having to go to work with his father at an early age. He thought of himself as quite manly, even though he was short (about 5'6"). He looked back upon his life and tried to focus on his contributions, believing that he had helped establish peace between the world's two superpowers with President Kennedy. He was proud of that despite being ignored in his final years.

As he matured, he appeared to have had unconditional love from his mother, which helped him develop intimacy with women. He developed the ability to be intimate with many people including his wife, Stalin's wife, his superiors, his peers and his underlings. He was emotional and warm toward those he cared about and pitied. But he could also order the murder of those he believed were enemies of the state or enemies of his leader. There is no evidence that he was unfaithful to his wife although he enjoyed paying compliments to the beauties married to heads of state.

He used some childish ways to reduce tension as well as healthy ways. Many believed he was out of control because he took his shoe and banged it on the podium at the U.N. But when the threat of thermonuclear warfare surfaced in the Cuban Missile Crisis, he wisely had Russian ships turn around rather than fire on American ships. This cost him dearly in his relationship with Castro and caused great criticism by his rivals. Overall, he retained his early ethical principles and valued the survival of his people while ridding himself of rivals. He was not one to take risky acts. He used humor, sometimes poking fun at others, but sometimes poking fun at himself and his own country.

Nixon gave an example of Khrushchev's humor. Troops were being reviewed in Moscow when a soldier in the ranks sneezed. The officer asked whomever it was to step forward. No one moved. The first row of soldiers was lined up and shot. The officer asked again who sneezed. No one replied so the second row of troops was executed. The officer asked again who sneezed. "I did," answered a timid voice in the back. "Gesundheit," said the officer.

Nikita and Nina lived a basically ascetic life for most of their marriage with few personal trappings, except when they used their dacha to entertain. He was basically moral, having learned early to please others and to value rules of the system, albeit the communist system, over his peer group. There is no indication that he used his power to obtain sexual favors or undue wealth. He was happy to have contributed what he could toward world peace.

He went through various stages in developing his final leadership style. Early, he was not particularly close to Stalin and focused on getting things done. That distance probably spared him during the purges of Stalin's enemies. During the war and the development of the Moscow subway, he probably would have been called a developer or a team manager showing as much care for his people as for the project. But the increasing power led to his unnerving outbursts and surprising frankness, traits that he probably learned from his hard-working, hard-drinking father and religious mother.

Although he did not have much education, he was a very quick learner and could eventually figure out how to handle most situations and most leaders except the most complex. Because he showed his feelings more directly, he was easier for other people to understand. But he could be cunning and deceptive when it served his purposes.

He believed early on that rockets were "the weapons of imperialist aggressors." After he approved the launching of sputniks in 1957, there was no way that any rival could overthrow him. This success pushed him more toward caring less about his people and more about his goals, thus making him a benevolent autocrat.

He took advantage of the capture of U-2 pilot Gary Powers to threaten President Eisenhower with broken promises and cancelled their summit. But he did not cancel "peaceful coexistence" plans with the U.S. because he saw that would be the greater good for the two world powers. At this time, he might have seemed tyrannical to the U.S. but was probably still a benevolent autocrat.

Some have said that Khrushchev was deposed as premier because of his inability to resolve the agricultural problems that gripped his nation. It is more likely that the changes he unleashed could not be contained and the old guard party members removed him. Toward the end of his political career, he became more aware of how he would be regarded by posterity. He became a peace advocate and uttered the famous statement that after the first exchange of missiles in a nuclear war, the ashes of communism and capitalism would be indistinguishable.

He spent the remainder of his years in retirement in a suburb of Moscow. Richard Nixon was on a personal trip to Moscow in 1965. He dropped by the shabby apartment where Khrushchev lived, but was told that Nikita was out by two "guards (?)" Khrushchev died on September 11, 1971.

5

FIDEL CASTRO

"Ambition is so powerful a passion in the human breast that however high we reach, we are never satisfied." Niccolo Machiavelli

1

Upbringing and Early Life

Fidel Castro was born August 13, 1926. His father came from northern Spain to fight the Americans in Cuba as a paid mercenary. He was hired to replace a wealthy young man who was called up to serve. After Spain lost Cuba, Angel Castro remained there working for the American-owned United Fruit Company as a laborer. He worked his way up to sugarcane contractor with a large staff of cane cutters, and eventually owned thousands of acres.

Angel married a schoolteacher and they had two children. When his wife learned of an affair with a maid named Lina, she left him. Angel and Lina had many children before they married. Fidel was their sixth child and he used to suffer when people made reference to his illegitimacy. Lina managed the Castro store where employees shopped and was described as messy and disorganized. She permitted chickens to live in their house. Unlike typical Cuban families, the Castros were not close and did not even sit together for meals. They ate on the run, standing up, a habit that Fidel was reported to have maintained later in his life. This was similar to Richard Nixon's family.

Cubans were angry that American troops, led by Leonard Wood and Theodore Roosevelt, claimed Cuba from the Spanish but did not give the Cubans total independence. Americans felt Cuba was important to their economy. They claimed the right to intervene if Cuba had civil wars, or tried to set up loans or treaties with other countries.

Fidel, like the other Castro children, was sent to a prestigious Catholic school where he was a good student though not particularly studious. He was a large, rambunctious boy compared to his quiet, small, younger brother, Raul. Fidel often got into fights with other students and sometimes had to be restrained by school authorities.

Fidel learned basketball by practicing day and night. The coach said Fidel drove him crazy asking questions about how he could become a leader. In the beginning, Castro was not a good speaker but he gradually became gifted in speaking simple Spanish and getting people to agree with him.

When Castro was in college, he walked around carrying Hitler's *Mein Kampf* under his arm. He mimicked Mussolini's speeches practicing with a recorder. He also studied the methods of other leaders such as Lenin, Stalin, and Juan Peron. He found that Hitler was the "mirror of every German's unconscious," according to psychoanalyst C. J. Jung. He learned that Mussolini used words about rich versus poor countries.

He studied Primo de Rivera, founder of the Spanish Fascist Party in 1933. De Rivera, whose father ruled Spain from 1923-1930, told people how to live and eat in addition to ruling. Castro imitated this when he set out rules and hours of when posadas were available to couples seeking a rendezvous place. The de Rivera father and son sought unification of Spanish-speaking countries. After the son was executed in the Spanish Civil War, General Francisco Franco made him a martyr.

When Castro was 18, Father Llorente wrote under his school picture in 1945, "Fidel distinguished himself always in all subjects related to letters. A top student and member of the congregation, he was also an outstanding athlete, always courageously and proudly defending the school's colors. He has won the admiration and affection of all. We are sure that, after his law studies, he will make a brilliant name for himself. Fidel has what it takes and will make something of his life."

Fidel and his father, Angel, didn't get along, like so many fathers and sons in this study. Their relations were cool and resentful. But his parents sent him to the University of Havana to become a lawyer. They also bought him a new American car that he wanted. Fidel, being Spanish, was taller than other Cuban students. He was also sloppy and earned the nickname "Bola de Churre" (grease ball). Sometimes he dressed up in a suit but he allowed his room to become disorderly. It was strewn with dirty underwear, cigarette butts and old newspapers.

Castro had a personal style of making people feel important. He used the Spanish familiar for "you" (tu) and spoke often with the phrase, "you and I." He wanted to be a leader of students but was so independent that he had trouble working and sharing with others.

When he joined other college mates to protest the increase of bus fares, police beat the students. They went to the newspapers to tell of this unfair treatment. The media attention was pleasing to Fidel and he sought more opportunities to make headlines. He planned his first speech on the anniversary of the execution of eight university students by Spanish colonial authorities in 1871. He gave the speech on November 27, 1946.

The month after his speech, he and two other students attacked and shot a rival student leader, injuring him seriously. His political activities in school displeased his father who cut off his allowance. However, his attempt on the man's life brought Fidel much attention and he relished more. When his parents heard that he was planning a coup of the Dominican Republic leader, Trujillo, they tried to divert him with a new car and the promise of a trip to the United States.

He abandoned the idea of the coup. But he faked injuries and donned bandages to get on the front pages of newspapers. He claimed that he was beaten when he led a demonstration against the American Embassy. This followed an episode in which U.S. Marines had relieved themselves on the statue of a Cuban leader. Needless to say, that incident stirred up anti-American reactions.

2

Love Life

At the age of 22, Fidel married a wealthy and beautiful woman named Mirta. Her father's wedding gift was a three-month honeymoon in New York. He enjoyed living off his family and his father-in-law and did not get a job. Mirta soon became pregnant and bore Fidel his only son, Fidelito. He took an inordinate interest in having a son who would become bigger than other boys. It was reported that he overfed Fidelito to the point of sickness. The marriage deteriorated as Fidel spent more and more time with his political friends and cared naught for work. In later years, Fidel tried to hide information about the marriage and many of his own people do not know about it.

Fidel began to carry a gun everywhere. He was seen shooting at animals, birds, and even playfully shooting at people. He and other Cuban students, including a communist named Alfreda (Che) Guevara, went to Colombia. They wanted to meet a popular Liberal Party leader named Gaitan. When Gaitan was assassinated a few days later, Fidel joined the mob that killed the assassin and overran the capitol. The uprising took 5,000 lives in April of 1948.

The Cuban leader, Eduardo Chibas, was an excellent speaker and often spoke to the public on the radio. He killed himself just after a radio speech August 15, 1951, in which he urged Cubans to clean up government corruption. Fidel was near enough to summon the ambulance and arrange for mourners.

By this time, Fidel had obtained a law degree but never tried more than a handful of unimportant cases. Batista took over the government with a coup on March 10, 1952, causing Fidel and his cohorts to flee because they had campaigned for election.

Frustrated by this, he conspired against Batista with political friends. Meanwhile, he met another wealthy beauty, Natalia (Naty) Revuelta. This young woman was something of a rebel herself and was attracted by the charismatic power-hungry young Fidel. She paid for Castro's needs as he found a leadership role among the young, angry, alienated Cuban revolutionaries. They never married but had one child, a daughter who came to denounce Fidel openly in later years. Eventually, Castro had five other illegitimate children by Dalia, a lady from Trinidad.

Castro had many affairs and women complained that he was very unromantic, often smoking cigars or wearing shoes in bed. He proclaimed that he could not marry because he was married to Cuba.

3

Path to Power

While many Cubans thought that Castro abhorred capitalism, he had several mansions with bowling alleys, heated pools, and hunting grounds. He entertained foreign visitors and dignitaries in sumptuous settings. This contrasted with his image of asking Cubans to join him in making sacrifices for communism against capitalistic Americans.

He led his first uprising in 1953. Like so many charismatic leaders, he appealed because he appeared strong, knowledgeable and decisive. Charismatic leaders are like a parent who knows how to fulfill the wishes of children. He was 26 and he had traveled over 30,000 miles in his car searching for money, arms and men. He asked his father for $3,000 to overthrow Batista and his father laughed him off, offering only $140.

Fidel loved uniforms unlike the leaders of most other "communist" regimes. The wives and women of his followers sewed uniforms for the revolutionaries to look like Batista's men. His mistress, Naty, typed his manifesto. She also got records to play over Santiago radio stations in case they were victorious. His wife, Mirta, waited at home until after the attack. One of his followers was engaged and Castro arranged a hasty wedding and honeymoon for him, in case he died during the attack. The man did die. Castro had a way of controlling the lives of his people on a very intimate basis just as had read that Primo de Rivera had done.

The night of the attack, they arrived in Santiago just as tourists descended upon the carnival. Castro forgot his glasses. He couldn't see well as he drove out in the line of cars prepared to attack at dawn. Because he was so big, the Cuban uniforms had sleeves and trouser legs too short for him. They sang, "To die for the Fatherland is to live." This song, reminiscent of Nazi Germany, was modeled after what he had learned about Hitler from *Mein Kampf.* After that, nearly 100 men and two women attacked Moncada barracks held by between 262 and 1000 Batista soldiers, depending on who was reporting it and which side they were on.

The element of surprise was lost when Fidel got out of his car and began firing his submachine gun. Then when the line of cars was to advance, he jumped back into his car only to find it would not start. Nobody gave any orders and there was no timed plan about how to proceed. Later Castro said, "History has never seen such a massacre."

After the fight, many tried to escape by taking off the hand-sewn uniforms and walking away in their regular clothes. Fidel and his main leaders were caught a few days later and tried in court. Meanwhile Batista had demanded that ten revolutionaries die for every one of his soldiers killed. Their barbarities and tortures were highly publicized by the time of Castro's trial on September 21, 1953.

Being a lawyer, Fidel chose to represent himself and had them remove his handcuffs. He donned an impressive lawyer's robe, which he took on and off as he changed places between the position of the accused and the lawyer's position. He described how revolutionaries were important to improve the country, pointing out that the rich capitalists exploited and oppressed the poor people. He called for new revolutionary laws for farm workers' rights to share profits and confiscation of property taken by politicians (such as the United Fruit Company). He ended the trial saying, "Condemn me. It does not matter! History will absolve me!"

The trial ended with 13-year sentences for his brother, Raul, and one other leader, 10 years for others, three years for some, and 15 years for him. He was sent to the Isle of Pines, the beautiful island depicted by Robert Louis Stevenson in *Treasure Island*. While there, he continued to write his "manifesto" in limejuice so prison guards could not see it. His followers smuggled it out and ironed the papers to bring out the writing. The works were copied, printed and distributed by followers who drove across Cuba to distribute them.

Castro used Hitler's trial words from 1924. "For it is not you, gentlemen, who pass judgment on us. That judgment is spoken by the eternal court of history. You may pronounce us guilty a thousand times over, but the goddess of the eternal court of history will smile and tear to tatters the brief of the state prosecutor and the sentence of this court. For she acquits us." Hitler and Castro charged their accusers with "betraying the true spirit and destiny of the Fatherland."

Inmates and prison workers called Fidel "Dr. Castro". In Cuba, people who completed a college degree were generally called "Doctor." He held school for his men, teaching them Cuban history, grammar, math, geography and English. He held his followers to stricter rules than the prison, such as having his men arise at 5:30am whereas the prison had inmates arise at 6:00am. He was again dictating the details of how his people should live.

Castro sued Batista for the tortures and killings resulting from Moncada. The cases were still being heard at his amnesty in 1955. He wrote Naty and Mirta from prison but their letters got mixed up. When Mirta received Naty's letter, she blew up and severed relations with her husband. Her family had connections with Batista, so his government gave her a small stipend to help her out and get her on his side.

In 1955, when Fidel and his Moncada followers were released on amnesty, they sailed back to the mainland. Castro was greeted in Havana with enthusiasts who hoisted him onto their shoulders. He went to the apartment of his sister, Lidia. He then went to Mexico City to dodge Cuban court warrants.

In Mexico, he solicited help to fight against another competitive revolutionary, Carlos Prio, who was also organizing troops to oust Batista. Fidel's group of 60-70 rented a few houses in Mexico City. They trained by running and rowing boats. He gathered four trusted men. Besides his brother, Raul, Fidel had a man who trained his followers in Spartan procedures; an Argentine physician named Bayo who had fought Franco in Spain. He also had Che Guevara and Frank Pais. Che and Fidel hated Americans and Che, a Marxist, convinced Fidel to become a communist. Pais was a poet and composer, and Fidel would eventually force him to lead another ill-fated uprising in Santiago in 1956.

Fidel spoke to an audience of 800 people in New York City on October 30, 1955. He was able to elicit contributions and support. But after the second failed uprising, in 1956 dictator Fulgencio Batista broadcast that Castro had been killed.

It was January 1, 1959, that Batista fled and Castro claimed victory as he marched into Havana with his rebels. It was not long before Castro clarified that he was going to be anti-American and aligned himself with the Soviet Union and communism.

The American government attempted to upset Castro's communist regime with the CIA-trained exiles at the Bay of Pigs in 1961. After the invasion, U.S. involvement was aggressively denied at the U.N. These untruths unraveled within hours. A band of half-trained Cuban refugees had been landed on a Cuban beach by some freighters. With little support, they were soon captured and the expected uprising of Cuban masses against Castro's communism did not occur.

During the Cuban Missile Crisis in October 1962, President Kennedy exposed the Russian missiles that were being mounted in Cuba. After days of intense negotiating, Khrushchev agreed to remove the missiles in exchange for American pledges not to attack and some other agreements undisclosed at the time.

Castro was angry that the USSR removed the missiles from Cuba. Mao, one of Fidel's heroes, told Castro that he wouldn't trust the U.S. agreement not to attack. Khrushchev wrote Castro that the U.S. wouldn't attack during Kennedy's term. The last conversation between Khrushchev and Castro involved Castro's wish to revolutionize Cuban agriculture to change it from dependence upon one crop (sugar).

Walter Cronkite interviewed Castro and mentioned that he had found that communist governments paid little attention to maintenance, leaving buildings unpainted, unrepaired and likely to deteriorate. Castro said that there were two reasons. Communists won power and built the working classes new apartments but had little left over to maintain capitalist structures. But he added that under communism when people didn't own things, they didn't seem to take care of them.

Castro could not convince everyone that his brand of communism was working. According to Georgie Anne Geyer, a French intellectual, Regis Debray, enchanted by Castro's ideas went to Cuba in 1965 to write for him. Twenty years later, he returned to France to work for French president Francois Mitterand. Debray, like so many young revolutionaries, had become disgusted with the unending sacrifice, inefficiency, dissipation, undisciplined youth, homosexuality, and suicides among the top-ranking Cubans.

In 1975, Cuba sent some 40,000-57,000 soldiers to Angola, backed by Soviet financing, airlift and support. By 1977, Cuban forces were in Ethiopia and they eventually numbered between 5,000 and 7,000. By 1989, Geyer wrote that Castro had hundreds to thousands of soldiers in South Yemen, Libya, Nicaragua, Mozambique, Syria, Equatorial Guinea, Tanzania, North Korea, Algeria, Uganda, Laos, Afghanistan and Sierra Leone. She stated that without Castro there would have been no Nicaraguan Sandinistas; no invasion of Grenada; no guerrilla movements from El Salvador to Uruguay and to Chile; no Marxist Angola, Mozambique and Ethiopia; and no "super-national drug state" spreading across Latin America defended by his trained guerilla fighters.

4

Leadership Style

Castro was one of those leaders who captured the public's imagination by making himself one with his people. Mao Tse-tung was another such. He made people think he was their friend. He might promise to visit them in the evening but kept them waiting for hours, thus imposing his power upon them. When he spoke, he often used self-deprecating jokes or comments. These gave the appearance of modesty or recognition of his own faults.

When he gave speeches, he combined flattery, flirtation, jokes, exhortations, denouncements, and commands. In 1989, he spoke to 200,000 Cubans in the Plaza de la Revolucion celebrating his 30 year old communist revolution. He ended his speech with the words, "Marxism-Leninism or death!" He was taking credit for making Cuba the true center of Marxism at a time when Gorbachev announced no more Soviet aid. During Gorbachev's visit to Havana on April 3, 1989, he urged Castro to imitate Americans and have open elections.

He dealt with other leaders by pretending to be so experienced in guerrilla warfare that they believed him. Between 1979 and 1989, he made deals with General Torrijos and General Noriega to get supplies, medicine, and drugs from Panama. He convinced Noriega that if the United States attacked, he would supply specially trained guerrilla fighters to lead the people into the mountains to hide and fight. He also promised to supply them with weapons. When the U.S. did invade Panama in a surprise attack on December 20, 1989, Noriega's people gave up quickly. American troops found 65,000 Cuban weapons still wrapped up.

5

Stresses

Each leader has a different way of reducing stress and handling failures. When Mao saw that his legacy was fading, he launched a cultural revolution. This revolution eliminated China's intellectuals and allowed Mao to write his own legacy in his own history books of propaganda. Hitler saw his Third Reich failing and instigated mindless attacks as if to end the world from his Berlin bunker. As Castro viewed the collapse of communism, he had his top military officers executed for "corruption" when in actuality he saw them as rivals.

Numerous assassination attempts against Castro have been tried. A U.S. embargo has been in effect ever since the Cuban Missile Crisis. The Soviet Union, long a dependable source for food and oil, crumbled in 1991 and has provided little help since. Cuba's financial crisis has worsened, yet Castro continues his "battle of ideas" against U.S. policies. His brother, Defense Minister Raul Castro, leads an anti-U.S. rally every weekend in a different community.

Castro continued to make headlines well into his 70s. In September 2001, he said that he believed western countries owed reparations to Africans for having made them slaves. He spoke of the slave labor on sugar plantations benefiting Cuba as well as the United States.

In May 2002, the United States undersecretary of state for arms control charged that Cuba had been developing biological weapons of mass destruction and collaborated with "pariah" states that have their own germ warfare programs. As ex-President Jimmy Carter arrived in Cuba, Castro denied the charges and invited Carter and American experts to visit suspected sites.

6

Accomplishments

It was not until Fidel Castro that Cuba made its final break with colonialism. In much of the rest of Latin America, the break is still incomplete. The U.S. has had a decisive influence over Cuba because they were the chief customers for sugar. From 1952 to 1959, the United States was favorable to Batista. Cubans saw them as supporting the Batista regime. Batista had used coups to assume power over the Cubans and his government was despised for its corruption.

When Castro's revolution succeeded, even John Kennedy wrote, "Fidel Castro is part of the legacy of Bolivar who led his men over the Andes Mountains, vowing 'War to the death against Spanish rule'." Although Castro was not a communist when he began the revolution, he became one and betrayed his promise that he would improve Cuba with democracy. Nevertheless he improved some things for his country.

According to Herbert Matthews, the reporter who gave the world the news that Castro was alive with his guerrillas in the mountains, the poor have benefited the most. All children are now getting some education, even in rural districts where most of them got none before. Poor children are better off in health, food, clothes, trades, and civic responsibilities.

The Cuban Revolution equalized the wealth by seizing the property and companies of the wealthy, restricting income, and improving the status of the poor and the Negro. The Castro regime tried to plan education, housing, public health, military buildup, and much more than was being done by previous regimes to aid the people.

At first Batista and his followers fled the island. Then the middle and upper classes fled. That included engineers, architects, doctors, teachers, journalists, lawyers, business managers and shop owners. Castro had to bring in technicians from the Soviet bloc, and have Cuban youths trained behind the Iron Curtain.

After the Bay of Pigs, he traded 1,300 Cubans who attacked for food and medicine, donated by American firms at the request of the Kennedy administration. During the Cuban Missile Crisis, Castro was not consulted while Kennedy and Khrushchev resolved the crisis through a series of deals. The Soviets had to make it up to Castro with apologies, economic aid, and a warm reception when he visited the Soviet Union in 1963.

Perhaps because of American support of a corrupt regime and exploitation of Cuban resources, a revolution was necessary. American errors led to the development of a Cuban Revolution. Matthews said, "It was Cuba's destiny to be to the Western hemisphere what France was to Europe with its Revolution of 1789."

Overall, the Cuban workers' paradise that Castro preached has fared no better than other communist states. The planned economy has led to chronic shortages and rationing. Dissident voices have been silenced and the media controlled over the 42+ years that Castro has ruled.

7

Summary

Fidel was raised in luxury compared to the peasants. He did not have doting parents but they gave him what he needed and he never had to worry about supplying his basic needs. He worried more about whether he could satisfy his social needs.

He had a good deal of basic trust that his parents would look out for him. But because he was called a bastard, he was somewhat ashamed of his heritage. He was an industrious and active young fellow, much larger than the average Cuban.

He became romantically involved at an early age and married Mirta. However, his proclivities to romance took him many directions and he was unfaithful. As time passed, he decided it was to his advantage to deny marriage to any one female and proclaim that he was married to all of Cuba. This allowed him to follow lust and disavow commitment.

He was able to achieve some intimacy with a few females. But for the most part, he valued power too much to sacrifice it for any single woman or for love and lust.

Castro has always been a reckless sort according to those who knew him. He used some amount of self-deprecating humor, modesty, and charisma to endear him to the public. He has not been one to avoid temptation but has used propaganda to depict himself as a man devoted to his people and to their good, rather than to his own personal agendas.

In terms of morals, Fidel always pleased his parents until he got into sports. Then he began to enjoy the adulation of his peers. His school authorities and peers made him feel that he could achieve great heights if he eschewed convention and risked his life to rid the country of bad people. He never gave himself over to the laws and rules of his society. But, he gave himself over to becoming a hero by bringing better management to Cuba. He didn't really care whether Cuba was communist or socialist or capitalist, as long as he was the hero who brought them some relief.

His management style was at first more dedicated to his people than it was to a cause. As time passed, he became more of a benevolent autocrat and sometimes even a tyrant. He cared little for the reactions of accusers. In recent years, many have accused him of not bringing relief for the poor and downtrodden through his communist regime. So he contented himself with becoming important as a leader who countered the powerful United States, ninety miles away, on the behalf of the little countries of the world.

6

JOHN KENNEDY

ο ο ο ο ο ο ο ο ο ο ο ο ο ο ο ο ο ο ο ο ο ο ο ο ο ο ο ο ο ο ο ο
"Man's chief pursuit is neither fame nor fortune; man's chief pursuit is woman." Anonymous

1

Upbringing and Early Life

John Kennedy was born June 19, 1917. He was born into an Irish Catholic family. His wealthy and ambitious father was usually gone, but left his mother continually pregnant. Housekeepers, governesses, and nurses had more interaction with the children than their own parents did. John, usually called Jack by friends and family, was a sickly youth, requiring frequent treatment that he greatly despised. His diagnoses were unclear until it was finally discovered that he had adrenal insufficiency.

John was second of the nine children eventually born to Rose and Joseph Kennedy. Rose gave firstborn Joe much authority because her husband was gone so much. Joe tended to lord it over Jack and the other children throughout their early years. Eventually, he and Jack stopped fighting and became very close.

In 1927, Joe moved his family to New York because Irish Catholics were so frequently rejected in Boston. He purchased a five-acre estate in Westchester and an 18-room summerhouse in Cape Cod. In 1933, he added a villa in Palm Beach, Florida.

John's father arrived to visit his father-in-law, former Mayor of Boston, with mistress Gloria Swanson and a number of reporters. His father-in-law said, "How dare you, you son-of-a-bitch, cavorting with that floozie while my daughter is at home."

Rose acted as if she was not disturbed by the presence of Swanson. She once even went sailing with her husband and Swanson, saying that they were trying to help her because her husband left her for another actress. Rose decided to compete with other women by improving her looks and her wardrobe. By seeming to permit her husband to have affairs rather than make an issue or divorce him, Rose may have suggested to the children that infidelity was acceptable.

John was sent to boarding school for four years. During that time, Rose maintained attitudes she had displayed during his home life. She warned him to take care of his health, posture, teeth, eyesight and diet. John's father wrote each child letters that rarely included moral principles but stressed the importance of winning at any cost and the pleasure of coming in first.

When he was ten, John went over his mother's head and wrote his father "A Plea for a Raise." He explained that he used up his 40-cent allowance on "areoplanes" but had become a scout and needed more to buy canteens, blankets and "searchliagts." Although not a very good speller, he convinced his father that he should have a 30-cent raise.

John was always poor in school, greatly overshadowed by his older brother, Joe, Jr. As his parents pleaded with the schoolmaster to allow John to skip summer school so he could travel with his family, the schoolmaster argued that he had sloppy work and personal habits and needed to learn that unfulfilled assignments and work must be made up during the summer. His poor performance caused a falling out with his father.

A psychologist saw him at age 17, and issued a report saying, "He has established a reputation in the family for thoughtlessness, sloppiness and inefficiency, and he feels entirely at home in the role. Any criticism which he receives only serves to confirm the feeling that he has defined himself correctly; in fact the definition is the best possible defense that could be devised."

An incident involving John and 12 other boys in a club called the "Muckers" landed him in danger of being expelled. The boys had designed a prank to bring a pile of manure into a dance for eligible and wealthy young boys and girls. This prank was hurting the expensive private school (Choate) at a time when the national depression and poverty in the country had made enrollment dip.

The schoolmaster summoned John's parents. Although it seemed that his parents sided with the school, Joe finally recognized that what he believed was a fun-loving, spirited son was quite acceptable even if he was not like his older brother.

Joseph Kennedy hired athletes and trainers to teach sports to his children. Rose was active herself, with swimming, walking vigorously and playing golf without the use of a golf cart.

In his late teens, John accompanied his father to England where Joe would be appointed ambassador in 1938. He enjoyed the pomp and circumstance that was afforded his father. Also during this year, John became 21 and like his siblings, received a one million dollar trust fund from his father.

John enjoyed England and traveled across Europe with a friend recording political events. He wrote about these to his father. Joe Kennedy, Sr. suggested that John write a thesis or a book about his observations. With the help of a professional writer and publisher hired by his father, John wrote *Why England Slept*. The book expounded the theory that England was too slow to respond militarily to the Nazi threat. To make it a best seller, his father bought 40,000 copies that were then stored in Hyannis port.

John's father did not favor declaring war on Germany so he differed from his son about that issue. Joe also differed with Roosevelt, favoring appeasement and peace, which eventually resulted in a falling out between the two.

John's slovenly habits continued and he was seen as a messy, fun-loving fellow who pulled pranks on others. He surprised his friends by never carrying money since his father paid for everything. When caught short by a cash need, his friends had to pay. His peers and family usually saw him as a "lightweight." He graduated from his first school, Choate, with the aid of tutors. His I.Q. was tested at 119, bright average, and interestingly was only one point over Lee Harvey Oswald who assassinated him in 1963. His atrocious spelling was seen in many sample letters and speeches before he hired speechwriters.

John enrolled in Princeton against his father's wishes because of friends who attended. However, he fell sick and had to withdraw. An unexceptional student, he admitted to friends that he wasn't as smart as his older brother, Joe, Jr. who had attended Harvard. After his health returned, John enrolled in Harvard and barely managed to graduate from Harvard Law School in 1940.

He didn't know what to do after law school but thought of writing. Toward this end, he audited some journalism and business courses at Stanford University in California where he roomed with actor Robert Stack. While there, he signed copies of his book and was something of a celebrity, making frequent trips to Hollywood to meet stars.

Between girlfriends, he had back surgery in 1944. At the same time, his older brother Joe was killed in a plane crash in the war.

A shocked and grieving Joseph Kennedy, Sr., asked Senator Harry Truman, "Harry, what are you doing campaigning for that crippled SOB (Roosevelt) that killed my son Joe?" Truman confided to a writer that "Old Joe Kennedy is as big a crook as we've got anywhere in the country." Shortly, Truman was asked to run with Roosevelt as his vice president.

A short time after the death of Joe, Jr., another tragedy struck the family. Kathleen, one of John's sisters, lost her husband, an English-man who was killed in the war. As Jack recovered from back surgery, still thinking only that he might be a writer, his father told him he was to replace Joe in politics. Jack resisted but his father demanded.

His father then got him a position with the Hearst newspapers as a political correspondent. John covered the Potsdam Conference after Roosevelt's death when Truman, Stalin and Churchill met. While there he became violently ill and received his first diagnosis of Addison's disease. He had to be brought back to the U.S. by Cabinet Secretary James Forrestal.

2

Military Service

John still had not found himself when his brother entered the military in 1941. So he entered the Naval Reserves in June 1941, because he was able to skip the physical examination with his father's help. Also John lied on his military forms, concealing his illnesses. He claimed to have had only the usual childhood illnesses.

With his sparkling looking record, he was granted a commission as an ensign in the Naval Reserves. He was assigned to a desk job in Washington, D.C. His father thought that military duty would enhance political possibilities for his boys and encouraged them to do this.

However, in 1942, John's health deteriorated and he was hospitalized during a six-month leave. When he returned, according to family values, he volunteered for the toughest assignment he could find; namely risky PT boat duty.

With his father's influence, he was sent to the Solomon Islands for more exciting duty. He was given a PT boat crew of ten men. A destroyer hit his boat. This was because of inattentiveness on the part of his crew or him. He managed to swim pulling a crewmate to shore. Then he swam again for help, a difficult chore for one in poor health. Expecting to be in trouble, he was surprised to receive a medal through his father's influence. Although his father wanted a higher medal, he was given an award for life saving.

His only other PT boat duty was when he was sent to help rescue a ship but ran out of gas on the way. By that time, his back trouble was so bad that he was relieved of his command by a physician. With his father's help, his illnesses were seen as connected with his duty. Writers such as Inga Arvad (who would become his mistress) glamorized his duty.

3

Love Life

John Kennedy carried on an extremely active love life throughout his short life, starting in his teenage years. Though he was often sick and away for treatment in places like Arizona, he had sex whenever possible according to letters to his buddies.

When he was 19, he wrote a friend the following letter with numerous spelling errors: "Got a fuck and a suck in a Mexican hoar-housse for 65 cents, so am feeling very fit and clean…Smoke and I set out yesterday, went over the boarder + arrived at a fucking Mexican town…Anyways Smoke + I ended up in this 2-bit hoar-house and they say that one guy in 5 years has gotten away without just the biggest juiciest load of claps-so Smoke is looking plenty pallid and even I occasionally think of it, so boys your roomie is carrying on in true 9 South style and is upholding the motto of 'always get your piece of arse in the most unhealthy place that can be found…your gonnereick roomie."

His father had affairs with many women, one of whom was Gloria Swanson, beginning when John was ten years old. Joe bragged about this affair and in later years John also had an affair with the older fading movie star.

When serving in the Navy, a twice-married Danish woman named Inga Arvad was sent to interview him. Being four years older and having interviewed world leaders, John was enamored of her and began an affair. The FBI suspected that she was a spy and bugged her apartment. Their tapes caught John in sexual adventures with her. This information was crucial in his relationship with J. Edgar Hoover of the FBI when he became president.

His affair with Inga continued from 1941 to 1944. He tried to persuade his father to permit him to marry Inga. However, his father argued against marriage with a divorced woman, saying it would damage his political potential. His relations with Inga were certainly not monogamous because he had enjoyed sex with numerous women, famous and infamous from his teens until his death.

In 1949, John's sister Kathleen died in a plane crash. John thought he was going to die soon also. He told friends, "They keep giving me these chemicals because I have this disease. It'll finish me off by the time I'm 45." He commented to George Smathers with whom he had numerous debaucheries, "The point is that you've got to live every day like it's your last day on earth. That's what I'm doing."

John's father thought he should marry for political reasons. In 1952, he met Jackie Bouvier, who was looking for a man with money since her father had lost all his. John was 36 and Jackie was 23. He liked her facility with foreign languages and she had been educated at the prestigious Vassar and Sorbonne universities. Her knowledge of ancient history and her love of the fine arts made her an interesting conversationalist. She was working as a correspondent interviewing famous people as Inga Arvad had done. This probably made John more interested in her.

John proposed by telegram. After the June announcement of their engagement, he took off for a European vacation with friends before his September marriage. He wrote her from Bermuda, "Wish you were here."

They married in 1953 at a wedding for a crowd of 3,000, designed by the "Ambassador." Jackie hated politics, the competitive roughhousing of the Kennedys, the constant presence of John's male friends, frequent stories of John's affairs, and the fact that she was left alone so much. She took out her frustrations by shopping binges and constant redecorating.

Caroline was born by Caesarian section in 1957. John was away and almost didn't return to Jackie's side at the time of the birth. George Smathers insisted that he do so. He was extremely emotional and happy when he saw Caroline. After Jackie's recovery, she kept herself busy by hiring and firing staff and perfecting her looks.

When John ran for President, Jackie dutifully traveled some with him, gave short speeches, and refrained from discussing issues or smoking in public at his request. John, Jr. was born in 1960. By this time, Jackie was so disgusted with the cavorting of her husband that they had little to do with each other and she kept very much to herself.

Throughout their marriage, John had sex with other women. Reporters, secret service agents, the "rat pack" and others often provided women. There was an endless succession of women in the White House and the White House pool where John liked to swim nude with women. Because of his clandestine activities, he twice or more lost contact with the man who carried nuclear codes handcuffed to his wrist.

John Kennedy was exceptionally bold in a conversation with England's Prime Minister Harold Macmillan. He told Macmillan, "I don't know about you, but I get sick if I don't have a woman every three days."

4

Path to Power

Ted Sorenson sat in the front row of all Kennedy's speeches, making notes of what the audience liked, and eliminating what they didn't. He included more quotes from famous people and John finally got the reputation of being an eloquent speaker and a learned, deep man. One writer said, "No national figure has ever so consistently and unashamedly used others to manufacture a personal reputation as a great thinker and scholar."

In 1957, Mike Wallace of ABC and Drew Pearson said that Ted Sorenson wrote Kennedy's book, *Profiles in Courage*, for which he won the Pulitzer Prize. Kennedy wanted to sue them. However, political advisor Clark Clifford said that immediate public apologies would be better if Kennedy could produce proof to show ABC and Pearson. He did and apologies were immediately issued.

Kennedy had a poor voting record in the House of Representatives, largely due to numerous absences for illness. His father had already begun to refer to John as the future president of the U.S., introducing him as such and calling him a war hero. He had John move to Boston to take over the congressional seat of a man who was going to leave it to run for Mayor of Boston. Joe Kennedy hired a staff, set up rallies, parties, dinners, forums, printed flyers, publicized appearances, paid for billboards, interviews, etc. to enhance John's political career.

Joe sent a $600,000 donation to Archbishop Richard Cushing for a Boston children's hospital through the Joe Kennedy, Jr. Foundation, listing John as president of the foundation. Therefore it seemed that John had funded the hospital program.

Joe Kennedy hired a man with the same name as John's rival to run so the public would become confused and the vote for John's opponent would be split. It worked and John won the election even though he refused to be pinned down to a specific platform.

This election revealed a pattern seen in all John's campaigns. It included control by his father, extravagant expenditures, shady tactics, fuzzy issues, and unlimited energy. John was not forced to devise a political agenda or to develop effective leadership skills. He supplied charm and others did the rest. His main goals were to win votes and please his father.

As a senator wanting to run for president, John pestered Lyndon Johnson for committee assignments but Johnson resented how Kennedy interfered in his areas. For example, Kennedy wrote and spoke about the South and ending segregation there. That was an area that Lyndon and Southern Democrats wanted to handle.

John was totally devoted to winning and didn't want his staff to arrange anything unless it helped him get votes. When he was running for re-election to the Senate, he was taken on a tour of a sausage factor and chatted with black workers. Later he chided his staff saying, "Well, you just wasted an hour of my time. They gave me a great reception but not one of them is a registered voter in Massachusetts who can vote for me."

When Kennedy was positioning himself to run for president, Lyndon Johnson said, "It was the goddamndest thing, here was a young whippersnapper, malaria-ridden and yellow, sickly, sickly. He never said a word of importance in the Senate and never did a thing. But somehow, with his books and his Pulitzer prizes, he managed to create the image of himself as a shining intellectual, a youthful leader who could change the face of the country. If he ever got elected president, Joe Kennedy would run the country."

When Kennedy was ready to leave his old Senate seat, his father had him put a former classmate in to hold the spot until Teddy came of age (30), even though John wanted to give the seat to his friend, Torby McDonald.

Kennedy ran for the presidency against Nixon with the help of his father's money, paid organizers, friends and show business cronies called the "rat pack." Part of the "rat pack" included Peter Lawford who married his sister, Dean Martin, Sammy Davis, Jr., Joey Bishop and Frank Sinatra. The rat pack arranged for girls to be available at various stops that Jack made. They all shared an endless pursuit of pleasure in sexual conquest, and when Marilyn Monroe entered the picture, even Bobby Kennedy was involved.

John's sense of humor made the public love him. When he was running for the presidency, he told an audience, "Do you realize the responsibility I carry? I'm the only person standing between Nixon and the White House."

As the campaign proceeded with jokes about his father's backing, he used self-deprecating humor to turn the accusation into a joke. He told a group, "I have just received the following telegram from my generous daddy. It says, 'Dear Jack, don't buy a single vote more than is necessary. I'll be damned if I'm going to pay for a landslide.'"

Walter Cronkite interviewed presidential candidates Nixon and Kennedy with the stipulation that it be unrehearsed and unedited. Nixon cooperated wholeheartedly. However, when Kennedy was asked the same question, "What single quality do you think will be the most important that you take to the White House?" Kennedy stumbled around. He requested that the taped interview be redone. His aides rejected all arguments about how unfair that would be. Cronkite went to Kennedy's room. Kennedy assumed he was coming to discuss re-shooting the interview. Cronkite told him "All right, but that is the lousiest bit of sportsmanship I've ever seen." At that point, Kennedy said to let it go.

President Eisenhower had little respect for Kennedy. After Kennedy won the presidential election, he referred to John as "Little Boy Blue," called Bobby Kennedy "a little shit," and called Teddy "the bonus baby." He was convinced that the ambassador's money was the chief factor in John Kennedy's success.

5

Leadership Style

Kennedy had Press Secretary Pierre Salinger arrange for transportation, accommodations and instant speech transcripts for the press. Kennedy aides saw reporters almost as battle companions. Most were male, and reporters often thought that if they were helped to cover newsworthy events, they would repay the favor by no reports on drinking, womanizing, and homosexuality. The liberal rather than conservative bent of many male reporters also helped Kennedy protect his image.

Through flattering press coverage of seeming interests in culture, the Kennedy wit and vitality transformed the view of the American presidency. Many Americans felt almost as if royalty presided with a mixture of youth and endless possibilities. Patriotism no longer had the appeal that it enjoyed during wartime. However, Kennedy's inaugural address inspired a slight resurgence of patriotic spirit with his line "Ask not what your country can do for you but what you can do for your country." That line was one of the most winning lines ever produced by speechwriter Ted Sorenson.

The full-time elite group of well-trained Secret Service men who protected the president was Kennedy's most intimate group. He saw them even more as comrades and pimps and expected them to provide the boss with a constant and steady supply of female sex partners. One Secret Service agent said, "He didn't want to know about security but about broads."

Kennedy told one new Secret Service agent, "You've been here two weeks already and still don't have any broads lined up for me? You guys get all the broads you want. How about doing something for your commander in chief?" The agents had little trouble recruiting women who felt it was their "patriotic duty" to oblige the president.

Kennedy cared nothing for classical music, opera, ballet or the arts. As Jackie once said, the only music he appreciated was "Hail to the Chief." However he wanted to create the impression that he was intelligent, cultured and profound. He had no policies, no long-term goals nor convictions, except to be elected. He fooled many intellectuals into believing he was one of them. Among those were Theodore White, Arthur Schlesinger, and John Kenneth Galbraith.

The power that his father held over him was clear in a conversation with Clark Clifford, presidential advisor for several administrations. John told Clark, "My father wants me to appoint Bobby as Attorney General but Bobby has never practiced law. My father said that doesn't make any difference. He wants Bobby to be Attorney General because he's a lawyer, is savvy, knows political ins and outs and can protect me. Would you go to New York and talk to my father about this but don't tell anyone else about it?"

Clifford did discuss this with Joe Kennedy. John's father said, "Thanks for your views but Bobby is going to be Attorney General."

Early in his administration, John suffered embarrassment during the Bay of Pigs invasion, which had been planned by the Eisenhower administration. Some said that he did not feel confident enough to ask strong questions of those planning the action. He learned to slow his advisors down and ask more probing questions by the time the Cuban Missile Crisis occurred eighteen months later. This was seen as his most important contribution to the presidency.

Despite seeming to value Martin Luther King's role to end segregation, Kennedy was more intent upon avoiding bad press coverage than ending racism. In 1961, critical news stories described the jarring and bloody confrontations of Freedom Riders. King had asked Kennedy to issue a second "emancipation proclamation." Kennedy refused. From his jail cell, King said he disliked leaders who felt that they could "set a timetable for another man's freedom."

Overall, Kennedy's leadership style did not contain a grand vision like Woodrow Wilson or Ronald Reagan. Many have assessed his style as crisis management from one hour to the next, focusing mainly on how he wanted to be seen and remembered.

6

Stresses

John could lie easily when it helped him get what he wanted. He suffered from Addison's disease but lied about it to get into the military and to be elected president. Addison's disease is eventually fatal but in 1940, it was discovered that cortisone could replace adrenalin, which was withering in his body. Cortisone was extremely expensive as well as having dangerous side effects. His father arranged for a supply of it to be held in safety deposit boxes around the world for his use when he traveled. Voters wanted to know the health of the candidates for the presidency. When reporters said that Kennedy used Cortisone and would die without it, he denied regular use and his aides denied it entirely.

His treatment for Addison's disease made Kennedy's face fill out from the thin boyish look he once had. It made his hair remain brown; his skin look tanned and heightened his sexual cravings. In addition to the failure of the adrenal glands to produce their important hormones, John had degenerative back disease. He used narcotics for pain and extended their use to sexual pleasure. Peter Lawford told of an incident when pain pills or experimental drugs were used to heighten sexual pleasure with two White House interns, aged 21 and 23. The girls were given the drugs and Kennedy and Lawford watched their sexual reactions and even watched them experience hyperventilation problems, gasping for air, but did not call for medical help. Risky behavior with sex and drugs had become a way of life early when John thought his life would be short.

When he didn't get the nomination as Adlai Stevenson's vice president in the run against Eisenhower, he ignored his wife's problems to drown his rejection in sex and male camaraderie. He flew to his father's French villa for a vacation leaving Jackie eight months pregnant. She had had a miscarriage in her first pregnancy and was very uncomfortable in this one, but he was selfish and tended to himself rather than to his wife and coming child.

He joined George Smathers for an orgiastic yachting trip on the Mediterranean with many women. He got word that Jackie had an emergency Caesarian and delivered a stillborn child, that her condition was critical and a priest had been summoned. When he did not rush to her side, Smathers convinced him that a shattered marriage would end his political ambitions. This was foremost of importance to him. So after three days, he left and joined her. She was furious, especially when she learned what he had been doing. Such incidents demonstrated his lack of commitment and intimacy with women.

In relationships with women, he lied and promised more than he could deliver to get his way. In 1960, Judith Campbell (Exner) was summoned to a hotel room where he was with another girl. He proposed a three way sexual event but Judith refused to participate. He

promised marriage if she would forgive him and continue the relationship. But, of course, he had no intention of fulfilling his promise.

When Kennedy carried out the doomed plot to invade Cuba on
April 15, 1961, which he inherited from Eisenhower's administration,
he had two main reactions. One was to call his father and ask for help.
After hours on the telephone on April 19th, his father became disgusted
and said, "Oh, hell, if that's the way you feel, give the job to Lyndon."

Kennedy tended to blame others in situations like the Bay of Pigs
fiasco. Despite public denial of U.S. participation, he had White
House officials give the press information that implicated the Joint
Chiefs, the CIA (he had Allen Dulles replaced), the Eisenhower
administration and even the press for publicizing anti-Castro activities.
The real cause of the botched operation was that Kennedy did not feel
qualified to question military and CIA experts in sufficient detail. In
his wish to be seen as strong and manly, he was afraid not to go ahead
with the attack. As Bobby said, if he had reneged he might have been
seen as cowardly.

Clark Clifford said that after the Bay of Pigs embarrassment,
Kennedy had decided it would never happen again. As a result, he used
intense questioning for other problems like the Cuban Missile Crisis.
The Bay of Pigs fiasco also caused him to pour more funds and man-
power into plans to assassinate Castro. This plan, called Operation
Mongoose, was abandoned only after the Cuban Missile Crisis.

Kennedy was pragmatic and amoral. He had good looks, youth,
wealth, recklessness, vanity, and lechery. He pursued and abused
power, indulged himself at the expense of others, and tried to fulfill his
father's image. He abused high position for self-gratification and irre-
sponsible encounters with women and mobsters, which had potential
for blackmail and scandal.

One of Kennedy's greatest gifts was his ability to use humor. He
first used it as a youngster when writing to friends about his life-threat-
ening illnesses, diagnostic tests and treatments. He turned this talent
for humor, and especially self-deprecating humor into a high art. Once

after a conflict with former president Truman, he said, "I guess Truman will apologize for calling me an SOB, and I will apologize for being one." Another time, he was describing his experience aboard the PT 109 when a reporter asked how he became a war hero. He said, "It was absolutely involuntary. They sank my boat." Shortly after his election, Kennedy was heard to say, "When we got into office, the thing that surprised me the most was that things were as bad as we'd been saying they were."

Kennedy, Johnson and Nixon were pragmatic, secretive, deceptive and insensitive toward others. All three were anti-communistic but used the F.B.I. and C.I.A. for personal advantage.

7

Accomplishments

The Kennedy administration enjoyed some firsts. In 1961, he established the Peace Corps of volunteers who were sent to aid impoverished areas of the world. By the end of the year, 1,000 citizens were involved. In 1962, he authorized the flight of John Glenn, the first American to orbit the earth.

In 1962, after reconnaissance revealed Soviet missiles being installed in Cuba, he questioned his advisors and listened to all, even Adlai Stevenson whom he personally disliked. He tempered the military proponents of force and argued for more careful steps and compromises. He felt personally that Khrushchev was testing him to see how tough he was, and worried about the possible danger to so many people across the world. Stevenson and others proposed that the U.S. offer not to invade Cuba but offer to withdraw missile bases in Turkey, England and Italy.

Kennedy finally decided on the plan to quarantine Cuba and negotiate terms, which produced the desired effect. The Soviets withdrew their missiles. He offered this deal to the U.S.S.R. through private sources (newsman John Scali). His back up plan was to offer the same deal through United Nations Secretary U Thant. It averted a possible nuclear war. Kennedy had learned from the Bay of Pigs disaster and Berlin Wall erection not to escalate crises.

In 1963, the U.S., United Kingdom and U.S.S.R. signed a Nuclear Test-Ban Agreement, prohibiting atmospheric testing of nuclear weapons. He had been moved to this goal because the U.S.S.R. had resumed above ground nuclear tests using 30 and 50-megaton bombs. The U.S. also resumed above ground tests. But after the Cuban Missile crisis, the world was ready for an end to nuclear face-offs. The world had watched in terror as the two leaders sparred in a macho contest of who would be the first one to back down.

In June 1963, a meeting was set for the two superpowers to discuss banning nuclear tests and weaponry. The U.S.S.R. stopped jamming U.S. news in their country. A hot line was established between the Soviet premier and the White House. The Russians agreed to inspection of nuclear facilities. In July, the Soviet Union agreed not to test above ground, under water or in outer space.

In November 1963, the U.S. supported or authorized the overthrow of the South Viet Nam President Diem. Although the U.S. had supported South Viet Nam leaders for nine years, stories were emerging of terrible persecution and murders of the citizenry. So the U.S. government supported a coup to overthrow the corrupt leader. However, his own bodyguards killed Diem instead before the U.S. plan could be carried out. Three weeks later when Kennedy was killed, he had not decided what to do about Viet Nam.

Kennedy did not live up to Truman's ideal. Truman said, "The president is the only person in the government who represents the whole people. When there's a moral issue involved, the president has to be the moral leader of the country."

8

Summary

Joe Kennedy made his wife, Rose, into a baby factory. She had four children in five years. She could not be as close to any one of them as they were to each other. The crowd of siblings was what Kennedy children had to accept in place of intimate relationships with their own parents. As a result, John preferred to be with many rather than one in his friendships, activities and often even in sexual encounters. Because he missed a one to one relationship with either mother or father, he did not know how to have a one to one relationship with women. His family was like a team with the coach being Joe. To this day, the Kennedy cult of the crowd is their favorite way to interact with others.

The family wealth meant that John never had to worry about physical or safety needs but cared more about social needs. He turned to his father for money, advice, direction and his very existence because of his father's preparations for medical care throughout the world. This caused him to conform to his father's expectations and lifestyle. The result was that he lacked the independence, industriousness and maturity to take on productive responsibilities and relationships.

His illnesses made him worry about whether he was on a par with his older brother. He was delighted in his teens to find that he was a real man because women would have sex with him. This success, which his father applauded, made him believe that his main contribution could be in the area of his love life. He never achieved any particular intimacy with his women or wife, but his risky sexual activities made him feel he was worthwhile as a man.

He had a particularly healthy coping technique in times of great stress. He used self-deprecating humor to win the favor of others and get himself out of jams. But he never succeeded in learning asceticism or resisting temptation. It is difficult to know if he might have learned it in later years. Lee Harvey Oswald assassinated John Kennedy on

November 22, 1963, as he rode in a motorcade through Dallas. Lyndon Johnson succeeded him.

Morally, he avoided punishment and was valued when he followed the precepts of his mother minimally and his father maximally. He loved being counted as okay by his peer group, which he achieved through being one of the guys sexually. In the end, he enjoyed acceptance by political peers and by his own father.

In terms of leadership, he was a minimalist. He trusted his advisors. That is why he got in trouble during the Bay of Pigs. He was only an administrator, with little concern for his people and little concern for the task. But during the Cuban Missile Crisis, he became the compromiser or even team manager as he asked his staff to consider all diplomatic possibilities. He was able to satisfy Cuba, the Soviet Union and the United States with a peaceful resolution to the threat of nuclear missiles being placed 90 miles from U.S. territory.

7

LYNDON JOHNSON

"Life's greatest happiness is to be convinced we are loved." Victor Hugo

1

Upbringing and Early Life

Lyndon was born on August 27, 1908. He was the first child and later had three sisters and one brother. His mother, Rebekah, married Sam Johnson, and was moved out to the boonies of Texas, without plumbing or books. Her minister grandfather had been president of Baylor University where she went to college. She earned a degree and taught Texas poor children for free about English, poetry, and public speaking. Her elocution gifts were seen in Lyndon who eventually was able to talk almost anybody into anything.

Rebekah loved Lyndon immensely and taught him how to read by the age of four. This allowed him to start school a year and a half younger than usual. Her own father had been a teacher, lawyer, newspaper editor and Secretary of State in Texas. However, he was unsuccessful in his effort to run for Congress. This caused Rebekah to be intensely interested in politics and in developing that desire in Lyndon.

Sam was an energetic, intense, enthusiastic persuader who grabbed people by their lapels and looked them right in the face as he talked to them. Lyndon learned this unusual trait from watching his father campaign and operate as a rancher and politician. Sam wanted to be a law-yer but couldn't afford college. So he became a farmer, bought and sold real estate, and finally was the legislative representative of his district in Texas.

Rebekah loved her husband and they laughed and talked politics together. Family get-togethers were noisy and Sam made all his children discuss, debate, and argue politics. He also had them do spelling and arithmetic, and think quickly.

Lyndon's mother had an interesting way of controlling the behavior of others. Whenever her students or her own children did not measure up, she stopped talking to them, ignored them, and talked to other people until they had suffered a while. Then she resumed talking to them as if nothing had happened. Lyndon came to use this trait. His friends and subordinates called it a "freeze-out."

Lyndon was a restless, inquisitive child who needed attention. He got attention by getting lost a lot, running away, and making people have to find him. When he began school, he liked to dress differently to get attention. When he had to go to the bathroom and write his name on the board, he took up two boards. He used to demand to sit upon his teacher's lap, being the youngest in the class, and did this without embarrassment. He craved attention for the rest of his life.

Open affection and kissing between father and children was common in the household. News photos showed Lyndon kissing his father on the mouth. Lyndon enjoyed physical closeness and invaded the comfort zone of distance between men conversing, often kissing men on their foreheads throughout his political career.

Rebekah poured her hopes and dreams into Lyndon. She started him in violin classes but showing no talent, switched him to dance lessons. He preferred to tease the girls but turned out to be one of the best dancers ever to be president.

Lyndon was always the leader in his group, despite the fact that he usually ran around with older children. Around age ten, he began doing shoeshines in barbershops where he joined in political conversations with patrons. He often argued or informed them since he talked so much about politics with his father.

Lyndon was 11 when his father went broke because of paying too much for his farm. He lost his high position in town and suddenly the family was the laughing stock. Whereas Lyndon had always over-dressed like his father, now he continued but people scorned them both. He lost respect for his father, whom he felt had made the whole family the butt of jokes. He reacted by becoming a juvenile delinquent who ran with a wild bunch, disobeyed orders and did what he wanted. He drove off and wrecked the family car. He stayed in California for some time until he returned at his father's strong invitation.

On one trip to California, he worked for a lawyer uncle who mentored him to some extent. His parents wanted him to go to college and begged him to return. He was dead set against college. This was hard, especially for his mother who had been one of the first women to get a degree in Texas. But he finally decided to try for college. He did, he said later, because everyone he knew had gone and he'd been unable to do anything other than manual labor. The labor, however, built up his frame. He had previously been a tall, skinny youth who avoided fights and was seen as a 6'3" coward.

His mother helped him cram facts to take the college entrance exam. He passed and entered Southwest Texas State Teachers College in San Marcos in 1927. At age 19, he got into campus politics. He was known as "Bull" Johnson because he bragged and people could not believe what he said. He complimented everyone unduly, but never took a real stand on any issue. He toadied up to the college president and developed a personal relationship with him.

His mother wrote him constantly saying "My dearest love" and "My splendid sweet son." He wrote her saying "Dearest mother, I love you so, don't neglect me." He wrote for the campus newsletter and, not surprisingly, developed a flowery writing style.

To make some money he became principal of a school for Mexican children in a small Texas town for nine months. He taught them history and public speaking following in his mother's footsteps. He later said that his Great Society program in which the strong must care for the weak came from his mother's ideals and this early experience.

But after nine months, he returned to college where he enjoyed campus politics again. He worked in a Houston high school for a short time where he taught public speaking and coached the debate team. He graduated at age 23 in 1930. Shortly, he went to Washington, D.C. to be the secretary for Representative Kleberg. He was for poor people and therefore was for Roosevelt who became president in 1933. In typical fashion, he toadied up to Roosevelt and enjoyed rapport as FDR's protégé.

2

Love Life

He proposed to Lady Bird the first day they met. He loved her, enjoyed talking to her as his father had his mother, and laughed with her. He realized her shyness and sometimes poked fun at her in front of others, even ridiculing her appearance and her clothing. Her wish to have a husband who would amount to something was important. She doted on him as his mother had, calling him "my dearest love."

Knowing that he was the pride and joy of his mother, he decided not to discuss Lady Bird with his mother and went off suddenly to marry her in 1934. His mother reacted wonderfully well. In fact, Lyndon kept a letter from his mother about his marriage framed on the walls of his boyhood home to show visitors. Written November 30, 1934, it said, "My darling boy, I rejoice in the happiness you so richly deserve, the fruition of the hopes of early manhood, the foundation of a completely rounded life. I have always desired the best in life for you. Now that you have the love and companionship of the one and only girl, I am sure you will go far."

Lady Bird set out to inform herself so that she could be a fitting wife for a man in politics. She learned how to take his constituents on tours, entertain them, and do his bidding. As time passed, if she knew of his many affairs, she kept it to herself.

In 1938, Lyndon met Alice Glass, a 26-year-old beauty who was the mistress of a Texas legislator. A cultured intelligent woman, she began to advise 30-year-old Lyndon about appearance, dress, public relations, and culture. He was a rapid learner and within a year they were deeply in love. Although they hid their affair from their spouses, the four of them were often together. Alice and Lyndon remained friends for 25 years. With her help, Lyndon was on his way as a man with great ambition.

Madeleine Brown met Lyndon in 1948 when she was 23. She was married to a mental patient and encountered Johnson at a reception for his radio station. After spending the night together, Lyndon, she said, hollered out the window "My God, I love Texas in the morning." He always stressed secrecy and she often came to him on short notice. When she became pregnant two years into their relationship, he was furious. He sent some financial help and purchased nice gifts, as they continued their affair fitfully for some years.

In the 1960s, she remarried and in 1967, was seriously injured in a car accident, which disfigured her face. During her painful recovery, he sent messages and warnings to keep quiet. She meekly responded to his wishes. In 1969, they met for three hours. They didn't have sex, she said, because Johnson seemed too frail. She asked him to acknowledge her son, Steven. But he declined saying "I've got the girls to consider, and Lady Bird."

In 1987, this woman's son (born in 1950), claimed to be Johnson's only male heir and filed a $10.5 million lawsuit against Lady Bird. He alleged that he had been deprived of his birthright and wanted to change his surname to Johnson. He was 36, he said, before his mother told him on her deathbed about his father and the 21-year love affair with Lyndon.

Lyndon had another affair with a well-known woman, Helen Gahagen Douglas, the wife of actor Melvyn Douglas. On the last day of his presidency, Lyndon reminisced on incoming President Nixon and his shabby treatment of Helen. He said, "She was a fine person and he destroyed her." The Congresswoman had been Johnson's advisor and probable lover during her 1950 campaign for the Senate. But Nixon defeated her by falsely implying that she was a communist. She never ran for office after that.

Johnson's attitude toward women was very chauvinistic. After a female reporter criticized Johnson, he told White House Counsel Harry McPherson, "What that woman needs is you. Take her out. Give her a good dinner and a good fuck."

A female Congresswoman opposed his educational programs. He told Joseph Califano "There's no point in my calling that woman. Gaither (Califano's aide) is a good-looking boy. You tell him to call her up and ask her to brunch this Sunday. Then he can take her out, give her a couple of Bloody Marys and go back to her apartment with her. Tell him to spend the afternoon in bed with her and she'll support any goddamn bill he wants. Now if he wants to help his president, that's what he should do instead of writing these whiney memos every night."

Johnson's press secretary, George Reed, wrote that Johnson sought new additions to his White House harem constantly. Doris Kearns, a reporter who later wrote a book about Johnson, became a steady admirer during the last years of his administration.

When he first became president, he told Lady Bird not to fritter away her power but to find a couple of projects. She selected Head Start and Beautification. But when Bob Dole began criticizing her Beautification Program (eliminating billboards, etc.), Lyndon had her retreat because he didn't want her to be hurt. Even though he had affairs and was chauvinistic, there were many signs that he cared deeply for his wife.

Lady Bird apparently cared deeply for Lyndon, as well. This care was demonstrated by a story from Joe Califano, a member of the Johnson cabinet. Joe had been invited to dinner with the Johnsons but declined because he hadn't been home in several days and wanted to see his children. Lady Bird said, "Joe, this is going to be a nice evening for Lyndon. This has not been a good week. You've been bringing a lot of bad news to him. I want Lyndon to see you in some pleasant circumstances. You know, Lyndon sometimes can confuse the messenger with the message and I wouldn't ever want that to happen to you." So Califano went.

After his heart attack in 1955, Johnson hated to be alone, especially at night. When Lady Bird was away, he would have a friend or aide sleep with him. Lady Bird was often in bed when Johnson began his morning meetings and she sometimes had to excuse herself to get up and dress.

3

Military Experience

Johnson had enrolled as a lieutenant commander in the Naval Reserve two years before Pearl Harbor. In his 1941 campaign for Congress, he said, "If the day ever comes when my vote must be cast to send your boy to the trenches—that day Lyndon Johnson will leave his Congressional seat to go with him." He promised, "I shall never vote for war and then hide behind a House seat where bullets cannot reach me."

After Pearl Harbor was bombed, he went to the White House asking for a job in Washington, D.C. But this time Roosevelt did not oblige. So for his political career, he drafted himself. He and his assistant, John Connally, traveled up and down the West Coast and Sun Valley, Idaho, visiting shipyards and movie stars. He also visited Alice Glass, his mistress of many years.

Soon he learned that Congressmen were going to be recalled to Congress to give up their military posts. He worried that a lack of military action would doom his career. Secretary of the Navy James Forrestal told him that Roosevelt wanted to send a three man survey team to observe and report on the war effort in the South Pacific. Forrestal suggested that Johnson be the Navy representative. Roosevelt agreed and on April 29, 1942, Johnson was ordered to Australia. He made out his will and prepared to leave.

Upon arrival in Melbourne, the observers met with General Mac-Arthur. They were told of the battle shaping up in the Coral Sea. The three were given the choice to accompany pilots on missions to rout the Japanese out of a base in New Guinea. They chose to fly with troops to see firsthand action. On Johnson's one and only flight, his plane was attacked and gunners responded. He remained cool. But another one of the planes was shot down.

MacArthur told the two surviving observers that he had awarded a posthumous Medal of Honor to the dead man. He awarded a Silver Star to the two survivors. Johnson modestly accepted the award.

Lyndon soon developed flu and a fever. Then he was recalled home along with other Congressmen who returned to their Congressional posts. He decided to return whereas four of the eight on active duty remained in the military. He thought he had enough active duty to satisfy future voters.

As time went by, Johnson exaggerated his military duty and his flu became Dengue Fever. His 25-pound weight loss became 40 pounds. The 20,000 miles he had flown became 60,000. The mission he flew became missions. The 13 minutes of actual combat became three months. He gave himself the nickname "Raider Johnson" but many realized this was still the same old "Bull Johnson." He wore the Silver Star as his regular attire, and during speeches often pulled his lapel to show the silver bar. He could make himself believe anything and he finally believed that he deserved more than the Silver Star for his service.

4

Path to Power

Lyndon was always good at developing close relationships with men in powerful positions. He became a protégé of Sam Rayburn, Speaker of the House. Johnson came to a point where he had to decide whether to go against Rayburn to side with President Roosevelt and thus rise in the ranks. At that time, Labor leader John L. Lewis accused Roosevelt's vice president, John Nance Garner of Texas, of being an enemy of labor and a heavy drinker. Rayburn asked Johnson to sign a letter of denial in order to unite the Texas delegation. Johnson refused in order to please Roosevelt and get ahead. This made Roosevelt indebted to Johnson and allowed Lyndon access to the Oval Office.

Johnson came in often and would type up whatever agreement he and Roosevelt drafted. For example, he asked that his Texas friends and backers (Brown and Root) be given the contract for construction of the Naval Air Station in Corpus Christi. Once Roosevelt agreed, Johnson typed it up and his Brown and Root friends paid his campaign costs after that.

John Connally was nine years younger than Johnson. He came to work as Lyndon's secretary in 1939 at the age of 22. A confident, handsome law graduate, Johnson saw him as an equal and a younger version of himself. Lyndon made staffers compete to see who could do the best job and Connally always rose to the task. Connally wrote Lyndon's letters to his mother unbeknownst to her. He was offered lifelong social security, medication, care, food, and shelter for the rest of his life if he remained loyal to Johnson.

Although Johnson helped others in his position as Congressman, he never got much out of it financially. But his chance came when an Austin, Texas, radio station was having trouble financially. This was due to the fact that the FCC had only let it operate in daytime hours. He bought it in Lady Bird's name at a low price. Then he "influenced" the FCC to let it operate for 24 hours. He then used his influence with

Texas businessmen to secure advertising. He became quite wealthy within five years.

Johnson was openly doting and obsequious first to Rayburn and then to F.D.R. Truman had seen this and when he succeeded Roosevelt, he allowed Johnson's career to stagnate. Lyndon decided to run for Senator. He had run against Pappy O'Daniel in 1941 and barely lost. He thought his loss was due to some fraudulent votes so when he ran again in 1948, he pulled every trick he could think of to win.

He smeared the opponent, Coke Stevenson, by saying he was a "front man" for communists. Lyndon hired sheriff's deputies to bring people in to vote, and paid people and politicians to have votes recounted and added. After the election, Stevenson was leading but votes continued to come in for *eight* days. In Duval County, for example, an impossible 99.6% turnout showed that almost every possible voter was listed as having voted. And almost all votes had been cast for Johnson! On the 8th day, Johnson was declared the winner by 87 votes.

After Kennedy's assassination, Johnson realized that he had to promise to carry out the martyred president's policies instead of his own. When he did this, he couldn't understand why Bobby Kennedy didn't like him. But to his credit, he didn't mind the fact that many of his staff maintained close relations with Bobby and Jackie Kennedy.

He went far beyond what Kennedy had proposed. He wanted to go down in history for helping to end poverty, end racial prejudice and elevate society as a whole. He was proud of placing Thurgood Marshall as the nation's first black Supreme Court Justice. He was proud of discovering Barbara Jordan. She was the first black elected to the Texas Senate; the first black woman elected to Congress from the South, and he put her on his Commission on Income Maintenance Programs.

Johnson's "war on poverty" required that he enhance Martin Luther King's reputation. He stopped J. Edgar Hoover's F.B.I. wiretapping of King in 1965, although Hoover had written him that King was "undermining the nation." Johnson had never been as close to King.

He was closer to other black leaders like Roy Wilkins and Whitney Young. After King's assassination, Lyndon tried to call black leaders together and offered to help King's family. He proclaimed April 7, 1968, the day of the assassination, a "Day of National Mourning." He immediately pressed the Congress for a National Fair Housing Bill to appease black leaders. The leaders had said there would be violence unless they had something to offer their people. The bill passed.

Johnson's "albatross" was the Viet Nam war. His advisors, the military, Defense Secretary Robert McNamara and others said that there was no way to know the total cost of the war. They advised Johnson not to alarm Americans or Russians by putting forth a dramatically high figure of money and troops needed for the war. They proposed that he put the budget information forward slowly by bits and pieces. As a result, the public was misled about Viet Nam. Johnson and others told the public that the U.S. would win the war.

Johnson frequently lied to win support and praise. He even suggested that others lie for him and about him. But he also wanted them to make him look good so he wouldn't have to lie. In 1965, Johnson told his advisors, "Remember, they are going to write stories about this like they did in the Bay of Pigs. Stories about me and my advisors. That is why I want you to think carefully, very, very carefully about alternatives and plans."

Trying to close his credibility gap, his January 1967 State of the Union speech left off predictions that the war would end by the close of the year. "I cannot promise that it will come this year or come next year." At this time, angry draftees were burning their draft cards. This was met with a new law to prosecute draft dodgers quickly. Johnson felt that justice did not move fast enough against draft violators and wanted the attorney general and the F.B.I. to assist with investigations.

By the end of 1967, 9,000 Americans had died and 60,000 were wounded. So Johnson permitted the military to bomb North Viet Nam, but many were skeptical of victory. The polls showed that only 28% approved of his handling of the war.

McNamara resigned in protest to Johnson's continuation of the Viet Nam war. This was the first step in the de-escalation of the war and cemented Johnson's decision not to run again. Johnson wanted to be admired by posterity. So he told many that he wasn't going to be the first American president to lose a war.

5

Leadership Style

Lyndon learned to manipulate people. He constantly told them "Do it now. Today. Not tomorrow. Not next week." He poked people with his finger and used his height and strength to intimidate them. He took people to the deep end of his pool where he could stand on the bottom and they could not. There he asked them for agreement of his goals as they struggled to stay above water.

Whenever Johnson became angry with someone, he stopped talking to him or her. He sidestepped them and dealt with their cohorts or underlings. This could last from hours to weeks. Joe Califano described how he prepared a memo about how the 10% surcharge tax should be extended for one more year. Johnson asked others what they thought. He said he didn't want "yes" men but when they agreed with Califano, he blew up. He took Califano off the list to come to meetings, receive drafts, etc. This went on for three weeks until one day Johnson acted like it had never happened. Califano was receiving Johnson's famous "freeze-out" which he learned from his mother.

Johnson made phone call after phone call to get agreements from people to back him on his causes and bills. He kept his staff working through meals, into the night, over weekends, and at his ranch as well as the White House. He told people they had to do things for him and he would not accept "no." A good example was Earl Warren who didn't want to head the Warren Commission on Kennedy's assassination probe.

Abe Fortas didn't want to be appointed to the Supreme Court. Johnson illegally used information from Abe Fortas about pending Supreme Court decisions to influence his presidential actions. He felt he deserved these opinions when Earl Warren resigned and wanted Fortas to replace him. Many objected to this improper liaison between Johnson and Fortas.

Richard Russell tried to block Fortas' appointment to replace Warren to the Supreme Court. Russell, a senator from Georgia, wanted a friend to be appointed. When Johnson ignored this, he earned the enmity of his life-long friend and mentor, Russell. He included a special tribute to "the good common sense counsel of his old mentor" in his final State of the Union address.

At meetings he had posters saying "House" and "Senate." Each major bill was listed on a card, which progressed from each side through passage down into a bowl, drawn on the board to signify final passage. He used it to persuade leaders to move each of his proposals through the legislative process. In this way, he was able to pass more bills in the shortest time than any president.

Some American Medical Association representatives came shortly after the passage of Medicare, complaining that it was "socialized medicine." He listened, and then said he needed physicians in Viet Nam to serve the civilian population. When he asked the AMA to help, they agreed. He immediately said, "Get a couple of reporters in here." The reporters were told of this then asked about Medicare. Johnson said, "These men are going to get doctors to go to Viet Nam where they might be killed. Medicare is the law of the land. Of course they'll support the law of the land." He turned to the AMA president and said, "You tell him." The doctor said, "We are, after all, law-abiding citizens and we have every intention of obeying the new law." The sly Johnson had ceded nothing and gotten something.

Johnson had boundless energy, which was hard for others to match. He used every waking minute and even conducted business while he shaved, while he sat on the pot, and while he was in the nude upon awakening or bathing. He wanted other people to be as devoted, and available to him by phone whether they were in church or on the pot or wherever.

Johnson believed in hands on, total control management. Despite his lack of military experience, he did not leave war to the military. In the Viet Nam war, he was personally involved in the selection of targets.

Military personnel were delighted in the 1990s to have a president like George Bush and a defense secretary like Dick Cheney who avoided political micromanagement of the battlefield.

6

Stresses

Lyndon had self-discipline and could use it when it helped him achieve his goals to be admired and get ahead. During the beginning of his senatorial campaign, his fits of rage turned off citizens in small towns. When his people told him he was ruining his chances, he brought his fits under control. When he was told to stop smoking after his heart attack in 1955, he wanted to live long enough to be remembered in history so he stopped smoking. He stopped drinking in 1966 except for an occasional drink because he wanted to be at "full capacity" to deal with Viet Nam. He could control his habits when it served his long-term goal. But he always missed these vices and smoked and drank the last four years of his life until his death in 1973.

He was capable of thinking things over and making changes. He sometimes did this after retreating and pondering, similar to Mao. The following incident demonstrates this ability.

Johnson was disturbed by black riots in Watts where 5,000 people rioted, four died, 100 were injured and 250 were arrested. The Los Angeles police chief said violence would occur "when you keep telling people they are unfairly treated and teach them disrespect for the law." Johnson took that as a criticism of his voting rights and civil rights programs. For several days, he withdrew from people, refused to take calls, walked around the ranch with Lady Bird, drove his car and golf cart alone, and saw only his closest friends and daughters. Then he returned to Washington, D.C. and complimented the police and governor for restoring peace.

Johnson pandered to whoever could help him. When Russell or Rayburn or Roosevelt could no longer help his career, he betrayed them or turned against them. Johnson ridiculed others who disagreed with him causing even some friends to desert him. About Gerald Ford, he said, "He is so dumb he can't fart and chew gum at the same time." He called Arkansas Senator William Fulbright "Senator Halfbright." Fulbright learned of various things Johnson had said about him. This caused a long-time rift that Johnson regretted. On Lyndon's last day of the presidency he told Joe Califano about Fulbright, "If only we had talked to him more, had him over here more, found some things to agree with him on. We never should have let the fight become so personal."

Johnson often relieved tension by humor, but it was often critical of someone or something. Rather than self-deprecating humor, he tended toward elevating himself in humor. One of his best-known quips was when he was pulled over for speeding. Recognizing Johnson, the officer said, "My God!" "And don't you forget it!" said Lyndon.

Johnson bitterly disliked Richard Nixon and this was intensified a few days before Nixon's election. Richard had interfered with Lyndon's efforts to negotiate peace with the North Vietnamese. A cable had been intercepted from Nixon instructing the South Viet Nam president to block peace negotiations until Nixon took the presidency because he might offer better terms. Johnson was furious because he learned that Nixon had talked to Anna Chennault, the Chinese born widow of WWII hero General Claire Chennault. She was critical of Johnson and urged Nixon to contact South Viet Nam himself.

Johnson saw this as treason but could not deal directly with Nixon without proof. So he placed a conference call to the three presidential candidates and said this to all of them. "The fate of our country lies in your hands over the next few weeks. There would be serious trouble if anything anyone said were to interrupt or disrupt any progress we are trying to make to bring this war to a halt." Then he offered candidate Hubert Humphrey the information and taped conversation between Anna Chennault and the South Viet Nam Embassy in Washington. Humphrey, a decent man, chose not to use it and lost the election against Nixon.

Johnson always imagined conspiracies were afoot. He feared for his life after Kennedy's assassination, believing despite FBI reassurance, that he would be targeted next. Johnson always felt that antiwar activities were controlled by international communist organizations. CIA information failed to substantiate his view but reported that while antiwar activists were not under the control of communist groups, their purposes coincided with those of the communists.

Disheartened by his criticism over handling the Viet Nam War, Johnson had declared that he would not run again. But he thought that Democratic leaders would rally to his defense and offer his name in nomination so he could turn it down. When they did not, he became depressed, self-pitying and humiliated. He even had to convince Hubert Humphrey to include one sentence in his nomination acceptance speech noting Johnson's contributions. The sentence was "Johnson rallied a grief-stricken nation when our leader was stricken by the assassin's bullet...and in the space of five years since that tragic moment, President Johnson has accomplished more of the unfinished business of America than any of his modern predecessors."

Then as people began to leave him to work on the Humphrey platform, he felt betrayed, abandoned, lonely, and talked of how difficult it was to run the government, pass legislation, and induce the North Vietnamese to negotiate without assistance. Those who saw him at the end of his term saw a man who lost control of his emotions and wept. This revealed how important it had been for him to be loved and admired.

7

Accomplishments

Johnson described his own accomplishments in his final State of the Union address. He focused most on Medicare, voting rights, Head Start, 8 ½ million new jobs, millions lifted out of poverty, 5 million trained for work, and aid to elementary, secondary and higher education. He cited his biggest failures as not achieving peace in Southeast Asia, and not getting a gun registration and licensing bill passed, which he wanted after Robert and John Kennedy were killed by guns. In addition to his own assessment, another contribution was his meetings with Soviet Premier Kosygin in New Jersey to reduce the tension between the superpowers. He also set up the Departments of Transportation and Housing and Urban Development. But he recognized in his final speech the ways in which he had been most important to the nation.

8

Summary

Johnson came from a family that was not wealthy but could supply him with basic needs. They would fall on harder times during his adolescence, however.

Johnson probably had the greatest need to be adored by others of any modern president. He wanted to be loved by all as his mother apparently loved him. But his mother's love was conditional. When he displeased her, she froze him out as he was later to do with colleagues. This intense relationship built sufficient trust in his caretaker that he was able later in life to trust others, and especially women. But the ostracism he felt when he displeased her made him long to do enough to receive her praise. This translated into doing enough to receive the public's praise and remain the center of their life, as he had wanted to be the center of his mother's life.

Early on, imitating his mother's flowery speech and fancy dress left him feeling sissified and cowardly. He avoided fights even though he was bigger than most boys. This gave him some doubts about his manliness, which would prove to be the secret of his unwillingness to pull forces out of Viet Nam.

He lost faith in his parents with his father's downfall. After his rebelliousness and disregard for college, his father had told him that he was a failure and would never amount to anything. Perhaps his return to the fold, his decision to attend college and become a politician was to show his father. But this criticism left him feeling inadequate about his own abilities. This inadequacy made him begin to brag and build himself up, so that he was labeled "Bull" Johnson.

He sought women who doted on him like his mother when he pleased her. He could develop intimacy with such women. He never reached the stage of love in which he could surrender himself or commit himself totally to fidelity. He made everything into a contest of wills because he feared he was a sissy, a mama's boy, and would some day be exposed as such. So he had to keep women in their place, beneath him. But he could care deeply about some, especially his wife.

Johnson relieved tension by doing risky things like driving fast, having sex indiscriminately, and shocking reporters by giving interviews in the bathroom or bed. He kept his health in check as long as he held office but lived his last years recklessly, allowing his health to deteriorate. He also handled stress by making humorous remarks. However, many of his jokes included criticisms of others which came back to haunt him as they ruined relationships with close friends.

In terms of his morals, Lyndon learned early to please his parents. He later learned to appear as if he pleased people to earn rewards. As his peer group became more important to him, he attached himself to men who had money and power. Then he manipulated them to get what he wanted. He used his intimidating size, his physical closeness, and his ability to talk them into doing his bidding. But he mistook their intimidation and awe for affection and loyalty. He was hurt when he learned they did not really care for him.

He manipulated women to get admiration, which he had apparently first done with his mother and teachers. He feared being alone which was brought on by his early fear of being ignored by his mother, and made to feel as if he did not exist. Thus, he made his wife promise to never let him sleep alone. However he died in his bed during an afternoon nap in 1973.

Johnson never replaced acceptance with allegiance to society's rules. He always selfishly cared more about getting people to like him than about doing for others. He could hardly be well liked when he sacrificed friends to rise on the ladder of importance. His quest for approval of the masses was bigger than life because he wanted to be remembered in history first as the greatest Congressman, then the greatest Senator, and then the greatest president. It was this wish for posterity that made him pass acts that benefited others for the Great Society. He was living up to his mother's wish to be important in politics, as she wished her own father had been.

His leadership style was unique. Johnson made mistakes about the conduct of the Viet Nam war. He tried to shield the American economy from the consequences of the war to avoid criticism of his leadership. Americans weren't asked to share in the costs of the war in terms of rationing, taxes, or shortages. Johnson did not talk truthfully with Americans about the extent of the war.

He made the war into a personal vendetta against the enemy. He made statements like, "I'm going to bring *my* ships in here, and then, with *my* airplanes up here, I'm going to send *my* troops in." This leadership style showed more concern for achieving his goals than for the reactions of his people, so he was a benevolent autocrat at best and tyrant at worst.

Johnson and Nixon both despised Ivy League types like Kennedy. Neither handled criticism well. Unlike Nixon, Johnson was not a loner fighting against everyone. Viet Nam was a problem for both Johnson and Nixon. But Johnson felt his aides turned against him. Nixon used Viet Nam as a reason to sanction crimes such as Watergate.

When Lyndon's people criticized his wish to win at any cost in Viet Nam, he felt they were traitors. Additionally, even though he could not stand to be ignored he punished others by ignoring their very existence. This backfired on him when he announced he would not run again and felt ignored by former aides and colleagues.

Johnson was tyrannical in his wish to get his way. He accomplished this by manipulations, bargains, rewards and promises with politicians, swapping favors to get what he wanted. He achieved passage of more bills than any congressman because of this dedicated energy to getting his way with his peers.

8

GOLDA MEIR

○ ○

"We may have come in different ships but we're all in the same boat now." Whitney Young, Jr.

1

Upbringing and Early Life

Golda Mabovitch was born in 1898 and lived her first eight years in Russia, first Pinsk, then Kiev. At the age of three, she heard that a pogrom was coming with hooligans wielding sticks to hunt Jews. Her father nailed planks on the door to protect the family. Fear dominated the Jewish population in her area of Russia.

She had a sister, Sheyna, nine years older, and would eventually have a younger sister. Her mother had five other children who did not survive. Her mother took a job as a wet nurse because she had constant breast milk with all her pregnancies. She gave her very body for the good of others and for the small pittance to help her family. This giving of the most basic kind would dominate Golda's life.

Golda's mother was a sociable lady who had frequent family gatherings and was determined when she set upon a course, another trait that Golda would demonstrate as well. Her father was a Ukrainian orphan who studied the Torah in a Jewish seminary. After he served in the military he became a carpenter and made furniture for school libraries. He opened his own carpentry shop but went broke. He tended to believe people too readily, and was easily duped, as Golda's mother was fond of saying. He decided to go to America to make a better living. He left his wife and daughters when Golda was five years old. They moved in with Golda's grandparents for the three years during which her father developed a job and home site in the United States.

Golda's older sister set an example of political awareness and independence. For instance, when Sheyna was 14, she refused to go to work and wanted to continue schooling to "change the world." She joined the Socialist-Zionist movement whose goals were to overthrow the tzar and to bring a Jewish Socialist state into Palestine. People got arrested for discussing such ideas in Russia. Zionism had to do with the return of the Jews to the land of their forefathers in Israel. Sheyna admired a reporter, Theodor Herzl. He was so shocked to learn of the injustice done to Jewish Captain Dreyfus at his trial in 1894 in France, that Herzl went on to found the World Zionist Organization.

When Golda was eight, her family moved to America to join her father in 1906. They made their life in Milwaukee, Wisconsin, where her father ran a small store. As a child, she worked in her father's store. At the age of 14 she became a sales clerk in a department store. She planned to be a teacher. Tragedy struck the family when Sheyna contracted tuberculosis and had to be treated in a sanitarium in Denver, Colorado. The family was poor and Golda's parents wanted her to stop school and go to work. Using her older sister's example, she wanted to continue school to attain her goals. In 1912, she defiantly began her first year in high school.

2

Love Life

Golda's parents sought a marital match with a well to do man in his mid-30s for her. Opposed to this, she wrote sister Sheyna in Denver of her wish to pursue a college education. Her sister and impoverished husband offered their home to Golda, and sent money for the trip to

Denver. Upon arrival, 15-year-old Golda made money by teaching English lessons to immigrants. She did not tell her parents because they would have disapproved of it. Her father wrote her only once but her mother wrote several times. In addition to attending school and teaching English, she joined political discussions with Sheyna's friends. Their house was a refuge for Russian Jews who went to Denver for TB treatment.

The Jews would talk about anarchists like Emma Goldman and Peter Kropotkin, about President Woodrow Wilson, Europe, pacifism, the role of women, and the future of the Jewish people. Golda listened avidly to Socialist Zionists who sought a Palestine for Jews to be free, independent and live without fear of persecution.

At these gatherings, she met Morris Meyerson when she was 15. He introduced her to music, poetry, and literature. At age 16, Golda moved into her own place and went to work for a clothes maker. She had found Sheyna to be exceptionally stern and wrote her parents of her move. Her father wrote her to come home if she loved her mother, who was very worried about her being on her own. She returned to her family in Milwaukee but promised to marry Morris when she was older.

She graduated high school in 1916 and registered in college. Meanwhile her mother was allowing Jewish boys to stay in their house if they had volunteered for the Jewish Legion. That legion was going to fight for the British to liberate Palestine from the Turks. Palestine was then part of the Ottoman Empire. It was at this time that she first met some Jews who later became important in the founding of the Jewish state.

Ben-Zvi and David Ben-Gurion came to Milwaukee to recruit soldiers for the Jewish Legion in 1916. She became the spokesperson for a small Labor Zionist literary group. Her father developed a lecture program and invited speakers from Chicago by charging attendees a small fee for seminars on Yiddish literature.

The American Jewish Congress was established in 1918. One part of it (Zionists) wanted a home in Palestine. The other part (Bundists) did not. Golda and her father were Zionists. Since women could not speak to the congregation inside synagogues, she put up a box and spoke outside as people exited. This was a disgrace to her father until he heard her speak, then he no longer interfered.

She began teaching the Yiddish language and literature to Jewish school children because it was one of the strongest links between Jews. She didn't like to mix Yiddish with English. Later in her life, she learned Hebrew. She, her family, some pupils, and Morris (who sometimes came to visit her) used to talk, picnic and sing songs.

After World War I, the anti-Semitic pogroms in the Ukraine and Poland did away with whole Jewish communities. When she learned of this, she organized parades and demonstrations to protest it. However, some Jewish business owners feared they would lose business with too much attention brought to them.

She decided there must be a place for Jews to go. She joined the Labor Zionist Party to prepare to go to Palestine and help build a homeland. She was admitted into the Party although she was just shy of the required age of 18.

She moved to Chicago and worked in a public library. Her older sister had moved there with her family from Denver. As time passed, Golda feared she'd have to choose between Morris, six years older than she, and Palestine. She raised funds for her trip to Palestine by making speeches.

In November 1917, Morris was impressed that the British government said they would support a national home for Jews in Palestine. The announcement came as British forces under General Allenby began to win the battle to free Palestine from the Turks.

Golda married Morris on December 24, 1917. She wanted a civil ceremony but her parents forced them to have a religious ceremony. They took a place of their own for two years while working, speaking and organizing to leave for Palestine. She was in demand as a speaker because she spoke good Yiddish and English. Her father was angry that a newly married woman would travel without her husband to give speeches. Morris, a sign painter, fixed up their house and helped Golda's younger sister.

In 1918, the American Jewish Congress held its first convention in Philadelphia to safeguard the rights of Jews in Europe. Their plea was to be presented at the Versailles Peace Conference. Golda was one of the Milwaukee delegates and was excited to cast her own vote before women could vote in the United States.

In 1920, she and Morris moved to New York and prepared their move to Palestine. This caused Golda's older sister Sheyna to want to go. This would be difficult because she had children of three and ten years and would have to be joined later by her husband.

On May 1, 1921, Arab riots and attacks against Jews in Palestine left 40 immigrants murdered and mutilated. This did not deter Golda and Morris. They left America May 23rd. Golda would return to the U.S. from time to time but never for very long.

When they arrived in Tel Aviv (founded in 1909 by 60 Jewish families) it had a population of 15,000. It was a booming town of Jews mainly from Lithuania, Poland and Russia. The British government permitted Tel Aviv to levy its own taxes on building and to run its own water system. Its main street was named for Theodor Herzl, the founder.

No one met Golda, Morris and Sheyna. Fleas and bed bugs were in the hotel rooms and flies were on the food at the market. The hot sun was unbearable. Some Jewish immigrants thought the new arrivals were millionaires from America. They soon applied to a kibbutz that was a commercial farming settlement.

Jewish people in America, Germany and Russia had dropped money in synagogue boxes since 1904 to buy land for Jews in Palestine. In fact many Arabs were becoming rich from selling the land. Golda soon learned that the myth that Jews stole the land from Arabs was false.

At first the kibbutz turned them down because they thought Golda was a spoiled American girl. They eventually convinced the kibbutz to give them a chance to work and show their toughness. They chose the

Kibbutz Merhavia, established in 1911. The kibbutz committee assigned jobs, eight hours a day, and all shared chores. Children were brought up together in dorms but shared their parents' room too. A few houses, clusters of trees and sun-scorched fields were all they had in 1921. She picked almonds and helped plant saplings for a forest alongside others.

Women hated kitchen duty because they thought it demeaning and wanted burdens equal to the men. They were the first "women's libbers." Golda tried to improve conditions by substituting oatmeal for the distasteful breakfast of oil, herring and tomato sauce. She made Saturday morning cookies twice a week instead of once. Golda tended chickens, served eggs, and prettied things with tablecloths and flowers. Morris painted crates to use for cupboards. But perhaps the biggest attraction for the other immigrants was the record player that Golda and Morris brought from the United States.

People tended to get sick with malaria, dysentery and sand-fly fever in Palestine. Despite anyone's condition, the custom was that nobody drank or ate unless everyone shared it. In addition to the discomfort and illnesses, Morris began to suffer because he had no one to talk with about books, art and music. This was because priorities were so very practical. He felt starved for humor and intellect.

Sharing was a way of life but it was not always good. Golda thought that the lack of private showers, private toilets and private tea-making facilities in their rooms caused many immigrants to return to their homelands.

She was chosen to be the delegate to the kibbutz convention in 1922 in Degania. They discussed things such as how often mothers should visit babies, how kibbutz applicants should be screened, and other concerns for the 83,000 Jews that composed 11% of Palestine's population at that time.

Guard duty was part of life, due to the anti-Jewish riots. But Golda found a better job when she was chosen to be the English-speaking guide for Mrs. Philip Snowden, wife of a British Labor Party leader.

As time passed, Morris was suffering recurring bouts of malaria and they had to leave the kibbutz. Also, Golda wanted to have a baby but Morris wanted them to raise it, not the kibbutz. So they left the kibbutz for Tel Aviv after 2 ½ years. Both became irritable in Tel Aviv and were frequently mad at each other. Golda felt this was because Morris was in poor health and she had lost the vital role she played in the kibbutz. They were invited to Jerusalem just about the time she learned that she was pregnant and their son Menachem was soon born.

When Menachem was six months old, Golda returned to the kibbutz without Morris. He was disheartened and no longer wanted to live in the kibbutz system. When he would not join her after some time had passed, she decided to return to him to try to maintain the marriage. She became pregnant again and Sarah was born in 1926. Golda and Morris had four years together in Jerusalem. She became more miserable because she couldn't participate in building the Jewish national home. Additionally, she felt she had to endure poverty to feed the children on their low wages.

Although Golda was not devoutly religious, she visited the Wailing Wall and saw that it was crammed with scribbled petitions. She observed people crying and praying, and was moved as she viewed what remained of Solomon's temple. Later, she was glad she had gone to see it because visiting Jews were banned from 1948 to 1967. It was only after the Six Day War that Jewish soldiers liberated the Old City of Jerusalem and Jews could visit it again. But in 1926, she wrote "Shalom" (peace) on a piece of paper and stuck it in a cranny just as other Jews did.

By 1927, some 7,000 people were unemployed and more than half of the arriving Jews returned home within a year. Many returned to the U.S. or the British Empire, but some who returned to Russia were executed or sent to Siberia. There were very few Jewish businesses in Palestine. It was hard to find jobs because Arabs would work for less than Jews.

Eventually, Golda's parents moved to Palestine and lived in Herzlia, where her father became a cantor. Golda prepared lunches for laborers. But Golda and her family dreaded holidays. Generally, there was no food at holidays when people were off work because everyone was so poor.

Golda began to work at the General Foundation of Jewish Labor to protect the rights of workers. When she took the job in 1928, she somehow knew it would end her marriage because of the time it took away from Morris. They separated in 1928 when she moved to Tel Aviv with the children to work. He joined them only on weekends.

She became the secretary of the Women's Labor Council. The Council provided vocational training for young Jewish girls without farm trades and taught Hebrew to immigrants.

Golda felt guilty about leaving her children for her work. She said, "At work, you think of the children you've left at home. At home, you think of the work you've left unfinished. Such a struggle is unleashed within yourself; your heart is rent."

Her older sister and mother chastised her for leaving her children when they were sick to go to America on a business trip. Though feeling guilty, she felt justified in working for the greater good of many.

In 1932, her daughter Sarah was ill so Golda brought her back to America along with Menachem. In Palestine, Sarah had been treated inadequately for kidney disease but in America got proper treatment. While in the U.S., Golda toured, spoke to raise money and recruits for Palestine, and her children learned English in addition to Hebrew.

She explained over and over to Americans the reasons that help was needed. She said, "If you had land and water and the misfortune of having extremely hostile neighbors, you also had to acquire arms and train an army."

Morris remained in close contact with his children. He was indescribably happy that Menachem learned to play the cello. Golda and Morris remained married until he died in 1951. He died in her house but, as fate and the history of their relationship would have it, she was gone.

3

Path to Power

Golda was asked to join the Executive Committee for the Histadrut (Jewish self-government) organization. She did this from 1934 to 1948. All employees were paid a fixed basic living wage according to seniority and the number of dependents. The janitor of Histadrut with nine children got more than Golda with two children, and she approved that plan. Histadrut dues were on a sliding scale according to income and dependents. The dues provided trade union, pension and sick funds, and eventually unemployment funds.

A growing friction between the left and right wings of the Zionist movement resulted in the assassination of one Jew by another. There were bloody clashes between workers all over Palestine and David Ben-Gurion proposed a cease-fire.

Hitler came to power in Germany in 1933 and began to strip German Jews of their civil rights. By 1934, Jews fled Nazism in Germany and Austria bringing only their intellect and energy. Another 60,000 Jews had to be absorbed by the Palestinian population of 400,000. This occurred at the same time Arab terrorism grew in an atmosphere of an indifferent English government.

In 1936, Arabs destroyed thousands of trees planted by Jews. They derailed trains and busses, burned fields, killed and wounded Jews in over 2000 attacks. The Palestinian pioneers worried that stronger Jewish self-defense might give the British more reasons to clamp down on immigration. Jews were determined to not simply retaliate but to defend themselves.

Arabs doubled the population as Syrians arrived to enjoy greater Palestinian opportunities. Arabs tried to stop Jewish immigration by not working and letting the Palestinian infrastructure deteriorate. Jews reacted by doubling their own workload.

In cabinet meetings, Golda sat as issues were discussed for hours and then voted. In 1937, after an Arab general strike, she was sent to America to raise funds to launch a shipping enterprise so that Jews might sail on their own ships.

In 1939, the British were ready to yield to Arab pressure and stop Jewish immigration to Palestine. Three years earlier, the Peel Commission recommended that Palestine be split into a Jewish state of 2000 square miles and an Arab state occupying the rest of the country. The Arabs turned that down.

Golda was invited to sit, but not participate, in the audience at Evian-les-Bains where 32 countries went to Franklin Roosevelt's International Conference on Refugees. Countries lamented that they could not take in more Jewish refugees. But Jewish representatives like Golda could only sit and listen. She decided that Jews should never depend on anyone else for permission to stay alive.

The British "White Paper" stopped Jewish land purchases in Palestine. It allowed only 75,000 more Jews to be admitted over the next five years, unless the Arabs changed their minds. The Jews thought that the pre-World War II appeasement of Germany had extended to appeasement of Arabs. They began to prepare to fight the British if necessary to defend their land and immigration privileges. They wanted to take in as many Jews from 1939-1945 as possible to save them from Nazism. When the British objected, they set out to develop the self-governing state of Israel, which they did in 1948. Golda wrote, "It was the Jews of Europe, trapped, doomed and destroyed, who taught us once and for all that we must become the masters of our own undertaking."

In 1941, an article in the *Jewish Voice* described German atrocities against Jews in Europe. Unaware of the true extent of those atrocities, the article described the treatment of Jews by American imperialists and British rule of Jews in Palestine as no different. But, of course, the true German atrocities were beyond belief.

After the war, Golda believed that Germany should pay reparations. These would build up Israel to absorb Jews who had remained alive and make Israel the strongest guarantee against another Holocaust. She witnessed Adolf Eichmann's trial when he was brought to Israel. She heard Eichmann's aide testify that he learned of Eichmann's order to exterminate and destroy the Jewish race in the summer of 1942. This made her feel justified in the illegal extraction of Eichmann from Argentina by Jews.

In 1946, Britain blocked ships bringing Jewish Holocaust survivors to Palestine, arguing that they should settle in Europe. That year, President Truman asked that 100,000 refugees from Germany and Austria be allowed to enter Palestine. She testified in 1946 to the Anglo-American Committee of Inquiry, saying, "I don't know, gentlemen, whether you who have the good fortune to belong to the two great democratic nations, the British and the American, can realize what it means to be a member of a people whose very right to exist is constantly being questioned."

Following this meeting, Golda and other Jews went on a hunger strike. This was in sympathy with refugees the British wouldn't permit to sail for Palestine, and who had threatened to starve rather than go elsewhere. She went 101 hours with only tea. On June 29, 1946, the British government said the refugees couldn't be admitted despite the report of the Anglo-American Committee. They sent 100,000 British soldiers and 2,000 policemen to imprison 3,000 Jews, including many Jewish leaders.

In November 1947, she flew to the U.S. to raise money ($50 million) to arm Israel. In 1947, she also flew to talk with Transjordan leader King Abdullah. She had to go disguised as a Muslim woman and traveled with an Arabic-speaking guide. She requested that the King not join in the Arab attacks against Israel. He had earlier agreed not to attack Israel but when he faltered, she felt she had to speak to him personally. It was not known that she clandestinely talked with the king, grandfather of King Hussein of Jordan, until after Abdullah was assassinated in 1951.

The Jewish state came into being with a population of 650,000. Golda cried as David Ben-Gurion read the United Nations proclamation. It said that Israel was now established and open to Jewish immigration. Eleven minutes past midnight on May 14, 1948 after the proclamation was read, President Truman recognized the new Jewish state. The American policy was that recognition would be an act of humanity. The murder of six million Jews by the Nazis had been the worst atrocity of all time and U.S. leaders said that every thoughtful human being must feel some responsibility for the survivors who had no place to go.

Two days later Golda flew back to the U.S. and raised another $150 million to aid Jews in Europe. While there, she was summoned back to be Israel's minister to Moscow because the Russians had also recognized the new Jewish state. A car wreck and fractured leg delayed her return and she was accused of "malingering" but arrived shortly.

She ran the Israeli Embassy in Moscow much like a kibbutz where the staff worked, ate and did chores together. On the Rosh Hashanah High Holiday, 50,000 Jews awaited her at the synagogue despite a warning in Pravda to dismiss the State of Israel. She met Molotov's wife, a Jew, who talked warmly with her. Despite being the wife of one of the highest-ranking Russian officials, Mrs. Molotov was arrested a few months later. In January 1949, the Moscow Yiddish newspaper and theater were closed. She was asked to return home to Israel because of growing anti-Semitism in Russia.

David Ben-Gurion asked her to be Minister of Labor and she served in that capacity for seven years. As the population of Israel doubled within two years, people had to be fed, clothed, housed, educated, employed and cared for. Some 200,000 lived in tents in close quarters. Housing and jobs became her priorities for the masses. She returned to America to raise funds to build 30,000 one-room units for families.

She also persuaded the Truman administration to start an Israel bond issue so Israelis might avoid living on just philanthropy.

While in America on this trip, she learned that her husband, with whom she had maintained friendship but had been separated from for many years, had died. She returned for his funeral only to find that her daughter was extremely ill. She stayed until Sarah recovered. She then returned to Israel and tried to help Ben-Gurion protect the holy places of Jerusalem that Jews had not been permitted to visit.

In 1953, the "Doctor's Plot" was invented in Moscow claiming that Jewish doctors conspired to murder Stalin. A trial was staged as part of an anti-Jewish campaign and Israel realized how badly relations with Russia had deteriorated.

Golda finally changed her Meyerson name to the nearest Hebrew equivalent, Meir. She met with various world leaders on Israel's behalf in this time of stress. This included Nasser in Egypt, and Bulganin in Russia. She spoke with President Kennedy who assured her, "Nothing will happen to Israel."

At Kennedy's funeral in 1963, President Johnson said, "I know that you have lost a friend, but I hope you understand that I, too, am a friend." At the funeral she talked with France's DeGaulle who pledged friendship if Israel did nothing but retaliate, but promised no help if Israel attacked Arab countries first.

She worked from 1958-1973 with Africa to develop votes at the U.N. by offering agricultural training, regional planning, and medical services. She described Idi Amin of Uganda as "quite mad."

He said, "I want a few Phantoms from you." She replied that they didn't manufacture Phantom jets but bought them from the U.S. He followed that request with another one saying, "I need 10 million pounds sterling at once." When she declined, he approached Col. Qaddafi of Libya.

In 1967, Israeli aircraft and torpedo boats strafed the American warship *USS Liberty* in error, thinking that it was an Egyptian attack in disguise. Within hours, Israel, believing that Egypt was about to attack, bombed Egypt first in what was termed an act of aggression. (Israel's attack on the American ship resulted in over 30 deaths and 171 wounded Americans.)

At first President Johnson thought the Russians had launched the attack against the *USS Liberty* but a "flash" within two hours from Tel Aviv notified the White House that Israel attacked the ship in error. Israel apologized saying that they mistook the ship for an Egyptian one. While the accident did not justify a break between the U.S. and Israel, many in the Johnson administration did not feel that Israel made adequate restitution or explanation for the action.

In 1965, she wanted to retire and felt she was "running down". But the Labor Party was split. Arabs were preparing for more war. Yasser Arafat's El Fatah became the most powerful part of the PLO. Nasser of Egypt was rousing the U.N. against Israel. So she stayed on. Then there was the Six Day War of June 6, 1967, to retake the old city of Jerusalem. The barricades that had separated Jerusalem were torn down but Arab leaders vowed to destroy Israel for that act. So she stayed on.

Levi Eshkol, prime minister of Israel, died in 1969. Meir was asked to become the fourth prime minister because she was the only acceptable candidate who would not precipitate a divisive struggle. She never sought the office and would not accept the role until she was pressed to do so. She soon returned to the U.S. where President Nixon helped to arrange a cease-fire with the help of Dr. Henry Kissinger. She served as prime minister for five years and encountered many problems.

4

Stresses

Golda always dressed plainly and wore no make-up. She kept her long hair tied up in a bun because her family liked long hair. But she knew that she was perceived as unfeminine and jokes were made that she was a man in disguise. She handled this by digging in harder to do her job and by being philosophical. She wrote, "I have never forgotten that I come from a poor family or ever fooled myself into thinking that I was honored anywhere for my beauty, wisdom or erudition."

Golda broke with her dear friend and older colleague, David Ben-Gurion, over an issue involving another colleague, Pinchas Lavon, who believed he was being conspired against. Her defense of Lavon caused Ben-Gurion to call her and others "corrupt." She could not tolerate that insult because she viewed herself as having the utmost integrity and broke with him. Although she refused to go to his 80th birthday party, he came to her 75th birthday party in 1973 in an effort to remain friends.

She had numerous frustrations. She was discouraged by the freedom of her ministers to leak information to the press. There was no privacy or freedom in her position. She tired of saying the same things over and over. Criticisms in the press seemed ever more vitriolic. The cease-fire was broken by horrifying events such as the gunning down of Catholics from Puerto Rico, the kidnapping of an Israeli scientist, the murder of Israeli athletes in Munich, and the slaughter of Israeli children trapped in a school. She handled frustration by working tirelessly night and day. When she could no longer control her emotions, she sometimes wept. But unlike many women, she never used her femininity to gain special favors.

She had a soothing effect on others, however. She often made soup and coffee for her cabinet members. Listening, discussing and mothering others was not only calming to them but to her. She found her greatest area of stress not to be her work but her family. She regretted that she had not given her family as much as she had given the state of Israel, but she subscribed to the principle of the greatest good for the greatest number.

She was sometimes able to use humor to reduce tension and lighten relationships. When she arrived shortly after Nixon had selected Dr. Henry Kissinger to be Secretary of State, Nixon greeted her. He said, "Madam Prime Minister, we are both blessed by having Jewish Foreign

Ministers." Mrs. Meir, whose Oxford-educated silver-tongued Foreign Minister was Abba Eban, said, "Oh, but Mr. President, I am doubly blessed: Mine speaks perfect English."

Nixon's daughter was doing a book called *Special People* and Golda granted her an interview. When Julie asked Mrs. Meir how it felt to be appointed the first woman Foreign Minister, she said, "I don't know. I was never a man minister."

5

Leadership Style

Richard Nixon described her because he dealt with her frequently. He said, "She was one of the most powerful personalities, man or woman, that I have ever met in 35 years of public and private travel at home and abroad.... She was absolutely straightforward. There was nothing devious about her." He went on to describe her leadership style. She read everything before she signed it. She took the death of each soldier personally, even leaving word that she should be called whenever an Israeli was killed. She was so adamant about this that she was once awakened with news that 25 sheep had been killed.

Nixon also described her way of dealing with business. He said, "She was always very gracious in her conversations with Mrs. Nixon, and she showed an obviously sincere interest in our children and in personal matters. But generally her approach was to make short shrift of the "getting-to-know-you" sort of icebreaking comments at the beginning of a session and go directly to the serious issues at hand. The first time we met in the Oval Office, there was the usual idle chitchat while the photographers clicked away. But as soon as they had been ushered out, she crossed her legs, lit a cigarette, and got right down to business, running through a list of equipment she wanted for her armed forces."

When she was 75, she tried to cut down her appointments and delegate more, but she felt she had to talk to those who wanted to talk and listen to those who had something to tell her. The press grilled her with questions and groups wanted her to speak and suggest things about problems that concerned Israel's future. It became more necessary to say "no" and protect her health and stamina. Age was taking its toll and there were foreign dignitaries who felt entitled to spend time with her. The more of them she saw, the later she had to stay up to read through things. She had a part-time maid who left at noon after fixing her lunch and placed food in the refrigerator for her evening meals.

Once when she was about to go to Washington, D.C. Israeli planes were on alert because they'd heard that a suicide attack was being planned with a plane loaded with explosives. They shot down a Libyan plane with 106 people, which strayed over the Sinai Peninsula. She felt that her visit was tarnished by having to explain to President Nixon that the "black box" showed the pilot had ignored all attempts to identify himself.

Her administration was beset by the Yom Kippur War of October 1973. Although Israel won, over 2,500 Israelis were killed in the war with Syria and Egypt. Yom Kippur, the Day of Atonement for sins of the past years, was usually spent in going to synagogues to hear Kol Nidrei and fasting until the blowing of the Shofar (ram's horn). But when she heard that the families of Russian advisers in Syria were fleeing the country, she worried that Syrians were planning to attack Israel. Military leaders like Moshe Dayan urged a pre-emptive air strike but she knew the world would be against helping them if they attacked first. She held off and in the afternoon, Israel was attacked on two sides from the Suez Canal and the Golan Heights.

She called Nixon and Kissinger and others to get an arms airlift and on the ninth day, planes arrived. Nixon said, "I ordered that everything that can fly should be used for a massive emergency airlift of supplies."

Golda wrote him later that the airlift was invaluable. She said, "It not only lifted our spirits, but also served to make the American position clear to the Soviet Union, and it undoubtedly served to make our victory possible. When I heard that the planes had touched down in Lydda, I cried for the first time since the war had begun…"

During the Yom Kippur War, she met with parents of soldiers when many details of their fate were still unknown. This was partly because the Egyptians and Syrians withheld POW lists out of spite. Kissinger came in to negotiate between Israel, Syria and Egypt. She said he had everything, "Intelligence, diligence, stamina, and the fact that he represented the greatest power in the world."

On October 31, 1973, she flew to the U.S. when Nixon and Kissinger thought Israel broke the cease-fire agreement to say, "We are not liars." She flew to Egypt and the Golan Heights to talk to soldiers and answer their questions.

She called Germany's Willy Brandt and said, "I need to know what possible meaning socialism can have when not a single socialist country in all of Europe was prepared to come to the aid of the only democratic nation in the Middle East."

She spoke to the leaders of the Socialist International in London saying, "Not one inch of your territory was put at our disposal for refueling the planes that saved us from destruction." They were refueled in mid-air. One man told her that the reason for this was the Arab oil cartel.

At the end of the war, her administration was blamed with a lack of preparedness. Moshe Dayan offered to resign but she did not accept it because she felt that a cabinet crisis was not needed at that critical time. However, by March 1974, she felt too tired to heal the rifts inside and outside her country and administration. When she resigned, Yitzhak Rabin became prime minister in June 1974. During her tenure, the Labor Party lost much ground and it was left to Rabin to try to heal rifts. Meir's "hawkishness" was blamed for missing many peace opportunities.

The Yom Kippur War of 1973 showed the results of modern armored confrontations. After the first Arab attack, the Israelis counterattacked with little attention to their own safety and therefore exposed themselves to the enemy. The Egyptians, who had a carefully planned defense, inflicted high casualties on the Israelis. Half of the Israeli tanks and armored vehicles were destroyed. A close study of this war taught military experts that defense should become their chief concern.

At an award ceremony for Golda Meir, Kissinger described the issue that has confronted world leaders in 2001-2002. He said, "A Palestinian state on the West Bank is bound to be an element of instability both for Jordan and for Israel; it will compound the crisis, not solve it." He commended Golda by saying, "Golda was a ferocious negotiator and a woman of powerful convictions. But when she gave you her word, you could absolutely count on it. Once she made up her mind to do something, even if it was difficult and painful, she followed through with enormous courage and extraordinary ability."

Shortly after the award ceremony, Anwar Sadat, the new president of Egypt, flew to Jerusalem. Meir was in the long line of dignitaries to meet him. She grabbed his hand and said, "Why didn't you tell me you wanted to come to Israel?"

As Walter Cronkite said, "One can only speculate about what might have developed in Egyptian-Israeli relations if the more liberal Meir had been in charge" instead of Menachem Begin.

She wrote in 1975 with words that electrified us after September 11, 2001. Speaking of the early Jewish leaders like Elaihu, founder of the Haganah, she wrote, "It is bitter to write about Eliahu now, in a world that has chosen to endow Arab terrorism with glamour and to admit to the so-called council of nations a man like Yasser Arafat, who has not one constructive thought or action to his credit and who, to put it plainly, is only a costumed multiple murderer heading a movement dedicated solely to the destruction of the state of Israel. It is not by killing or maiming children, hijacking aircraft or murdering diplomats that real movements of national liberation accomplish their aims".

6

Accomplishments

Golda brought in Israel's first national health insurance bill. It served Arabs as well and reduced the infant mortality rate. Despite this, Arab atrocities provoked Israeli retaliation and world censure followed. Ben-Gurion wanted her to be the foreign minister in 1956, with Shimon Peres director of defense and Moshe Dayan chief of staff. But she did not seek that role and it was thrust upon her from 1969 to 1974.

Her tenure was notable because she strengthened the rapport between the U.S. and Israel and brought about much financial and material help for her struggling country. She also added determination that Israelis would not deal with terrorists and would retaliate fiercely against anyone who attacked. Meir's position was that giving in to terrorists would lead to more terror so their demands were declined.

When she met Pope Paul VI in 1973, he began by saying that Jews should have more mercy and had behaved harshly in their own country. She told him that it was true that they jailed terrorists and blew up the houses of Arabs who sheltered terrorists after repeated warnings. She added, "Let me assure you that my people know all about real 'harshness' and also that we learned all about real mercy when we were being led to the gas chambers of the Nazis." She wanted to speak for Jews who had perished while the Vatican maintained its neutrality during World War II.

Dr. Henry Kissinger spoke in appreciation of Golda Meir on November 13, 1977, when she was given the Stephen Wise award. The award was because the 20-year-old Golda attended the very first convention of the American Jewish Congress in 1918 in Philadelphia. As a Milwaukee delegate, she was honored with a medallion reading, "For a lifetime of courageous and inspiring leadership of the Jewish people."

Kissinger said, "I have always admired Golda and loved her for her strength, for her wisdom and for her humanity…She reflects a universal conscience—the need for a world in which the weak are protected by a general order." Kissinger described her leadership as a turning point in which crucial negotiations began with Egypt and Syria. But he added, "I will not insult your intelligence by pretending that Golda was always easy to deal with."

7

Summary

In Golda's early years, her family lived as poorly as any Russian peasants and also suffered the attacks of Jewish pogroms. Thus survival and basic needs were always in doubt.

Golda was loved by her parents and grew up learning to trust others. She was a confident little girl who followed her older sister's example and used initiative and industry to take her farther than girls used to venture in those days.

She fell in love with Morris but it turned out that her love life played a secondary role to her interest in being important in politics. The same was true of many other leaders such as Hitler, Castro, Kennedy, Nixon, Hussein, and bin Laden. While she could be intimate with her husband, and she was probably faithful to him, she did not live with him during her most important career years as she helped to develop Israel.

Golda had mostly healthy coping techniques. She could never be accused of using denial or risky acts to relieve tension. She had a good sense of humor and could make light of serious issues quite often. She prided herself in avoiding temptations by using asceticism in the pioneer years of Israel and she lived minimally to the last years of her life. She planned for problems well and her working years gave her numerous opportunities to serve others in altruistic ways.

Golda's moral development went through the usual stages of controlling her actions to please first her parents and later her peers. She was not one to flaunt rules but believed in societal conventions and actions that benefited more people. She was ready to see and say that all people had equal worth. She believed in fairness and equity, and she was uncomfortable with dishonesty and disregard of rules. Overall, her integrity was as intact as was Harry Truman's, a rare trait among politicians.

Golda's leadership was almost equally concerned with her people and the tasks to be done, with a little more attention to the goals. She varied between being a compromiser and being a team manager. There were times when she went against the advice of her own experts and became a tough negotiator. At those times, she might have been called a benevolent autocrat.

9

RICHARD NIXON

"So it is more useful to watch a man in times of peril, and in adversity to discern what kind of man he is; for when at last words of truth are drawn from the depths of his heart, and the mask is torn off, reality remains." Lucretius

1

Upbringing and Early Life

Richard Nixon was born January 9, 1913 in Yorba Linda, California. Richard was the second of five boys. His older brother Harold was 3 ½, the favorite son, and a bold and delightful child. After Richard was about six months old, his mother also nursed her sister's baby because her sister was ill, thus reducing the amount of interaction with baby Richard. When Richard was one year old, his mother went to the hospital for a mastoid operation. Richard cried incessantly and clung to his mother upon her return. Thus his first year did not produce a child who trusted those responsible for him. He would forever find it hard to believe that they or anyone else really cared much for him.

When he was nearly two, his brother Don was born. Don would prove to be not particularly bright and generally was a disappointment for the Nixon family. However, when Richard was five, his brother Arthur was born. This child would die when Richard was twelve years old. Don and Harold were closer to each other as the years passed than either of them was to Richard.

When Richard was 17, his parents had a surprising addition to their family. Edward was conceived during the terrible turmoil of Harold's terminal illness. Harold died of tuberculosis when Richard was 20. Edward and Richard had little interaction due to the 17-year difference between them.

Although the family was poor, Richard grew up in a part of California where many had found oil on their property and became rich. But his father Frank was a streetcar operator, carpenter, grocer and butcher. Frank had a hard life because his mother had died when he was seven. He ran away from a harsh stepmother at age 14 with only a fourth grade education.

When Frank was 18, he shook hands with presidential candidate William McKinley, who complimented Frank's horse. It changed his life and made him interested in politics. Frank felt proud to hate people and things. He told the press in 1952, "Truman hates Dick like a rattlesnake" and beamed. He was chronically angry, bellowing, crude, brittle, and had little room for love in his life.

Frank married a Quaker when he was 30. Jessamyn West, Nixon's novelist cousin, said there was little hugging or kissing in Frank Nixon's family. Frank, she said, adopted the Quaker lifestyle of his prim and proper wife. West wrote *Friendly Persuasion*, which was eventually made into a movie, and used her own Quaker family as the model.

Frank made enemies because he usually thought he was right and others were wrong. Dwight Eisenhower, who knew him, described him as "the breadwinner, Supreme Court and lord high executioner." Richard tried to be different from his father by being quiet and studious. But his father's personality characteristics finally emerged in his personality in later life.

Many said that Richard tried to be the "coolest" man in the room. His father was the loudest man in most rooms. Richard dressed neatly whereas his father was sloppy. Dick refused to repair things because his father had been a handyman. Nixon never embraced women, possibly because his father had been flirtatious and lecherous. Frank even hollered when his wife tried to give money to charities and made her account for every penny.

Richard's mother, Hannah, had to be secretive and manipulative to live with vociferous Frank. She schemed to do things her own way behind his back. She lied to Frank. She also lied to reporters when Richard became famous. She told reporters that her husband was descended from Philadelphian John Nixon who gave the Declaration of Independence its first reading. This was not true because Nixon was dead by 1774 and his sons were children at the time. She told reporters that Richard was the first child born in Yorba Linda and that the day after his birth there was a solar eclipse, though neither item was true.

Hannah exaggerated to make Richard's life sound miraculous. She said that it was a miracle he survived a cut at age three, pneumonia at age four, and undulant fever in his teens. Even though she lied to reporters, she told them that she punished her children when they lied. This is reminiscent of Nixon lying to the public, yet proclaiming to be an honest man in his "Checkers" speech and in the Watergate affair.

Like his father, Richard had rage. At age seven, he wanted a jar of pollywogs captured by a six-year-old boy in a canal. He hit the boy on the head with the blunt end of a hatchet and left a lifelong scar.

Richard, his brothers and his father bonded somewhat by discussing politics from the age of seven. They discussed why Warren Harding should be elected, the Teapot Dome scandal, and various other items. But Frank was hard on his boys and Richard may have thought his father's punishments were out of love. He once said, "It's good to have the whip at your back." Richard also said the boys had to be pretty smart to avoid punishment.

Richard laughed little as a child, and was first called "Gloomy Gus" by his own brothers. But he began to excel in school, having been taught to read early by his mother. At age six, he won a church recitation contest in which he bested his nine-year-old brother, Harold.

Richard's mother was often away at her parents. It is unclear whether this was due to depression or to escape her own family. At age ten, on November 12, 1923, Richard wrote his mother a very strange letter in which he adopted the personality of a dog writing to his master (his mother).

> "My dear master: The two dogs you left with me are very bad to me. Their dog, Jim, is very old and he will never talk or play with me. One Saturday the boys went hunting. Jim and myself went with them. While going through the woods one of the boys tripped and fell on me. I lost my temper and bit him. He kicked me in the side and we started on. While we were walking I saw a black round thing in a tree. I hit it with my paw. A swarm of black things came out of it. I felt a pain all over. I started to run and as both of my eyes were swelled shut I fell into a pond. When I got home I was very sore. I wish you would come home right now. Your good dog, Richard."

It is surprising that his mother saved this letter and showed it to the press. Perhaps she thought that it showed his creativity or was cute. The letter suggests that Nixon was so sensitive to hurt that he lost track of reality and exaggerated the viciousness of those who hurt him.

A psychological interpretation suggests that Richard felt like a dog, left by his mother for a while with an old dog (his father) that would not talk or play with him. He may have felt like a dog instead of one of the boys with playmates. When he got mad at them for hurting him, perhaps he wanted to bite them. Then they kicked him (as his father did). Then he became hurt by a swarm of bees and was on his own to defend himself. In the story, he came home very hurt. He seemed to wish his mother were home to protect him from loneliness and problems, which was probably his real wish.

Richard's mother wanted him to be a musician like her brother. At age seven, he took piano and violin from her brother who taught music. At age 12, dissatisfied with his progress, Hannah sent Richard to live for five months with her sister, "Aunt Jane", who also taught music. This immediately followed the sudden death of Arthur from a brain fever like meningitis. Hannah may have sent Richard away because she was depressed over her loss, as much as for his musical improvement.

Aunt Jane did not feel that Richard had much musical talent. In an interesting sidelight, when Nixon was president, he brought Aunt Jane to the White House to hear pianist Andre Watts. She said, "If thee had practiced more on the piano, thee could be down there on the stage instead of up here." This typical Quaker denigration of his abilities gives some clue to Nixon's drive to excel and show his family and others that he was really worth something.

Writing to his mother from Aunt Jane's house, Richard complained that his father kicked him. But in later life, he kicked others. He kicked protesters in Peru and Major Don Hughes for arranging a stressful speaking schedule. He told the press they wouldn't have Nixon to "kick around any more" so it was obvious that kicking was an important punishment in Dick's life.

His father had given up on making money with a lemon grove. He bought a gas station and eventually expanded it into Nixon's Market. Ordinarily, his wife made pies that sold well in the store. Dick had to pick out produce for his father's grocery at 4 a.m., then get to school, then come home to work in the grocery. When he made his runs to the Los Angeles produce markets, he bargained with farmers to get the best prices for produce to bring back to their market. He did all that and yet maintained very high grades.

Because of the family demands of running a grocery, the Nixon family did not eat meals together but each ate on the run. Nixon, as president, always made eating on the run a virtue saying that he cost taxpayers less than other presidents. He said that they took more time to eat and therefore did less work.

Dick's mother kept her boys in line by rejection. She loved Richard only if and when he was neat, clean, and obedient. She was never one to compliment. Later when reporters asked whether she thought her son would be a good president, she said, "If God is on his side." Contrast this with Rose Kennedy who, when asked the same question about John said, "He'll make a wonderful president."

When Dick was 12, his young brother Arthur died of a "sleeping sickness" or "encephalitis" or virus. Dick once told a reporter that Arthur died from a concussion caused by a boy throwing a rock at his head on the schoolyard. Perhaps he felt that story would yield more sympathy. Much later, he told a reporter that his father should have had the family cow tested for tuberculosis, a common source of the illness. His family, like many Quakers, wanted fresh milk. Dick blamed his father for being too stubborn to have the cow tested. He thought that might have prevented Harold's later death from TB, Arthur's death, Don's lung illness, and his own illnesses as a child.

The impact of Arthur's death on the family was great. Hannah sought solace in her Quaker church. Frank thought the death was a sign of God's displeasure and began to be fanatically religious. He sent the oldest boy, Harold, to an evangelical Bible school in Massachusetts. Harold came home in 1927 with severe tuberculosis. His mother attributed this to cold early morning showers.

When Richard was 15, his mother took his oldest brother to a tubercular colony in Prescott, Arizona. She rented a cabin and nursed three other boys with tuberculosis to afford Harold's treatment for three years. But when she left the family and the market in favor of the older brother, it probably felt like rejection to the family and particularly to Richard.

In the summers, Dick visited his mother in Prescott. While there, he worked as a janitor in a country club and was a barker at a carnival. He kept his distance from his brother and the other dying boys. These young boys who coughed up blood still fell in love with local girls. They tried to live their short lives intensely and developed a morbid sense of humor much like John Kennedy who also felt his life would be short.

Feeling abandoned by his mother and less loved than brother Harold; Dick found it hard to trust that others would really like him. He dated rarely. He focused more on building up his self-respect by aiming for higher educational achievements. He loved applause and was particularly outstanding in debate and acting.

When Dick was 17, he wrote a poignant high school essay about the death of his brother Arthur, who died five years earlier. He wrote, "We have a picture in our home which money could not buy. It is not a picture for which great art collectors would offer thousands of dollars. The first thing we notice is that this particular boy has unusually beautiful eyes, black eyes which seem to sparkle with hidden fire and to beckon us to come on some secret journey which will carry us to the land of make believe. Money could not buy that picture for it was the last one ever taken of my brother, Arthur."

At first glance this seems like a very sensitive essay, but it had a quality seen in the earlier letter to his mother as if he were but a dog. This letter displayed how Nixon tried to use words to make people feel sorry for him. He described some pitiful situation to evoke a sympathetic reaction, a trait that he was to use over and over in his political life.

This was also the year when his parents had a surprise birth. Edward was too much younger than Dick for them ever to be close. Dick was class valedictorian but lost an election to be class president in high school. This hurt him deeply and he was seen as prickly, aloof and argumentative. Those adjectives could have described his father. His forte was debate but his debate coach was bothered by his tendency to slide around an argument instead of meeting it head on. Students said they hated him because he would twist the truth to get a point across.

His high grades earned him a scholarship to Harvard, but his family could not afford to send him there. So he went to Whittier College and majored in history. Whittier probably allowed him to be more of a standout than he might have been at Harvard.

He graduated from Whittier College in 1934. He lost out as valedictorian to a woman. While in college, his oldest brother died of tuberculosis. The money that his family had spent on Harold could now be given to him as a loan for his college education. Both Nixon and Kennedy moved ahead when the favorite older brother died.

Nixon went to Duke University where he was still called "Gloomy Gus." He was closer to male than female schoolmates. The boys worried about their grades since they were essential to getting a job as a lawyer upon graduation. He and some other boys broke into the Dean's office to see their grades one night. In later years he told John Dean, "There are ways to sneak into offices in the middle of the night."

Although third in his class when he graduated from Duke University Law School in 1937, he was unable to get a law job. He applied to the F.B.I. but they never responded. His mother intervened and asked a friend to hire him. Once hired, he quickly found that he hated law practice. He began to consider politics and orations against Roosevelt and Democrats.

2

Love Life

Dick met his first girlfriend, Ola, while acting in a high school play with her. She later said he didn't know how to be sexy, was an awkward dancer and embracer, and wasn't really personable with girls. He was smart but seemed apart from others in an insecure way. He dated her throughout Whittier College. She broke it off when he went to Duke. She met another man and married. She said Dick acted hurt and talked as if they were closer than they really were. They did not have sexual relations by the time they broke up, according to the woman. However Nixon may have felt as if still another person besides his parents rejected him.

He didn't date at Duke and didn't join beer parties with fellows saying he didn't have enough money. After graduation, he met Pat Ryan at a football game. They were both in a play at Whittier Community Playhouse. She was then a high school typing teacher. She gave up an interest in being a Hollywood starlet and accepted his marriage proposal after 2 ½ years of dating.

Perhaps one of her attractions was that she had nursed her mother who died when she was 14, and her father had died of tuberculosis when she was 18. She had gone to New York City to work with tubercular patients for two years. Thus she may have reminded Dick of his mother in her care for such people and her humble origins.

They married on June 21, 1940, at the Riverside Inn in California, a hotel that had hosted several presidents. Dick required that Pat be quiet, supportive, voice no opinions of her own, and praised women who did likewise like Mamie Eisenhower. Pat once said to Gloria Steinem, "I'm not like all of you—all the people who had it easy. I've never had it easy."

Nixon despised Eleanor Roosevelt, Indira Gandhi and once slapped a female reporter who had exposed his dirty tricks in an early campaign. He disliked addressing women's groups. Once when talking to a group of female reporters, he talked of kitchen matters as if he were unable to realize that working women had other pressing issues besides cooking.

Nixon lauded Pat's strength, moral character and her willingness to lie for him to shield his whereabouts. She had grown up in an era when women were devoted to men upon whom they depended, and women did not try to carry on a career once married.

Ten years after their marriage when Dick was a Senator, he sought relaxation without Pat. He met Bebe Rebozo, a Cuban divorcee, and a poor boy who had worked his way up to chauffeur, gas station owner, investor, and flier. He became a confidante who helped Nixon in numerous ways.

Dick never touched Pat in public. He told others how nauseated he was when parents and children hugged and kissed. He proudly said that his mother never told him she loved him, adding, "She didn't have to."

Just as he shook hands with his mother after long absences, he shook hands with Pat after long trips, a spectacle which astounded reporters covering his trips. In 1952, Pat leaned over to kiss him after he received the vice presidential nomination but he turned away. However, she reached up and kissed him twice on the cheek. On her 61st birthday, he played "Happy Birthday" on the piano at a huge celebration She rose and went to him with outstretched arms but he ignored her and left her looking hurt and bewildered.

After his loss to Kennedy in 1960, he went to California alone for six months. He wrote, "I preferred to be alone. Everything I did seemed unexciting and unimportant." Then he decided to write *Six Crises* (deaths in his family, the Hiss case, nearly becoming President three times when he was vice president, a stoning in Venezuela, and his loss to Kennedy). He was inspired to write because of Kennedy's *Profiles in Courage* and Eisenhower's *Six Decisions*. Then in 1962, he decided to run for Governor of California against Pat Brown. A reporter overhead Pat tell Dick when she learned of his gubernatorial interest, "If you ever run for office again, I'll kill myself."

Obviously, Nixon did not listen to his wife and ran again but she did not carry out her threat. When they lived in the White House, Dick and Pat occupied separate wings. They saw each other for 30 minutes a day at dinner where they spoke so little that waiters rushed the food courses. Pat told her physician that they had not been intimate since the 1962 gubernatorial defeat. Rebozo was the closest person to Nixon from 1956 on.

There have been rumors that Nixon saw a Japanese woman when he served in the military but if true, this is likely to have been for a very short time.

3

Military Experience

In 1942, Nixon applied for a navy commission. He served in the Navy as Operations Officer in the South Pacific for ten months from October 1943 to July 1944. He saw casualties but was not under fire. He got merit citations and medals but not the battle stars, which he wanted. Although half of the Quakers were pacifists, Nixon wanted to serve to further his political ambitions.

Nixon rose from Lieutenant. Junior Grade to Lieutenant Commander doing things like bargaining to get snacks and liquor for the men in his outfit. He became an excellent poker player and began to drink and cuss more.

4

Path to Power

Before the war, Nixon's first case as an attorney where his mother got him hired was a disaster. He cost his firm $4,800 in an out of court settlement. The judge threatened Nixon with disbarment but his Quaker boss stood by him. He took a vacation to Cuba after the case and seriously considered setting up a practice there. But he returned and decided that he would rather be in politics than law.

After the war in 1946, the California Republicans were looking for a candidate to oppose long-time incumbent Jerry Voorhis. On a suggestion by the Whittier College ex-president, they contacted Nixon. He gave a rousing speech about returning veterans who wanted jobs, not government handouts. They picked Nixon and he boned up on Voorhis and hired Murray Chotiner.

Murray Chotiner was an associate and manager of Nixon as he began his political career. Chotiner had been Earl Warren's campaign manager but was quickly fired when his tactics were revealed. However, Nixon took his campaign formula to heart. The main aims were to discredit the opponent, associate the opponent with an unpopular idea that had a suggestion of treason, if the opponent calls you a liar attack and never defend, and organize a group of the opposing party to support your candidate.

Dick smeared Voohis as a dangerous socialist with ties to the Communist Party and Voorhis never returned to politics. Nixon's posters read, "Remember Voorhis is a former registered socialist and his voting record in Congress is more socialistic and communist than democratic." Later when Nixon became Vice President, 2000 Whittier residents remembered his dirty campaign against Voorhis and refused to have a street named after him.

When Nixon replaced Voorhis, Congressmen warned him that they knew Voorhis was not communist and that he was well loved and would be missed. So Nixon shifted his maiden speech in Congress from partisan politics to communism. He attacked Gerhart Eisler, who fled the country because his communist connections had been exposed.

Nixon was the only freshman Congressman to accompany Christian Herter's committee to Europe to study the Marshall Plan. He came back an internationalist, committed to aiding Europe to block communist expansion.

Nixon told an aspiring young associate, "You don't know how to lie and if you can't lie, you'll never go anywhere." He credited Chotiner with this philosophy. In his early campaigns, Nixon's denials of lying were very calculated but they later became routine. To cover lies, he acted like a "moralizer." If he had an inner voice of conscience, it may have told him he was bad or unlovable but it never stopped him from lying.

Whittaker Chambers and his family were Quakers and so was Alger Hiss's wife. Rumors of homosexuality and sudden deaths made tantalizing hearings as they came to light under Nixon's investigation. Hiss, an F.D.R. aide at Yalta, was a spy who urged pro-Soviet diplomacy. Chambers and Hiss had worked together but Chambers left the Communist Party in 1938 and became an editor for Time magazine. Despite Chambers telling the F.B.I. about Hiss in 1945, Hiss had continued to be promoted, a fact that intrigued Nixon. Hiss had been questioned by the F.B.I. but denied being a communist.

Nixon spent much time with Chambers to see if he could trust his account of Hiss. Richard became convinced that Chambers was truthful and Nixon's investigation led to the imprisonment of Hiss.

In 1950, Nixon ran for the Senate against Melvyn Douglas's wife, Helen Gahagan Douglas. She was the first to call him "Tricky Dick" with good reason. He linked her with a communist sympathizer (Vito Marcantonio) and with the State Department's appeasement of the Soviets. Joseph Kennedy sent Nixon $1,000 for his Senate campaign through John Kennedy as the Catholic Democrats supported Nixon. Nixon won and Douglas spent her later life in obscurity after being branded with Nixon's label "the Pink Lady."

At one low point in his career, Nixon sought a specialist in Internal Medicine, Dr. Arnold Hutschnecker, for stress. He had read his doctor's 1951 book called *The Will To Live.* This physician treated Nixon for stress and possible sexual impotence. In a 1974 book called *The Drive for Power*, Hutschnecker referred to patients indirectly. He wrote, "A sexually inadequate man may seek power as a substitute for poor sexual performance. An excessive drive for power is born out of weakness." Was he speaking of Nixon?

Because Nixon had slain various opponents, he earned the nickname "giant killer," and "dragon slayer." He was suggested as a good candidate to be Dwight Eisenhower's vice president.

Nixon looked upon Eisenhower as a masculine war hero and didn't know that Ike had many reservations about him. The first time they met, Ike had read about the Alger Hiss case and complimented him. In the 1952 campaign as vice presidential candidate with Ike, 72 businessmen contributed regularly to a fund to cover Nixon's travel and business expenses. If it had been acquired openly through direct requests for contributions, there would have been no problem, but it was secret. News of it brought accusations of improper financial support.

Eisenhower probably had some influence on Nixon. They were linked by the marriage of Ike's grandson David to Nixon's daughter Julie in 1968. However, the influence of Nixon on Ike is clearer because Nixon protected his communist-hunting friend, Joe McCarthy, far longer than Eisenhower liked.

Nixon and Senator Joseph McCarthy were cordial friends and both loved to ruin their rivals by labeling them as communist sympathizers. But in 1954, when McCarthy attacked Ike, Vice President Nixon could not keep quiet. He supported the investigation and censure of McCarthy, which was conducted by Joseph Welch, a gentle but effective Boston lawyer.

While vice president, he nearly became president three times: after Ike's heart attack, ileitis and stroke. He was very correct each time, however.

While vice president, he endured mobs, stoning, car attacks and jeers in South America. When he came back to good press praising his toughness, he looked for new challenges to become president. One of these was confronting Khrushchev in Russia shortly after the Soviets had crushed the Hungarian Revolution.

In July 1959, Nixon went to the American Exhibition in Russia and met Khrushchev. Nixon had just pushed the Captive Nations Resolution and urged a week of prayer for the enslaved people behind the Iron Curtain. Khrushchev told Nixon, "This resolution stinks like fresh horse shit and nothing smells worse than that." Nixon told Khrushchev whom he heard had been a pig herder, "There is something that smells worse than horse shit and that is pig shit." Then Khrushchev asked a laboring woman nearby, "Does this look like a slave? The vice president of the United States says you are slaves. Are you a slave?" The woman responded "Nyet" (no).

In the "typical American home" exhibit in Moscow, Nixon conceded that the USSR was superior in rocketry but the US was superior in other ways. "We too are giants. You want to threaten—we will answer threats with threats." Nixon turned the argument aside with a soft word and it ended amicably and with good press coverage in *Time* and *Life* magazines.

After being vice president, he wanted to be president but lost to Kennedy. At the time of the Kennedy assassination, he had planned to write another book but on November 24, 1963, decided to run for the presidency again. He sensed that the country's mood needed law and order to quell the violence of assassinations, race riots, and the Viet Nam war.

By October 1968, he felt confident of becoming the next president. Although Johnson was trying to reach a truce with North Viet Nam, Nixon and John Mitchell sent word to President Thieu of South Viet Nam that the Republicans did not agree with the administration's view on the peace accord. This obstruction of security affairs caused North Viet Nam to decline to sign peace agreements with the Johnson administration.

Nixon wanted the blue-collar votes of people like himself. Harry Truman, who had been criticized by Nixon, tried to warn the public about him. He said, "If Nixon had to stick to the truth, he'd have very little to say."

Once elected, Nixon announced his goals during his inaugural speech in 1969: "The greatest honor history can bestow is the title 'peacemaker'…Let all nations know that during this administration our lines of communication will be open."

He announced more goals at his second inaugural speech in 1973: "This past year saw far-reaching results from our new policies for peace. By continuing to revitalize our traditional friendships and by our missions to Peking and to Moscow, we were able to establish a base for a new and more durable pattern of relationships among the nations of the world…. We shall answer to God, to history and to our conscience for the way in which we use these years".

5

Leadership Style

Nixon tended to brag and exaggerate his accomplishments. He made himself famous by bragging that he cracked the Alger Hiss case when it was actually Whittaker Chambers whose admissions cracked the case. Nixon leaked stories to the press about the case and had himself photographed with the microfilms, which Chambers kept in a pumpkin (so they were called "the Pumpkin Papers").

He lied to preserve his good name. When reporters talked to some soured contributors, the story of the slush fund by the 72 contributors leaked out. Politicians turned against Nixon, as did reporters who had previously supported him. Ike was disheartened and never believed Nixon's innocence plea. Nixon denied using the money for his own purposes and denied granting favors to contributors, but he did. Many asked him to resign. Eisenhower urged him to go on TV and plead his case to the public but withheld public approval of Nixon.

Nixon went on television and gave the "Checkers" speech on September 23, 1952, so called because he said he was not going to return the little dog named Checkers that had been a gift. However he lied when he maintained that he never profited from or gave favors for the money. He bought his house with cash instead of a check, an issue that caused Eisenhower some concern. He lied about Pat's real name and birth date to make a sympathetic point for both of them.

He said, "I'm not a quitter and Pat's not a quitter. She was born on St. Patrick's Day (in actuality she was born the day before) and her name is Patricia Ryan" (it's really Thelma Catherina and was later changed). He ended with "And you know how the Irish never quit." He lied when he said the fund was not secret because it was.

Eisenhower had not decided whether to keep Nixon as a running mate. But Nixon took the decision away from Ike. He told the TV audience to send wires to the Republican National Committee. When Nixon told Ike to "shit or get off the pot" about whether to keep him as a running mate, Eisenhower never forgave him this crudity. But Ike overlooked this and several other slights and allowed Nixon to remain his running mate even though he came to distrust him.

Nixon wanted to use insider information to defeat Kennedy in the presidential election. As vice president, he had a major role in pushing for the invasion of Cuba and the assassination of Castro once it was suggested by the C.I.A. During the briefing with Kennedy before their televised debates, Nixon asked Ike and the C.I.A. to keep these plans secret so Nixon could be one up on Kennedy in the debates. Surprisingly, Kennedy suggested in the debates that he would push for intervention in Cuba and support Cuban rebels to upset Castro's regime. Nixon was shocked and thought he'd been double-crossed.

Nixon asked favors and granted favors in return. His brother, Donald, wanted a loan of $200,000 to buy a restaurant chain. At Nixon's request, Howard Hughes loaned it to Donald. Hughes wanted his medical institute to be classified as tax-exempt and Nixon pressed the I.R.S. to grant this and they did. This information came out eight days before the presidential election against Kennedy. When he lost to Kennedy, the press let it die.

When Nixon first won the presidential election, he came out as the candidate for a return to law and order. His stand against drugs was well known. Elvis Presley wrote in December 1970 and asked to be made a "Federal Agent at Large" to help in the fight against drug abuse. Nixon invited Presley to the White House. Elvis presented him with a commemorative World War II pistol and hugged Nixon. Nixon provided Presley with an honorary badge but never gave him "Federal Agent credentials."

He took revenge on those who publicly shamed him. When Nixon finally became president; he sought revenge against Tom Braden, a reporter who had questioned a loan eight years earlier in a campaign conference. Nixon had the I.R.S. audit Braden every year during his presidency.

When Nixon won the presidency again in 1972 by a landslide, the attitude on the night of the win was "We showed our enemies" instead of enjoyment. The next morning he asked everyone for resignations so he could start fresh. Then he left for two months of isolation at Camp David.

According to tapes released by the National Archives in February 2002, on April 27, 1972, Nixon considered the use of a nuclear bomb against North Viet Nam. Henry Kissinger dismissed the idea. Nixon said, "I'd rather use the nuclear bomb…You're so (expletive) concerned about the civilians and I don't give a damn."

"That, I think, would just be too much," said Kissinger. Nixon responded by telling Kissinger that he just wanted him to think "big."

One of Nixon's biggest contributions was to open up relations with China. That goal arose because of his view of leadership. A few weeks before the Watergate scandal broke, Nixon told Theodore White that he didn't like details and left them to others. He added that he didn't like domestic issues because you can't win them but you can win in international issues and those were important. Therefore he created the China initiative, the peace initiatives with Russia, and initiatives to improve relations with the Southern blacks and whites.

Another example of his leadership style could be called C.Y.A. or "Cover your ass." When he learned that the Watergate burglars had also been involved with the C.I.A. in the Cuban invasion, he wanted them kept quiet to conceal his role in that failed invasion. He thought that would tie him to the Kennedy assassination. He thought Oswald killed Kennedy because the government was trying to assassinate Castro after the Cuban invasion failed. Nixon encouraged and even pushed the administration to develop a covert plan to assassinate Castro, Oswald's hero. Nixon's handling of the Watergate burglars showed how he lied and encouraged his staff to lie.

Nixon would not have become president but for the assassinations of John and Robert Kennedy, his main rivals. He would not have had to resign if the break-in clues had not been found at the Democratic

National Headquarters at Watergate. He might not have had to resign if Butterfield had not answered the accidental question about the White House taping system. But his way of handling these situations was to try to keep covering up.

Nixon probably kept the tapes rather than destroying them for a variety of reasons. He began to keep them partly to copy Churchill who kept a diary of his administration. Nixon started a diary but it was hard to maintain and he resorted to tapes. He also taped people, as a form of surveillance of his own staff since he often perceived that people were against him or his policies. He could have doctored his tapes to reflect well on himself, much as he doctored the 18-minute lapse in the tape, which he denied that he erased.

There may have been psychological reasons that he didn't destroy the tapes, which caused his downfall. Perhaps he wished that people would see his dirtiness out of some twisted guilt feelings or some self-destructive urge. It is also possible that his lies and crimes had become so commonplace that he did not recognize them as such and forgot how many would be on the tapes. On one tape, he wanted to avoid being caught when he said, "I believe somehow I have to avoid having the president approve the break-in of a psychiatrist's office."

Perhaps the most stunning realization about Nixon after release of the tapes was his crudities and prejudices. He was heard to say, "What about the rich Jews? The I.R.S. is full of Jews, so go after them like a son of a bitch."

When defending himself, he used a crude reference, "It's the responsibility of the media to look at the president with a microscope, but they go too far when they use a proctoscope."

In the end, Nixon was defeated by his paranoia, his own fear that he was disliked. He retaliated against those who disliked him, over-bombed Cambodians to show his might, and sponsored a break-in to spy on those who opposed him. Then, he covered it up and lied to keep from being caught.

6

Stresses

Nixon's rage was well known to his staff. One of his points in his debate with Kennedy was that he was cooler in dealing with a crisis (or with Soviets like Khrushchev) than Kennedy would be. But when his aides overscheduled him during the Kennedy-Nixon campaign, he began kicking the back of the seat in a car his aide was driving. He kicked it hard and repetitively. The man he was kicking stopped the car, stalked off, and returned only when Haldeman pleaded with him.

Nixon's most common coping method was to blame others for his own problems. Before the first debate with John Kennedy, Nixon hurt his leg and was hospitalized for two weeks for an infection. He lost 20 pounds and looked exhausted when he was to appear on the television debate. He declined make-up in his wish to look natural. Kennedy looked tanned (a side effect of medicine used for Addison's disease). He later blamed cosmeticians for making him up poorly compared to Kennedy.

When Nixon lost to Kennedy, he felt that he was sabotaged by his own staff and by the media. During the campaign, his staff put him on a television program with students whom he later called "shitty ass liberal sons of bitches." He accused his staff saying, "You tried to destroy me in front of 30 million people."

An aide told Nixon, "What scares the hell out of me is that you would blow sky high over a thing as inconsequential as this. What in God's name would you do if you were president and got into a really bad situation?" Nixon responded that he would think about that.

Nixon was stoic about his loss to Kennedy but a deep rage made him lust for revenge and power when he finally became president. His first response to the loss was to write his book *Six Crises* as therapy but also to appear as smart as Kennedy. He wrote of a dream in these memoirs. "I had a rather curious dream of speaking at some sort of rally and going on a bit too long and Rockefeller stood up and took over the microphone on an applause line." This dream suggested a fear that a handsome and wealthier competitor (similar to Kennedy) would take away the applause, which Nixon craved.

Nixon felt unable to trust that anyone would like him since his earliest years. This gradually took the form of paranoid ideas that people were out to get him. It made him a very sore loser, ready to criticize and blame others for his failures.

When he lost to Pat Brown in the California gubernatorial race in 1962, he refused to concede. Finally he appeared and said, "Now that all the members of the press are so delighted that I have lost, I'd like to make a statement of my own. I believe Governor Brown has a good heart, even though he believes I do not. And as I leave the press, all I can say is this. For 16 years, ever since the Hiss case, you've had a lot of fun—a lot of fun—that you've had an opportunity to attack me and I think I've given as good as I've taken. But as I leave, I want you to know—just think how much you're going to be missing. You won't have Nixon to kick around anymore, because gentlemen, this is my last press conference."

Turning to press secretary Herb Klein he said, "I gave it to them right in the ass. It had to be said, goddammit, it had to be said."

Walter Cronkite wrote, "The Nixon policy was based on a simple formula: If it could bring down the press' credibility, it might improve its own." He added that when the Watergate tapes were released, they revealed that Nixon said, "The press is the enemy."

When Nixon thought his misdeeds would be discovered, he used government agencies to protect himself. After Kennedy's assassination, Nixon had always feared that his role in the Cuban invasion and plans to assassinate Castro would be discovered. Therefore, when he became president he had all files connecting him with the plans to invade and to assassinate Castro removed from C.I.A. files and destroyed. Only thanks to C.I.A. Director Helms and Nixon's aides (Haldeman and Erlichman) did the public learn of the major role played by Nixon.

When he was faced with accusations that he lied, he pleaded innocence and tried to make others feel sorry for him. He gave the "Checkers" speech proclaiming his innocence. He gave numerous speeches
proclaiming innocence in the Watergate break in. When accused of
illegal wiretaps, Nixon ordered the F.B.I. to reveal illegal wiretaps
requested by Kennedy and Johnson in order to say, "I'm not the only
one."

He tried to use government agencies to punish his enemies. He was
furious when the I.R.S. would not give his office damaging information on a contributor to the campaign of George McGovern. He said
he would fire the I.R.S. commissioner and the Secretary of the Treasury, George Shultz, and appoint those who would be more coopera-
tive. But he told the public, "I have never obstructed justice." He
added, "I welcome this kind of examination because the people have
got to know whether or not their president is a crook. I am not a
crook."

But when the special prosecutor demanded his tapes, Nixon ordered
Attorney General Elliot Richardson to fire the prosecutor. Richardson
refused and resigned. So did his next in line, Ruckelshaus. Robert Bork
did not resign and as third in line to the Attorney General, tried to
carry out the order in what was called "the Saturday night massacre."

Nixon lied to get sympathy as well as to keep from being caught.
On his last trip to France as president, he spoke at Orly airport to
appeal to the public. He lied saying 40 years ago he majored in French,
whereas he majored in history. When he appeared on television with
British newscaster David Frost, he defended himself saying, "If the
President does it, that makes it legal."

He lied to his family and encouraged them to lie about him. Nixon
let his daughter Julie make 150 speeches on his behalf during Watergate because he had lied to her about his guilt. He never admitted his
guilt to anyone. In his retirement, he asked an old friend, "What did I
do wrong?"

Elected on the issue of limiting federal powers, he had abused them and extended them beyond any president in history.

He was emotional and self-pitying in the last two days before his resignation. Alexander Haig feared that he might kill himself because he had said, "You fellows in your business (the Army) have a way of handling problems like this. Somebody leaves a pistol in the drawer. I don't have a pistol." Haig called Nixon's doctors and ordered that all pills be denied the president and the sleeping pills and tranquilizers he already had were taken away.

Kissinger was sent in to remind Nixon of his accomplishments. Nixon said, "Henry, you are not a very orthodox Jew and I'm not an orthodox Quaker but we need to pray." They both got down on their knees. Nixon prayed for help, rest, peace and love. He began to cry and pounded his fist on the rug saying, "What have I done? What has happened?" Kissinger held him until he got through and poured another drink. As Nixon became drunk and slurred his words, he said, "Henry, please don't ever tell anyone that I cried and that I was not strong."

His final farewell to his staff showed his paranoia and his willingness to lie in order to gain sympathy. He said, "Always remember, others may hate you but those who hate you don't win unless you hate them and then you destroy yourself." He spoke of the deaths of his two brothers, and of the four tubercular patients that his mother cared for in Arizona. He spoke of how his father's lemon grove in California never made a profit but oil was discovered on it after his father sold it, even though the nearest oil was on land owned by others.

After his retirement, Nixon told former aide Kenneth Clawson, "What starts the process really are laughs and slights and snubs when you are a kid. But if you are reasonably intelligent and if your anger is deep enough and strong enough, you learn that you can change those attitudes by excellence, personal gut performance, while those who have everything are sitting on their fat butts." Nixon was admitting that when people laughed, slighted and snubbed the little poor boy, he developed a deep anger and a determination to outdo those "who have everything" whom he stereotyped as "sitting on their fat butts."

Was Nixon unbalanced? The Smothers Brothers comedy act used to say, "Mom always did love you best." Nixon assumed others and the media felt the same way and loved Pat Brown or John Kennedy best. Nixon had no real sense of humor and was unable to laugh at himself, because he was so intent on trying to measure up and look as good as the rich and powerful people he envied. One of the rare humorous comments he ever made was when old political enemy Harry Truman accepted a bourbon and water from him at a Gridiron Dinner. He described the incident to the audience saying that love was bursting out all over when Harry Truman accepted a drink from Richard Nixon without having it tested first. Nixon did not seem to enjoy many jokes, either, but used expletives regularly. Aides said that his two favorite jokes were crude sexual jokes about farmers.

He tried to follow his parents and his Quaker religion to seek no personal profit but his envy of wealth and privilege became too strong. This quest to outdo the wealthy, the attractive and the privileged made him sacrifice morals to win. He felt that he was a "have not" and took on the "haves." He probably classified the "haves" as Jerry Voorhis, son of a millionaire banker; Helen Douglas, wife of actor Melvyn and friend of Eleanor Roosevelt and Lyndon Johnson; Alger Hiss, elegant diplomat and aide of Roosevelt; and John Kennedy, rich and popular.

7

Accomplishments

Nixon ended the draft, introduced new anti-crime laws, supported a broad environmental program, appointed conservative justices to the Supreme Court, and recognized the first moon landing of American astronauts in 1969. He brought stability to the country by reducing the tension between this country and China and the Soviet Union. He signed a Russian treaty to limit nuclear weapons in 1972. He signed the accord to end American involvement in Viet Nam in 1973. He allowed blacks to achieve integration through busing but he disdained human rights in general.

His secretary of state, Henry Kissinger, helped Israel and Syria end disagreements. The administration mishandled Cyprus and supported the Shah of Iran and other repressive regimes in Chile, South Korea, Romania, Greece, Brazil and the Philippines. All of these caused problems for the Reagan administration later. However, many international agreements were in jeopardy because of Watergate.

Kissinger stated that the erosion of executive authority after Watergate prevented a trade and missile-limitations agreements with the Soviet Union from being implemented. He added that Watergate might have tempted the Soviet Union into "an adventurous course" before they helped the Cubans enter Africa from 1975 to 1977.

Clark Clifford felt that he could not question Nixon's three major foreign policy achievements: the opening to China; his attempt to reduce nuclear tragedies by establishing relations with the Soviet Union; and his effort to bring peace to the Mideast. But he said, "Nixon's removal from office for cause, through orderly and constitutional processes, was a triumph for the genius of the original founding fathers—but at what cost in the spread of cynicism, the legacy of recrimination and myths, and the loss of respect for the noblest institution in American life."

In his later years, Nixon wrote books on foreign policy as an elder statesman. He died in 1994.

8

Summary

Although poor, Nixon never had to worry about survival or basic needs. But social conviviality was another story. His parents were not particularly close to anyone. An angry man raised Nixon and he picked up many of his father's characteristics of kicking, criticizing, and crudity. His mother, a Quaker, believed in proper behavior and displayed a rigidity and lack of warmth, which Dick took into his own personality.

He grew up feeling inferior to other boys with more money, more education, better looks, more self-esteem and athletic ability. He also realized his parents favored his older brother who died. He tried to strive to finally reach acceptance in their eyes and the eyes of others. Therefore, he grew up without the basic trust that children experience when they are certain that their parents love them.

Without a basic sense of trust, he felt he had to look out for himself. He thought he could expect little from others. To gain approval, he gave the outward appearance of diligence and religiosity, but inwardly felt he must claw his way to success with little help from anyone. Elliot Richardson, the Attorney General who resigned rather than fire the Watergate prosecutor, said Nixon's "inner core of insecurity" led to his great drive to be accepted.

Although he wanted to be accepted by men and women, he worked much harder for acceptance by men. Women were secondary to him, as they may have been to his father. He appears to have tried to court only one or two women in his life. Once married, he spent little time in developing the trust or intimacy that makes a couple close.

George Gordon, Lord Byron, once said, "Love is of man's life a thing apart, 'tis woman's whole existence." Love was a thing apart for Dick and he never reached the level of compromise or surrender that some reach in loving relationships. Nevertheless, because it was a thing apart and not important to him, he may or may not have been faithful to his wife. There is no absolute evidence that he was unfaithful but he may have had a short relationship with a Japanese woman during World War II. Overall, his relationship with his Cuban friend and backer might have been more intimate and committed than that with his wife.

Nixon used some unhealthy or childish coping techniques when he was under stress. He denied emotions and facts when he was under stress. He was not one to perform very many personally risky acts but enjoyed them vicariously by authorizing his underlings to carry out risky maneuvers. He was unable to relieve stress by joking and tended to rationalize and intellectualize to cope. He took pride, however, in avoiding temptations and lived a basically ascetic life following the mold in which he grew up. He was inhibited and tended to regress under stress, as was evident in his farewell speech and in the recollections of colleagues like Henry Kissinger.

Finally, when under stress, he was more likely to blame others for his problems and to distort facts than to face up to them. He imagined that politicians, the press and the public had as little love for him as his own parents had. As with people who feel shortchanged, he felt that he could bend the rules to make up for what he had not received earlier. As he began to bend the rules and rise above the law, he became convinced that others did the same and that he should not be penalized just for having been caught doing what others did.

Although he considered suicide, he had the courage to continue living for many years amidst the greatest criticisms any ex-president has ever endured. He was the only ex-president in modern times that decided to do without personal secret service protection to save money for the taxpayers. However, his resignation allowed him to receive the presidential pension which would have been lost if he had been impeached and removed from office.

Nixon's moral development went astray from the usual path early in life. He tried to please his parents to avoid punishment and win their love. But they were unloving parents and he diverted his wish to please others to his peers. While not successful with the many, he began to focus on the few. In one-to-one relationships, he found some who professed to see some greatness in him. While no great genius, he learned how to please those who mattered and cared little for the rest. Thus he never arrived at a true loyalty to social conventions. The main thing that kept him out of more trouble was fear of being caught and humiliated.

His leadership style was more like an administrator with little interest in achieving particular goals, and actually little interest in developing his people. He found people who needed little approval and set them up to carry out tasks that would bring him fame and importance. Even if his parents ignored him, he wanted to be sure the world would not ignore him. He was not ignored. He was castigated.

10

RONALD REAGAN

1

Upbringing and Early Life

Ronald Reagan was born in Tampico, Illinois on February 6, 1911. He was such a fat little baby that he reminded the family of a little Dutchman and was nicknamed "Dutch." He was the second son, the first being Neil, two years old when Ronald was born. His father Jack was an alcoholic Irish shoe store salesman. Jack was an inactive Catholic who could not hold jobs for long and the family moved frequently. They moved to Chicago when Ronnie was three, to Galesburg when he was four, to Monmouth when he was seven, back to Tampico when he was eight, and to Dixon when he was nine. As a result, the boys found it hard to make and keep friends.

Ronnie hated his father's drinking binges and when he was 11, he found his father lying in the snow drunk. He wrote about this, "I wanted to let myself in the house and go to bed and pretend he wasn't there. Oh, I wasn't ignorant of his weakness. I don't know at what age I knew what the occasional absences or the loud noise in the night meant but up till now my mother or my brother handled the situation. But this time I pulled him into the house and put him to bed."

However, Ronnie's interest in politics came from his father. Jack was opposed to stereotypes such as the way blacks were depicted in the movie *The Birth of a Nation.* He bragged that he had spent the night in a car rather than stay in a hotel that wouldn't accept Jews.

His liberally oriented father believed that people should stand on their own two feet. He thought that although everyone was created equal, ambition determined what each person would make of himself. Ronnie took this to heart. He wound up describing his father's weakness and alcoholic dependence as "a black curse." He never wanted to be weak and dependent like his father. This determination played a major role in his decisions to never subsidize the weak, the sick, the homeless, and the needy and to make them work to stand on their own two feet.

The family was very poor and Neil was often sent to the store for a soup bone and liver "for the cat." The family ate the liver and managed to make the soup bone last for a number of meals.

His mother Nelle, an ever-optimistic Bible-thumping Disciple of Christ church member, was a do-gooder who ministered to the sick and incarcerated. According to older brother Neil, "Ron was mom's boy and I was dad's boy." She nurtured Ron when he had bronchial pneumonia at age three. She valued prayer and dreams and believed they would come true. She helped him learn to read. She organized a local drama group where Ron had his first experience at memorizing parts. Eventually, he and his mother, who picked banjo, entertained people and patients at places like the Dixon State Hospital.

His mother's hero was a fictional character in a book called *That Printer of Udell's,* by Harold Bell Wright of the Disciples of Christ denomination. Nelle told Ronnie about the hero who discovered that he was an outdoorsman, orator, and wandering evangelist who created a social movement in Washington, D.C. Ron wanted to be like this man and made the decision to be baptized in the Disciples of Christ church at age 12. Ron began to teach Sunday school, give talks, and get into plays. The children were encouraged to attend traveling Chautauqua programs that offered plays, music, learning and moral guidance.

At 13, it was discovered that he couldn't see the blackboard at school. His photographic memory had helped him get along until then. His mother appreciated his excellent memory and gave him many assignments to remember for her. His black horn rimmed glasses were later replaced by contact lenses in Hollywood.

Ronnie wanted to be like his older brother, good at football and active in church plays and variety shows. While he finally grew better at football, he was outstanding as a Drum Major who led the YMCA band and twirled batons. When he gave talks or tried out for plays, the applause made this lonely boy feel extraordinary.

Dutch, as he was often called at home, was proud of being a lifeguard for six summers. He rescued 77 people and described that role as being someone that everybody looked at and looked up to. His eventual theme of rescuing people seemed to stem from this early experience.

In later years, he wrote that he realized some people hated to be rescued because it was like admitting their weakness and their need for help from others. He was acutely aware of this resentment because he hated to admit weakness, himself. That reminded him of his father. He also worked as a circus roustabout during his late teens.

When Reagan entered the Disciples of Christ-supported Eureka College in Illinois at age 17, the country was going through the Great Depression. He was lucky because his football career in high school led to a partial football scholarship, which helped pay his tuition.

He joined a strike committee to oppose the college president's plan to economize by firing instructors and cutting programs. He described giving a speech to the college and said, "For the first time, I felt my words reach out and grab an audience and we were one together." By his senior year in college, he was elected president of his class and had decided to become an actor. Little did he know that his college acting and orating would determine the rest of his life.

Ronald encouraged his older brother to enter Eureka College. Neil did so and left behind his work as a mechanic to become later a major advertising executive. He helped Ronald out later when his movie career floundered by connecting him with General Electric where he became their TV host and public spokesman. It was this move that led to his career in politics.

After graduation in 1932, having majored in economics and sociology, he tried to find a job. Finally he landed a job as a sportscaster with a radio station in Davenport, Iowa. He moved on to Des Moines and spent four years as a colorful sports announcer who made the audience feel they were watching a football game.

He learned to ride horses during this time, and remained a horse lover ever after. He finally convinced his station to send him to California for a radio stint. While there, he went for a screen test and was hired to play an announcer in his first movie, *Love Is On the Air.* Shortly after his movie career began, he made enough money to bring his parents to Hollywood and paid for their house.

2

Love Life

Perhaps because of his good relationship with his mother, he thought of women not as sex objects but as friends. He looked to them for approval and emotional support. He first dated Margaret, the daughter of a pastor, for eight years and always thought they'd marry. But she broke it off when she found someone else in college. After that he went to Hollywood.

His first real girlfriend in Hollywood was Jane Wyman. He treated his "pal" Jane in a casual way, taking her rather for granted. After dating for a year, she had minor surgery and was surprised that he only sent a formal, non-personal get-well card. When he went to visit, she refused to see him. He went in anyway, and she confessed her frustrated feelings. They became engaged and married in 1940.

During 1939, he had his first big role in a movie, *Dark Victory* with Bette Davis and Humphrey Bogart. He was to play a homosexual role but seemed unable to follow the director's advice because he was so disgusted by the sexual ambivalence of his character. He had difficulty dealing with the demands of a complex role and resisted the passion and sensuality of this and later roles. Directors finally found him unable to grow and cast him only in roles that were idealizations of his own self-image. He only played a villain in one of his 50 movies, the last one. When he ran for political office, he made sure that movie never showed again.

Ron and Jane made a "nice" Hollywood couple. They had daughter Maureen and adopted a son, Michael. Ron's first major film, *Knute Rockne*, featured him as George Gipp. He was in "feel good" movies, including *Santa Fe Trail* with Errol Flynn and *King's Row,* his best film. His autobiography, *Where's the Rest of Me?* comes from a line in *King's Row.* He woke up to find his leg had been amputated by a cruel doctor and said, "Where's the rest of me?"

Ron became president of the Screen Actor's Guild in 1947. He testified before the House Un-American Activities Committee during the search for communists, and was an informant for the F.B.I. As he described it, "I joined any group that promised to stop the threat of communism."

Between 1947 and 1948, he suffered severe viral pneumonia and broke his leg, resulting in a weight loss, brace and crutches for nearly a year. Also Jane had a child who died within 24 hours and the marriage simply could not survive the stresses. In 1948, Jane and Ron separated and would eventually divorce. Each had different stories of the problem. Jane said that Ron had gotten too involved with saving the world from communism and had too little interest in her.

Reagan began to cut a heroic figure, battling communism for Hollywood and the country. He began wearing a gun and some called him a fascist. However, he was so hurt by his divorce that he denied it by saying, "I didn't want a divorce. I didn't initiate it or pursue it, in fact I don't consider myself divorced."

Two years after his separation from Wyman, he was in London making *The Hasty Heart* with Patricia Neal. She was disappointed in his total lack of romantic interest. "Although I was a young, pretty girl, he never made a pass at me," said Neal.

Eddie Bracken who starred with Reagan in *The Girl From Jones Beach* said, "He was never for the sexpots. He was never a guy looking for a bed. He was a guy looking for companionship more than anything else."

After World War II, Reagan's movie career began to sag but his political experience had increased by the time he met Nancy Davis. Her father had abandoned the family and her mother toured the country trying to work as an actress. Eventually, her mother married a physician and entered the world of privilege.

Nancy and Ron met when she was receiving mail from communist sympathizers and was afraid of being accused as a communist. She was told to see Ron who might be able to help. They hit it off immediately and Ron later said, "Nancy Davis saved my soul." She appreciated his efforts and they married in 1952 with actor William Holden as best man. Seven months later, their first child, Patti, was born.

In 1957, Nancy and Ron made a movie together called *Hellcats of the Navy*. After this and another bad movie, he could find no parts and went to Las Vegas to sing and dance at the Frontier Hotel. After a short stint, he was offered the chance to host the General Electric (G.E.) Sunday Night Theater, thanks to a connection from his brother.

As a celebrity spokesman, he traveled the country giving talks and meeting workers. It was there he learned of the interference of big government in business, and changed his political focus to stopping communism*and* big government.

Nancy's support and ability to size up who could help or hurt Ronald's career has been of primary importance in his life and success.

Many say that except for Woodrow Wilson's wife, Nancy has wielded more power than any other first lady.

Their children and others attest to the fact that neither Ronald nor Nancy were very good parents. In an interesting aside, Ronald tended to call Nancy "Mommy." She was, of course, his major supporter, problem solver, and finally caretaker as he descended into Alzheimer's, a disease that apparently also afflicted his mother.

3

Military Experience

When he was a sports announcer, Reagan began taking home U.S. Army extension courses to study. He enrolled on March 18, 1935. He then joined the Army's Enlisted Reserve Corps in 1937 as a private but quickly became a second lieutenant when called to active duty after Pearl Harbor. However, he was rejected for combat because of his limited eyesight. He was assigned to the public relations branch and his unit made over 400 training films. He served as Personnel Officer, Post Adjutant, Executive Officer and even Commanding Officer from April 1942 to July 1945. He became a captain before his discharge, and was recommended for promotion to major but there was no major's vacancy in his unit at that time. He completed his commission in the reserves in 1953.

Among the films he made, some that are known to the public include *Air Force, Target Tokyo, For God and Country, Jap Zero, The Rear Gunner* and *This Is the Army*. He narrated many military training films. He had to recruit technicians and artists from the movie business for some films. He also had to view films and musicals to judge whether they were good for the morale of soldiers. He especially liked the music of Irving Berlin and was happy that some of Berlin's WWI songs were reprieved during WWII.

4

Path to Power

Reagan was unlike most other politicians who had a mentor or a person who helped and encouraged them in their first 30 years. He was a self-made man and disliked depending upon others. It was not until he was 53 and was asked to run for governor of California that he received any serious help from others.

While in Hollywood, he served five terms as president of the Screen Actors' Guild. That made him the only U.S. president who had been in charge of a labor union. He was notable in the 1940s and 1950s because of his obsession with ridding Hollywood and the country of the threat of nuclear weapons and communism.

He was a Democrat for Eisenhower. By 1960, he had changed his political orientation and gave over 200 speeches for the Republican presidential nominee, Richard Nixon, running against John Kennedy.

Even when his movie career failed, he did not consider politics. After his years with G.E. doing talks and hosting their show, he knew a great deal more about business and their views of government suppression. He saw governmental suppression of big business as a violation of the American dream of capitalism. This caused him to finally switch from his father's party to Republican in 1962. That change made him a prime choice for the party when they wanted an eloquent speaker for Barry Goldwater's run for the presidency.

In 1964, his "Rendezvous with Destiny" speech was so good that many believed the wrong man was running. Bucking the tide of the JFK-LBJ big government campaign, he wanted to reduce the size of government and the budget. He appealed to people's optimism and had none of the negativism that surrounded the Nixon image in the Republican Party. In his speech, he said, "Public servants say, 'What greater service we could render if only we had a little more money and a little more power'. But the truth is that outside of its legitimate function, government does nothing as well or as economically as the private sector...The taxpayer? That's someone who works for the federal government but doesn't have to take a civil service examination."

Reagan was then encouraged to run for governor of California. For the first time, he developed political goals. When he ran for governor, aides helped him fashion the image of a cowboy coming to rescue those in trouble. They photographed him on horseback, and created the straight talking, straight shooting image that served him so well. His parents and his religious convictions, however, had already created his inner belief system. In 1966, he ran against Jerry Brown and defeated him in a landslide. At the age of 55, as California Governor, he wrote all his own speeches. One famous line was, "I know 28,000 things that won't work and they're all on salary."

When he left the gubernatorial office, he had reduced the government budget by 10%, balanced the budget and reformed the welfare system. He had accomplished many goals he set for himself. Those who worked with him in California now encouraged him at the age of 65 to run for the presidency. Except for an ulcer, which he believed prayer had cured, growing deafness, and severe allergies, he felt healthy. He immediately challenged Gerald Ford to receive the Republican nomination but lost in 1976.

When he ran against Ford, Bob Hope said, "Ronald Reagan is not a typical politician because he doesn't know how to lie, cheat and steal. He's always had an agent for that."

As the Republican nominee for the 1980 campaign, he debated the beleaguered President Jimmy Carter and won a landslide victory a few days short of his 70th birthday. He came to office believing that Russia was getting away with murder and thought the U.S. military posture was only second best. He also thought government was too big and wanted to cut welfare programs. In addition, he wanted to rescue Americans from poisonous self-doubt with his infectious optimism and trusted others to work out the details.

Clark Clifford, an aide to former presidents, said, "Reagan's economic policies are contradictory. It's impossible to cut taxes, increase the defense budget and balance the federal budget by 1984 as he promised. We're going to face budget deficits larger than any in history. Unless these policies succeed, Reagan will be seen as 'an amiable dunce'."

Reagan was shot by John Hinckley, along with Press Secretary James Brady, a policeman and a Secret Service man on the 70th day of his presidency. Ron's reactions aroused the admiration of the public and Congress passed everything he asked for during the next three months. This was similar to the "honeymoon" period of Lyndon Johnson when he was able to pass everything in the name of John Kennedy.

Shortly after his recovery, Reagan gave a prophetic speech saying, "The years ahead will be great ones for our country. The West will not contain communism, it will transcend communism. We will not bother to denounce it, we'll dismiss it as a sad, bizarre chapter in human history whose last pages are even now being written."

Two years into his first term, he addressed the National Association of Evangelicals where he expounded his religious interpretations of world events. "Let us beware that while the Soviet rulers preach the supremacy of the state and predict its eventual domination over all the peoples of the earth, they are the focus of evil in the modern world. I urge you to beware the temptation to ignore history and the aggressive impulses of any evil empire, to simply call the 'arms race' a giant misunderstanding and thereby remove yourself from the struggle between right and wrong, good and evil."

His political goals for his second term of office were similar to his first but he pushed the Strategic Defense Initiative (SDI) to build expensive shields to protect the U.S. from Russian nuclear missiles. He called Russia the "evil empire" and was convinced by the C.I.A. that the U.S. could spend Russia into oblivion on nuclear build-ups. His views of big government were still the same but he added to big government by his defense spending. He believed that Armageddon (the final decisive battle between good and evil before Judgment Day) was near. After talks with evangelist Billy Graham and Mother Teresa, he was convinced that he was shot because God had a plan for him. He moralized about the "cold war" with Russia and saw himself leading a crusade against heretics. He wanted Russians to be able to worship God.

5

Leadership Style

Reagan was a loner to a certain extent because he was uncomfortable in close relationships. He could never fire anyone. Nancy and his staff maneuvered people out when they needed to go. He was optimistic, likeable, kind and generous to individuals, handing them a check or helping despite eschewing government welfare programs.

When a staff member was blatantly misbehaving, he demanded their resignation. An example was when two California aides participated in a homosexual orgy during a government summit. When a staff member's misbehavior was subtle, he left the handling to others.

Reagan used humor and aplomb when he was shot in 1981, telling Nancy that he forgot to duck. He also became quite serious following his close call and wanted to reduce the threat of nuclear war. About three weeks after he was shot, he wrote to Soviet President Leonid Brezhnev. He recalled their meeting when he was Governor of California and how they promised to try to fulfill the hopes and dreams of people throughout the world. He concluded by discussing the grain embargo saying, "Perhaps this decision will contribute to creating the circumstances which will lead to the meaningful and constructive dialogue which will assist us in fulfilling our joint obligation to find lasting peace." Reagan's hand-written notes of this letter were declassified in 1995. Brezhnev died before they were able to meet.

Reagan used his excellent speaking style and his wit, a combination that made him extremely popular. For example, in 1986 he said, "If it moves, tax it. If it keeps moving, regulate it. And if it stops moving, subsidize it." He could also use self-effacing humor. He criticized his own fund-raising abilities and went on, "That's why I got into government, because we don't ask for it. We just take it."

The military felt revitalized under President Reagan. His administration placed a heavy emphasis on defense, so the military became more attractive and commanded bigger budgets and a bigger share of attention.

General Vernon Walters, Ambassador at Large, said of Reagan, "He communicated deeply felt values and his oratory skills helped him ask for sacrifices to bring down Soviet expansionism."

Donald Regan wrote, "Kennedy might call up a minor bureaucrat to check on a detail; Johnson might twist a Senator's arm; Nixon might discuss the tiniest details of China policy with his staff; Carter might micromanage a commando raid in the Iranian desert from his desk in the Oval Office. But Reagan chose his aides and then followed their advice almost without question. He trusted his lieutenants to act on his intentions, rather than on his spoken instructions."

Nancy's concern with image had created a negative first impression when the public thought she was interested in expensive dresses and dinner parties. Her crusade against drug use by children ("Just say no") rehabilitated her image for many Americans. But she played a large part in his administration because he did not like to fire people. She took on the role of removing people who might disturb or embarrass her husband during his term of office. Unfortunately, she was ill equipped for the task and sometimes consulted an astrologer for advice on what days to travel or handle things.

Donald Regan, Reagan's first Secretary of the Treasury and then Chief of Staff said, "A generation from now, Reagan's homely understanding of the importance of small things and his sound judgment and good instincts in large issues will be more clearly seen and better understood."

Reagan aide Marty Anderson said, "He was genial and easygoing but warmly ruthless. He would do in the nicest possible way what had to be done but he knew where he was going and if you were in the way, you were gone."

One of Reagan's Chiefs of Staff, James Baker, called Reagan the "kindest and most impersonal man" he'd ever known.

Howard Baker who participated in the Tower Commission to expose the Iran Contra scandal said, "He knew who he was, what he believed and where he wanted to go, and could communicate these ideas to people."

When Americans were taken hostage in Iran, Reagan negotiated for their release and once achieved, never bragged about it. When a Korean airplane strayed over Soviet airspace and was shot down, 269 civilians died. He could have broken off talks with Russia. He did not.

Margaret Thatcher said, "It was clear from our very first meeting that Ron Reagan was in politics out of passionate belief. This is the century when we have had the biggest battle of ideas in history. Between totalitarianism and freedom, coercion versus liberty. Ron Reagan was a passionate warrior in this battle as I was."

6

Stresses

During his Hollywood years, other actors accused Reagan of being a snitch to the F.B.I. He stuck by his guns because he considered the threat of communism so abhorrent. He was not about to pander to others out of fear of ostracism. He handled the criticisms of his fellow actors by believing in his own religious views, which assured him that God was on his side.

When Reagan ran into problems, he often learned new skills to find his way out. When his acting career languished, he was determined to learn what was necessary to become a song and dance man in Las Vegas showrooms. He then learned a new set of skills as he became a spokesman for G.E. to businesses across the country.

When he was governor of California, he supported the unpopular move of making students pay tuition to the University of California. They revolted and gave him the silent treatment as he walked about the campus. After walking through a long string of students—a gauntlet—he turned around and said "Shhh!" They all laughed and his wit had removed the tension without the need for him to change his position.

He joked about California students in revolt saying that one male demonstrator "had a haircut like Tarzan, walked like Jane and smelled like Cheetah." But he didn't hesitate to call in the National Guard for 17 days to quell violence.

When he didn't win the Republican nomination against Ford for the 1976 presidency, he modestly said he wasn't ready and returned to his ranch where he built fences, wrote columns and gave speeches. When he debated Carter in the next presidential campaign, critics focused on his age. He used humor and said, "I promise not to make age an issue. I will not focus on the lack of age and experience of my opponent."

When he was shot, his humor eased the country. He told Nancy, "Honey, I forgot to duck" and said to his doctors, "I hope you are all Republicans" to which they replied, "We're all Republicans today, Sir."

When daughter Patti Davis became a teen speaker for world peace at odds with her father, he said, "Our daughter has been taken over by that whole gang" rather than blaming his daughter for her actions. But when his son, Ron, became a ballet dancer, he denied responsibility by saying, "I raised him to be all man." He was sorely disappointed in this son until he developed a talk show, developed a political philosophy, and followed somewhat in his father's footsteps.

During his presidency, world events were changing almost daily. Three Russian presidents died in quick succession until Gorbachev. Then terrorists hijacked a plane and held seven Americans in Beirut. Reagan did not cancel a meeting with Russian premier Gorbachev. However he did approve a shipment of arms that in the end led to the release of the seven hostages. This was a practice (appeasing the hijackers) that he publicly opposed.

Reagan was a quick learner about diplomacy and despite his age, could continue to change his approaches depending on what was needed. When he met Gorbachev in Geneva in 1985, he began, "Let me tell you why we fear you."

Gorbachev said, "You're not a teacher, I'm not a student."

Reagan then suggested that they meet in private and began to tell Gorbachev about movies and Hollywood. Liking Reagan's sincerity, Gorbachev accepted an invitation to Washington, D.C., and Reagan accepted an invitation to Russia. Gorbachev asked Reagan to stop the S.D.I. "Star Wars" program but he did not. The result was that in 1986, Gorbachev offered everything to stop the arms build-up. Both agreed to destroy half their missiles, they agreed that human rights could be discussed and they banned space defense for ten years.

Reagan's political stance was constantly being illustrated by action. When Reagan visited Russia, he was told of Russian protocol. But he chose to visit the house of a Jewish couple that had been denied immigration papers on the basis of religion. He also held a party for 100 political dissidents in the American Embassy in Moscow, which shocked Soviet politicians.

When Reagan suffered his "Watergate" over the trade of arms to terrorists for hostages, his staff told him to sacrifice Donald Regan. He refused to do that but Regan heard and left abruptly. The Tower Committee investigating that matter was shocked at Reagan's lax management style and lack of curiosity about details of his administration. When he finally apologized and said, "It was a mistake," they forgave him and took no action against him.

Reagan depended more and more upon his staff as his age, dwindling memory, and deafness increased. Reagan's aides helped him prepare for what appeared to be off-the-cuff conversations in the Oval Office by putting notes in his desk drawer. When he was about to meet with people or broach a new topic, he quietly slid open the drawer and glanced down at those notes.

On December 8, 1987, Gorbachev came to Washington, D.C. to sign the treaty to eliminate missiles in Europe. Reagan deliberately invited a whole range of people to meet him, including Joe Dimaggio, Saul Bellow, Pearl Bailey, James Stewart, Claudette Colbert, Zubin Mehta, David Rockefeller, Armand Hammer and Van Cliburn. When Van Cliburn played the Russian folk song *Moscow Nights* Gorbachev broke into song, as did some of the other Russians present.

There were many jokes about Reagan during his administration, especially about his age, but he was able to handle them with humor. He sometimes told jokes on himself and this self-deprecating humor added to his charisma. He said, "I have left orders to be awakened at any time in case of national emergency, even if I'm in a cabinet meeting."

When he heard that actor Clint Eastwood was running for mayor of Carmel, California, recalling his own movie *Bedtime For Bonzo*, he said, "What makes him think a middle-aged actor who's played with a chimp could have a future in politics?"

When he finished his last term, he spoke at the Republican National Convention in 1992. Referring to Bill Clinton who was saying he had not inhaled marijuana, Reagan said, "When you see all that rhetorical smoke billowing up from the Democrats, I'd follow the example of their nominee; don't inhale."

Paraphrasing Lloyd Bentsen's comment to Dan Quayle, "I knew John Kennedy and you're no John Kennedy," Reagan said about Clinton, "This fellow they've nominated claims he's the new Thomas Jefferson. Well, let me tell you something. I knew Thomas Jefferson. He was a friend of mine and, Governor, you're no Thomas Jefferson."

Amiability and humor did not help in his closest relationships because he was always distant from his own children. After Reagan announced that he had Alzheimer's disease, his wife continued to take him to his office in California, the office building that was used in the movie *Die Hard.*

7

Accomplishments

On Reagan's inauguration day, January 20, 1981, 52 Americans held as hostages in Iran since November 1979 were released.

Reagan appointed Sandra Day O'Connor of Arizona to the Supreme Court as the Court's first female.

He sometimes allowed his staff to persuade him to act precipitously. He sent U.S. troops to Lebanon in a multi-nation response to terrorism, after 241 Americans were killed in 1983. He also sent troops to Grenada to restore order in 1983 but did not first discuss this with Britain's Margaret Thatcher despite the fact that Grenada was in the British Commonwealth. This strained his good relationship with the Prime Minister. He also authorized sending troops to Libya to bomb terrorist targets in 1986.

He enjoyed great successes in some areas. His meetings with Gorbachev led to a major arms control agreement in 1987. For the first time in history, the Soviet and American leaders discussed how to have a world without nuclear arms. Many argue that his willingness to commit a huge budget to the defense spending on the Strategic Defense Initiative paved the way for the Soviets to give up the arms race. This was part of the shift in Soviet leadership that led to replacing enmity with amity.

He reduced nuclear arms and reversed double-digit inflation. Some of the difficulties of the Reagan administration policy in Central America resulted from propaganda portraying the Nicaraguan Sandinistas as social reformers. But unfortunately the Iran Contra scandal will reduce his image in history as president.

Reagan understood that he and his fellow leaders were heads of government with whom he could interact sociably. The leaders of Canada,

France, Germany, Britain, Italy, and Japan were personal friends of Reagan and on a first name basis.

8

Summary

Reagan's family was on the edge of poverty and, like Hitler, had to move frequently when "Dutch" was a child. Frequent moves keep children from attaching themselves to others in close friendships to avoid the hurt when relationships must be interrupted by more moves. Reagan developed the ability, therefore, to meet people well but not to become particularly intimate. However, Reagan 's mother was very devoted to him and he was attracted to women similar to her. His father was closer to his brother.

His mother held up to him a Christian literary hero, orator and social reformer. He began early to model himself after that man by saving lives as a swimming pool lifeguard, then saving Americans from Godless communism. Reagan probably became a man of good character, courage and conviction, because of this upbringing.

His unconditional acceptance by his mother formed a great trust in women who appreciated men with the qualities of a social reformer. His natural optimism allowed him to trust in people from a distance but he avoided closeness with most people. When he formed love relationships with his two wives, he was committed and unlikely to stray, to the dismay of many beautiful Hollywood stars that expected to attract him.

Reagan was able to pass through all the stages of maturation including trust (within limits), autonomy, initiative, industry, identity, and intimacy with Nancy. When it came to generativity, his fear of possible hurt when relationships cease prevented him from being close to his own children. He could be close to the masses but not to the individual, except for Nancy. His ego integrity, however, was in good condition because he had an altruistic life. Then he tragically descended into Alzheimer's disease.

Reagan had a variety of coping techniques when he was under stress. He could suppress problems up to a point but was sometimes known to totally deny some part of reality that he found distasteful or to distort reality in the direction he wanted to believe. He was not a man who needed to do risky things to relieve tension because he had a great many hobbies (song, dance, horseback riding, farm chores, reading, etc.) that relaxed him.

One of his greatest attributes was his ability to defuse tension by using humor including self-deprecating humor. He was not ascetic but he also did not require a great number of material possessions, and tried to share his wealth with family and unfortunates on a personal basis. He found great satisfaction in serving others and altruistic endeavors and rarely blamed other people for his own problems.

Early in life, he tried to please his parents and was never a rebellious or anti-social youth. Although his father had trouble holding jobs, it was his father's dependency on alcohol that disappointed him most. It convinced him that people should strive to be independent and should not be subsidized.

Unlike Kennedy who had no vision or agenda when he entered the presidency, Reagan knew that he wanted to recover vanishing freedoms for business, for progress, and for individuals. This interest showed that he had risen above just pleasing parents and peers. He wanted to act in such a way as to be loyal to higher concepts of society and religion that would benefit more people. Reagan reached the highest moral level when he tried to create programs with fairness, equity and worth for the greatest number.

Johnson desired fame and wanted everyone to like him. Reagan had no need to receive recognition at the cost of his morals and could swim against the tide when he thought he was right. This showed his integrity. Like Truman, he was a personally scrupulous man and educated himself whenever he encountered difficulties. Unlike presidents Nixon,

Kennedy, Johnson and Clinton, he did not abuse his power or use his position to get what was not his.

World leaders found him to truly believe in American values and morals. They appreciated his genuineness and admired his lack of guile. He was not a faker and that is why he frustrated Hollywood directors. He could not act a part that he didn't believe in, nor could he say something he didn't believe.

He thought that the country needed him to save them from evil. In this sense, he lost touch with reality slightly. He was perceived as distant in personal relationships but considered himself a savior in many regards. Fortunately this Christ-like self-image was combined with an ability to use humor. Only people who have a tremendous sense of competence can take themselves as lightly as he was able to do. Nixon was never able to do this. He lacked confidence in his own competence and thought he had achieved success through tricks instead of genuine ability.

Reagan's leadership style, however, left much to be desired. He was extremely kind but not close to his subordinates. While he never really helped them to progress like a developer or team manager, they did progress if they were able to handle things for him and help him. As a much older man and possibly one with some diminishing abilities toward the end of his presidential tenure, he needed more help from others. If left to his own directions, he would have been a benevolent autocrat trying to rid the world of evil and of communism. But because of his shortcomings, he was more of a compromiser than anything else.

11

MARGARET THATCHER

"Why can't a woman be more like a man?" Alan Jay Lerner

1

Upbringing and Early Life

Margaret Roberts was born October 13, 1925, in Grantham, Lincoln-shire, England. She was the second daughter of Alfred Roberts, a local alderman and grocer, and his wife, Beatrice. Her father bought a gro-cery shop and his daughters were born above it in Grantham, a small town near Nottingham. He was a thrifty, hardworking man and loved to read. The girls helped out in the grocery as well as doing household chores like ironing, sewing, and beating the carpets. Their meals were "waste not want not" and leftovers were always used in future meals.

They were avid Methodists who attended church on Sundays. Alfred disliked selfishness and the family values were orderliness, duty, and asceticism. However, Maggie did like the cinema and played piano well enough to win several prizes at local music festivals.

When her father was nominated to be the local councilor, at age ten she carried messages from the polling stations to the party headquar-ters. In 1945, her father became Mayor of Grantham. Margaret went to a school where her father was on the board. She was no genius but she was very industrious. At age 11, her teachers wrote, "Very definite ability and her cheeriness makes her a very pleasant member of her form." By age 15, they recorded that she had "intelligence and determination."

Her father realized her political interests early on and encouraged her to pursue education in that direction. Her mother was a practical woman, a dressmaker and housewife. At the time of her mother's death years later, Maggie would say, "She managed the household, stepped in to run the shop when necessary, entertained, supported my father in his public life and as Mayoress, did a great deal of voluntary social work for the church, displayed a series of practical domestic talents such as dressmaking and was never heard to complain."

Her older sister, Muriel, would go on to become a physical therapist. Maggie was never as close to her mother and sister as to her father and said when inducted as prime minister, "I owe almost everything to my father." But there was little humor in the family household. Margaret was never known for much humor but instead for her seriousness.

She was a confident debater in school. She had no scholarship and had to wait until there was a vacancy at Oxford University. Her father had scraped together tuition. She took the entrance exams, passed, and was allowed to enter. She had hardly been away from home before going to Oxford. She had visited London, seen the Changing of the Guard, rode an elephant at the zoo, and took in a Sigmund Romberg musical.

She majored in chemistry but was an undistinguished student. Oxford was filled with political ideologies and she quickly followed in her father's footsteps and joined the Oxford University Conservative Association. During World War II, there were many debates about what the party should stand for. She took up issues of equal pay for men and women and war profits. She did volunteer work to aid the war effort and made speeches for her association. She was noted for her strong convictions. She went through career paths similar to Harold Macmillan and Edward Heath by attending Oxford.

After she left Grantham, she rarely returned. Her father remained a supporter and guide until he died in 1969, so that he never saw her reach the cabinet level. Years later, she wept during a TV interview when recounting an election her father lost when he ran for alderman.

Margaret had to earn a living when she left Oxford. She first worked as a research chemist for a British plastics company producing glasses frames. So many members of parliament were working class that the Labour Government raised their wage from 600 pounds sterling to 1,000 per year. Margaret said that after that, it became possible for her to think in terms of a political career. Additionally, the practice of putting Member of Parliament seats up for sale to the highest bidder ended in 1948 and that helped the poorer candidates.

As the representative for the Oxford University Graduates Association, she received an invitation to run for parliament. She was the youngest (age 24) woman to run in the 1950 General Election. She left her plastics jobs and worked in London testing the quality of cake fillings and ice cream. She described the election as a contest between slavery and the proponents of freedom. She argued, what good was welfare if people had no freedom to "fly out" and live their own life.

Aware that her chemistry degree and the analysis of cake fillings was not a respectable vocation for a politician, she studied to be a lawyer. She enrolled in a part-time program first in patent law but later switched to tax law. She passed the Bar exam in 1953. She practiced tax law for less than five years. She then joined the Society of Conservative Lawyers and met many who would serve her later on. This training allowed her to understand finances and law language.

2

Love Life

She met Denis Thatcher on a blind date in 1949. His grandfather had made weed killers and sheep dip that expanded into prosperous paint and chemical companies. Denis directed them. He had served as a major in the Royal Artillery in World War II. After several dates, Denis introduced her to his colleagues at a dinner dance and they encouraged him to marry her. Denis had married before just as the war was starting. When he returned, he and his wife had grown too far apart and divorced. With Margaret's Methodist background, it took her a while to accept the divorce.

They married December 1951. Denis would become the first male consort for the first female prime minister in Europe.

Denis and Margaret shared interests in politics and the Conservative party principles. After her marriage, Margaret did not have to support herself and was able to devote her time to completing her law degree. She has always been grateful to Denis for his financial support. She described him thusly, "Being prime minister is a lonely job...But with Denis there I was never alone. What a man. What a husband. What a friend."

He once quipped that he was his wife's "eyes and ears to the world," a role that he felt was "an exercise in love and loyalty." Denis loved golf and absorbed the mood of the people through his social interactions.

As biographer Hugo Young said, Margaret spent little more than three years working in chemistry before she was in a position to tell businesses what to do.

Denis and Margaret had twins, Carol and Mark, born August 15, 1953. She continued working and had a nanny care for the children after their infancy. Denis retired just as Maggie reached party leadership, so he was able to travel with her as she met various world leaders. Margaret once said that when she was upset, she turned to Denis who usually embraced her and said something funny to make her laugh and relax.

Denis has endured criticisms and spoofs of the press for his careless remarks. Their daughter, journalist Carol Thatcher, wrote a book about her father called *Below the Parapet: The Biography of Denis Thatcher.* This affectionate biography also offers interesting accounts of the interaction between world leaders and the Thatchers as well as a more balanced picture of the inner life of her parents.

3

Path to Power

After having her children, Margaret sought office but had no success until 1958, when she was elected to represent Finchley north of London. She spoke brilliantly at her adoption meeting, and at age 32 was able to sum up Britain's economic problems, Middle East challenges and Soviet issues. Her conservatism matched Finchley residents. The 1959 election also brought a landslide victory to Harold Macmillan who had succeeded Anthony Eden in 1957.

Having arrived in the House of Commons, she had no particular cronies. She delivered her first speech without notes, using statistics and presented a bill to give reporters access to public meetings (similar to the U.S. Open Meetings law.) She argued beautifully that the public had a right to know what they were paying for. Because of her outstanding debating skills, fellow Conservatives frequently called upon her to debate the policies of the opponent Labour Party.

She also was appointed as Parliamentary secretary to the Ministry of Pensions, which she served from 1961 to 1964. This banal position dealt with details of national insurance and national assistance. She dug in to this unimpressive post and never complained. The experience led her to realize that civil servants wanted to keep their power even though they were not very capable or decisive.

From 1970 to 1974, she served as the Minister of Education and Science under Edward Heath. There, she earned the nickname "Margaret Thatcher, Milk Snatcher" for her efforts to expand nursery schools by saving money on such things as free school milk. She was dubbed the "most unpopular woman in Britain" in a 1972 newspaper article but she succeeded Edward Heath as the leader of the Conservative Party in 1975. In that role, she formed a plan to reverse Britain's perceived economic decline and to reduce the role of government.

After the Conservatives won a decisive victory in the 1979 general elections, she became prime minister. Her platform was limiting government control, ending government interference in business, and reducing public welfare costs. These were very similar to Ronald Reagan. She later added helping Zimbabwe (formerly Rhodesia) establish their independence.

Britain gained international respect during the 1980s because they sent forces to take the Falkland Islands back from Argentina. They also were in the news because their economic recovery improved Britain's level of prosperity, mainly because they had reduced the power of trade unions and had adjusted well to de-regulation.

The 1980 election of right wing Reagan followed and the victory of Margaret Thatcher's Tories over the British Labor Party suggested a trend toward conservatism in Western democracies.

In 1982, the Britain's elite Special Air Services Regiment was sent to Afghanistan. They instructed Stinger pilots that the Reagan administration had sent to fight the invading Russians. Unfortunately, Soviet forces found the passports of two British instructors in a training camp and tried to turn the event into a diplomatic incident blaming Americans and Britain for interfering in their war. British forces withdrew, but the C.I.A. persuaded Thatcher's government to continue training the rebels in secret encampments in the Scottish borders and highland regions.

When Reagan was shot, Donald Regan told Reagan that Thatcher had called to ask about his condition. Regan wrote, "Mrs. Thatcher's thoughtful gesture pleased Reagan; he and the Prime Minister, both conservatives and both political dark horses who have won office and the grudging respect of their enemies against the odds, truly like and admire each other."

In Reagan's final appearance in London in 1986 after two summit meetings with Gorbachev, Thatcher gave a moving speech thanking Reagan for all that he had done to improve East-West relations and remove the threat of nuclear war.

During her third term, she set historic precedents by returning education, health care and housing to private control. She resigned on

November 22, 1990. This followed heated debates about her creation of the much-hated poll tax. This charge resulted in people going to jail to avoid payment on principle, mass demonstrations and some riots. She was also reluctant and even adamant against economic integration with Europe, which brought criticisms at home and on the European continent.

4

Leadership Style

Thatcher dealt with all problems and details. She was an analytical, detail-oriented person. According to Young, she would "order Europe, instruct Reagan, see off the Russians, direct the Commonwealth, take charge of football hooliganism, the drugs crisis, and the precise configuration of the customs hall at the British end of the Channel Tunnel." She was essential to all decisions and none could be made without her.

Young said that her most important qualities were her "moral rectitude" which accounted for her "fiscal rigor," her "appeal to righteousness" or "inspirational certainty," and her pragmatism, which touched the people. But in actuality, she was often criticized as not being in touch with her people. She didn't really love people and they didn't really love her, say many political pundits. She was considered too arrogant to try to understand people unlike herself, which included the young, the minorities, the wealthy, and the sexually liberated.

The Queen of England, very unlike the working class that produced Margaret Thatcher, sometimes used the royal "we" in speeches. Eventually, Margaret used it quite often. In 1987, she said, "We are in the fortunate position, in Britain, of being, as it were, the senior person in power." When she visited Russia, she said, "We have enjoyed ourselves immensely." When she learned that her son's wife was pregnant, she said, "We are going to be a grandmother." This invited accusations of arrogance.

Thatcher loved Rudyard Kipling and poetry in general. She also read widely in politics, self-improvement, Marxism, religion, and other areas. Despite this, some of her cabinet complained that she didn't discuss things but stated opinions. Because she was so emphatic, many foreign ministers dreaded dealing with her.

She sometimes said that she thought welfare recipients were better off than her family had been in Grantham. She argued that if she achieved great things against difficult odds, anyone could. But she was lucky enough to marry a wealthy man. Not everyone could do that.

A recently published memoir of former Swiss foreign minister Edouard Brunner gave an interesting insight into the Thatcher marriage. During a 1984 dinner, the Swiss president asked Mrs. Thatcher how to cope with immigration from outside Europe. She chose not to reply and passed the question to her husband. Denis advised them to "keep Switzerland white" and said that he believed his wife felt likewise. Perhaps Margaret shared opinions with her husband that he occasionally voiced. In that way, such views would not be held against her.

After she resigned as prime minister in 1990, she was still in the House of Commons. It was not long before she issued a statement that included the following words. "I had been used to making decisions, and it took me a time to get into the understanding that I was not making the decisions...And so I didn't want to carry on in the House of Commons...I think the prime minister will find it easier if I'm not in the House of Commons and in a position to return. So I will accept the offer to go up to the House of Lords. It's so much more gentle in there, and you don't get the quick flash of the quick wit and the give-and-take of debate, which you'll get in the House of Commons."

5

Stresses

When she was nicknamed "Maggie Thatcher, Milk Snatcher," one newspaper called her the "most unpopular woman in Britain." Most newspapers supported her during that time but some did not. She weathered the storm by granting regular press briefings to those who supported her. This led to a protest song sung during that time called "Maggie Out!" She always had trouble with critics and negative press. When the public joined in this outcry, she said that she had to "build an armor" around her.

During her years as prime minister, unemployment rose and doubled, many did not like her acceptance of American missiles on British soil, and many disliked her permission for the U.S. to bomb Libya from bases in Britain. She advocated privatization of state-owned industry and utilities, strict trade union restrictions, and reduced social expenditures. While the economy grew, between 1979 and 1981, the economic output declined by 15%. These programs brought criticism and she probably would not have been re-elected but for the 1982 Falklands Islands War.

Her economic policies emphasized reducing the national budget. To demonstrate that she meant business, she forfeited much of her salary after 1979, refusing to accept over 11,000 pounds sterling a year. This meant that she gave up over $150,000 in American monetary terms.

She supported the campaign to keep Northern Ireland within the United Kingdom. In retaliation, on October 11, 1984, the IRA set off a bomb at the Grand Hotel in Brighton where the Tory leadership was having a Conservative party conference. It missed her but killed five others and made clear the dangers that British politicians faced. Unruffled, she carried on with the conference next day. However, this incident made her determined never to deal with terrorists.

Her work experience enabled her to tell Ronald Reagan in later years that because she was a chemist, she knew his Star Wars (Strategic Defense Initiative) would not work. But she accepted an invitation to help him work out a more palatable version of the SDI at Camp David. She was ready to support the SDI if Reagan stated that the West was not seeking nuclear superiority, that SDI production and use could be negotiated, that deterrence was not to be undermined by SDI discussions, and that arms control talks should continue. These talks and the ideological similarities between Reagan and Thatcher about Soviet issues provided a unified British-American position that forced the eventual dissolution of the U.S.S.R.

Margaret knew herself rather well. She once said, "I am not by nature either introspective or retrospective. I prefer to look forward. I feel easiest dealing with immediate practical problems."

On BBC interviews, Thatcher used her feminism to display her wardrobe and describe herself shopping like other British housewives. She always kept her hair, clothes, skin and appearance in good condition. She allowed herself to cry when her son disappeared for six days while in a car race across the Sahara and required an international rescue. Mark, who has had a somewhat strained relationship with his father, went on to become an accountant and has resided in the United States, mainly Texas.

She had problems with the young and reckless. She opposed a free festival at Stonehenge and enacted laws to counter New Age travelers. She opposed a movement to teach what tabloids called "Gay Sex Lessons in School." In 1979 she dismissed the Home Office Williams Report, which said that pornography does not harm adults or children. She feared that allowing pornography and sexual teachings about homosexuality in schools would cause "immorality" to increase.

When Reagan authorized the invasion of Grenada without informing her, she was furious. She called him and vented as he apologized and fumbled for reasons. She told her staff that U.S.-British relations would never be the same. Grenada was part of the British Commonwealth and when the Marxist leader was removed and killed, Britain and America were asked to help quiet the riots. The U.S. responded almost immediately and lied to Britain about the purpose of their fleet near Grenada.

Thatcher often visited her son's family in the United States. She happened to be in downtown Dallas, Texas, on October 19, 1987, (where the author was as well) the day that the stock market "crashed." She dined with several important American businessmen that evening and was reassured that there would not be a "meltdown of the world economy." Even so, she quickly approved two successive half percentage point cuts in interest rates to help restore business confidence. Always ready to listen and learn, she was a quick decision maker once she set a course.

Thatcher, however, shared some moral and religious ideas with Reagan. A speech on May 21, 1988, was controversial because she was using the Christian economic framework for the country.

> "The truths of the Judaic-Christian tradition are infinitely precious, not only, as I believe because they are true, but also because they provide the moral impulse which alone can lead to that peace for which we all long…Ideally, when Christians meet, their purpose is not to ascertain what is the mind of the majority but what is the mind of the Holy Spirit. Nevertheless I am an enthusiast for democracy. And I take that position, not because I believe majority opinion is inevitably right or true, indeed no majority can take away God-given human rights, but because I believe it most effectively safeguards the value of the individual, and, more than any other system, restrains the abuse of power by the few. And that is a Christian concept."

Occasionally she could use humor to lighten her usually somber countenance. Perhaps her funniest comment was, "Being powerful is like being a lady. If you have to tell people you are, you aren't."

6

Accomplishments

Thatcher was the first woman in European history to be elected prime minister. She became the first British prime minister in the twentieth century to win three consecutive terms, and was the nation's longest-serving prime minister since 1827. She broadened the base of the Conservative Party to include the middle class along with the wealthy aristocracy.

She changed the rules of political debate, transformed her own party, and altered aspects of British life that had seemed fixed, said Stephen Davies. The power of trade unions that had so dominated British political life before 1979 was sharply curtailed. The privatization of state owned industries, unthinkable before, became commonplace and has now been imitated all over the world.

When she became prime minister, 2 million people in her country owned stock. When she left office, there were seven times that many, said David Rothkopf in a *Time Magazine* article in February 2002. He said that shift "transformed a nation that had viewed itself as consigned to stagnation and frustration into a world leader in innovation regardless of the political party at the helm." That was because she championed the idea of a "nation of shareholders."

She was a hard-nosed debater and a woman of strong convictions. The Soviets, among others who found her hard to deal with, nicknamed her the "Iron Lady."

She had the ability to present the views and beliefs of ordinary people as opposed to those of a detached elite. Her criticism of the creation of a federal European state voiced the fears of ordinary people. She could face tough decisions such as Bosnia about which she held a series of television interviews to highlight the issues.

Current British Prime Minister Tony Blair has been one of Thatcher's greatest supporters. However, he became upset with her constant harping behind the scenes against economic integration with Europe. On the tenth anniversary of her resignation, November 22, 2000, he said that she had done much that was necessary in her time. But he believed that she also bore responsibility for four great errors that hurt Britain badly. These were boom and bust economics, social division, the neglect of public services and a stubbornly hostile attitude toward Europe. He added, "It really is time…that we moved British politics beyond the time of Margaret Thatcher."

In December 1990, she was awarded the Order of Merit by Her Majesty the Queen. On June 30, 1992, she became Baroness Thatcher of Kesteven and entered the House of Lords. In April 1995, she was made a member of the Most Noble Order of the Garter. She was also chancellor at Buckingham University, England, and chancellor of William and Mary College, in Virginia. She is a patron of a number of charities and has established her own foundation. She wrote *The Downing Street Years, The Path to Power* and other works.

Her husband was given a Baronetcy, which is a rare kind of hereditary knighthood. Thus when he became Sir Denis Thatcher, this assured that their son, Mark, would inherit a title.

She continued to give speeches until March 2002, when her doctor ordered her to make no more public speeches for health reasons after some small strokes. Her husband had suffered a small stroke on vacation the previous year. Some observers believe Margaret's cessation of speeches may help the current Tory (Conservative) leadership to escape claims that she was still directing policy.

7

Summary

The household in which Margaret grew up was never lacking in basic needs for the family of four but neither were there any excesses. Extreme self-discipline created a decent family life with few frivolities. Her family was sociable but even more, her father and she longed for respectability and prestige. They wanted to be looked up to and admired. These goals guided their parallel lives.

Margaret matured along the usual and expected paths of achievement. She knew that her parents loved her but from the beginning was closer to her father than her mother. She learned to trust others because she could trust in the love and nurturance of her own parents. She was a little girl with more initiative and industriousness than was seen in many of her gender at that time. She was never one to date much and held men up to the ideal her father had set as alderman and mayor.

She could be intimate with men of a certain type and age and found her husband to be the supporter that she needed so desperately. By the end of her life, she felt satisfied that she had left a legacy of which she felt justly proud so that she achieved a sense of generativity and ego integrity.

She was able to enjoy the ultimate stage of love, commitment, after having been raised with acceptance and unconditional love by her parents. There is little information about the stage of romantic love or lust, and it is likely that she had a prim and proper view of sexual relationships. There is little doubt that she had a close and intimate relationship with her husband. The two somehow avoided the conflicts and power struggles that many couples have when a woman outdistances a man in prominence.

Thatcher coped with stress in mostly healthy ways. She was able to suppress her emotions when others criticized or blocked her. She had some sublimations and fulfillments in other arenas of life such as reading, poetry, music, and constant learning. She was intellectual without intellectualizing, because of her analytical orientation. She loved to dissect subjects and discuss the kernel of issues in common down-to-earth terms.

She had no problem resisting temptation after her ascetic upbringing, and even eschewed her full salary. Her planning and anticipation of problems made her constantly prepared for obstacles in her path. She was altruistic and while sometimes minimizing social services for the needy, intended to serve the whole public in better ways.

She was never as humorous as many leaders. This was due not only to the lack of humor in her parents but due to her serious dedication to make herself knowledgeable and respected. She wanted to be listened to, but not because she was funny.

She developed a moral framework for her life beginning with a great wish to please her parents, and her father in particular. She acted in ways to be rewarded by him and this led to rewards from her peers. Never one to be out of line, she heeded the laws and rules of her society and always abided by them. In fact, many saw her as rigid and old-fashioned in her morality.

She had some moral shortcomings in race relations possibly, believing that the immigration and integration of non-white races should be blocked. That, however, can be found in almost all of the white leaders in this study. She saw the social utility of enacting laws and societal rules that benefited the most people. And while she might have had some prejudices, she made most decisions dispensing justice fairly for all.

Her leadership showed much greater concern for achieving particular goals than for pleasing or developing her subordinates. In fact, she could be courteous but somewhat cold-hearted toward colleagues. She had good working relationships with many but infuriated them by her unwillingness to hear them out or act on anything they offered. Her leadership, as so many in this study, falls into the category of benevolently autocratic. As she aged and enjoyed power for a prolonged period of time, she shifted into a mind set in which she overvalued her own opinions and thought her ideas were superior to others. She found it hard to be humble after she retired.

12

SADDAM HUSSEIN

o o o o o o o o o o o o o o o o o o o o o o o o o o o o o o o o o

"It is well that war is so terrible; we would grow too fond of it."
Robert E. Lee

1

Upbringing and Early Life

Saddam Hussein al-Tikriti was born April 28, 1937, in the tiny village of Al-Auja (Ouja) which had no running water or electricity. This hamlet of mud huts, tents and unpaved roads is near the small town of Tikrit, home of Saladin who fought against the Crusaders in the 12th century. It is approximately two hours from Baghdad, the capital of Iraq.

Saddam's father died before he was born, and it is possible that his mother never actually married his father. Saddam's mother turned Saddam over to her brother to be raised in Tikrit. This maternal uncle, Talfah Khairallah, was a soldier and he raised Saddam as his own son along with his other children. When Saddam was five, his uncle arranged for him to marry his cousin, the uncle's daughter, when he came of age. Saddam played with Sajida as he grew up but the marriage did not take place until 1963 when he was 26.

When Saddam was five, his uncle was sentenced to five years in jail for trying to overthrow the Iraqi government with the Ba'thists. Saddam grew up using his uncle as a model. His uncle thought the

Ba'thists were correct in their beliefs that Arabs should be unified. He also thought that colonialists and those who were aided by outside influences should be thrown out of office.

Saddam was returned to his mother for the five years his maternal uncle was imprisoned. His mother's new husband humiliated and beat the boy mercilessly. She had married the brother of Saddam's father who was considered a liar by the townspeople, and who did not permit Saddam to go to school. It is said that he made the boy go out and steal for him, frequently calling him the son of a whore.

Despite this, he apparently remained close to his three stepbrothers, born of the union between his mother and his paternal uncle. Saddam provided well for them when he came to power later. However, Saddam has said that he grew to hate foreigners. Perhaps this was because they occupied his land, imprisoned his mother's brother (his uncle Talfah Khairallah), and that made his own life miserable.

Other boys teased Saddam for having no father, according to accounts he told associates. He carried an iron bar to protect himself and sometimes used it on animals and watched them suffer. He was, however, very close to his horse and claimed that his hand was paralyzed for several days after his dear horse died.

After his maternal uncle was paroled, Saddam went back to live with him in Tikrit. He was then allowed to go to school although he was much older than the other students. This humiliation caused him to yearn for acceptance through pranks and jokes on the teacher. One day, he embraced his teacher and surreptitiously put a snake under the man's robe.

Talfah's son, Adnan, younger than Saddam, acted as a tutor so Saddam stayed with his studies and learned to read and write. Years later when he gained power, he rewarded cousin Adnan by making him Secretary of Defense.

After his release from prison, Saddam's uncle was deprived of his military career and became a school headmaster. Saddam admired his uncle who had been an Army officer and thought he would follow in his footsteps by applying to the Baghdad Military Academy. He failed the entrance exam and was not eligible for admittance. Perhaps because of this, Saddam was rumored to have killed a teacher and was arrested for this crime. He may have served time in juvenile detention but he has been careful to expunge old records and create new myths about his background so that much information is in the form of rumors.

When he was 21, he formally became a member of the Muslim sect called Ba'thist (which means resurrection) which wanted to remove foreigners and foreign influences from Iraq and unify all Arabs. Saddam began to incite protests against the Iraqi ruler, General Abd al-Karim Qassem. He tried to get other high school students to join in anti-government activities. In 1958, he was jailed for the murder of a government official from his area but was released after six months for "lack of evidence."

Saddam was involved in a Ba'thist attempt to kill General Qassem on October 7, 1959. He was to provide cover for the actual assassins but things backfired. Qassem's car got caught in a traffic jam. Then the coup leader tried to fire but his pistol jammed, and another had forgotten to insert the magazine into the gun. A third could not get a hand grenade out of his pocket. Saddam had his gun out and shot Qassem's driver and was himself shot in the leg. Qassem was wounded in the shoulder and arm, and as the perpetrators fled, he walked to a hospital to be treated.

Saddam created a myth about himself saying that he escaped by swimming up the Tigris River to his village. But others have written that he simply rode a horse until he crossed the Tigris to Damascus. He eventually went on to Egypt where he was brought under the protection of President Nasser in Cairo. Nasser was happy to help because Qassem whom Saddam had tried to assassinate was Nasser's enemy.

Meanwhile, Qassem ordered the Ba'thists to be imprisoned and Saddam came to light as the most wanted man. It was known that he fled the country to Syria first and then to Egypt. He attended school there and in 1961, finally graduated high school in Cairo at the age of

24. He may have attended some law university courses; at least he claimed that he did so. In his privileged status, he ran up bar and café bills and was known as a drinker and brawler.

He returned to Iraq in 1963 when he heard that Qassem had been overthrown. Qassem had been pro-Soviet so the U.S. aided the Ba'thists in a coup in which 5,000 were killed. The new Prime Minister replacing Qassem was another cousin of Saddam's named Ahmed Hassan al-Bakr. Saddam returned to Iraq as a hero of the revolution. First he was given a lowly position, but soon was placed in charge of security.

2

Love Life

When he returned from Cairo, Saddam married his cousin, Sajidah, with whom he grew up. They had five children, two sons and three daughters. But there is a rumor that his first son was born to his wife from another man. The Ba'thists who overthrew Qassem were themselves overthrown a few months later. Saddam, who supervised security and created a torture chamber unequalled in present times, was put in jail yet another time. His wife was supposed to have been used sexually and made pregnant by a jailer and his first son is said not to resemble Saddam. After the Ba'thists regained power in 1968, Saddam is supposed to have killed the man who raped his wife.

Saddam had many liaisons with women over the years but usually kept it from the public eye. However, when he had an affair with a well-known beauty, he forced the husband to step aside and made him president of the Iraqi Airline. Several of Saddam's family members became irate. His son, Uday, killed the man who introduced his father to the mistress. The son was arrested and as his trial was being planned, Adnan (Saddam's younger cousin and mentor) argued for mercy along with Saddam's wife. The son was sent to Switzerland and lived splendidly until he was returned to the fold in recent years. However, Adnan died in a "helicopter crash" soon after siding with Saddam's wife.

Over the years, Saddam has abused power by sexually using the wives of many of his associates. Few complain because he rewards them so well. But he can be vicious with women who resist him and at least one biographer knows of a sexual partner he personally killed.

3

Path to Power

During Saddam's prison term in 1964, he used self-discipline, hard work, reading and rising early to build himself up. He claimed to have been one of the chief debaters in the prison commune. He sent messages to al-Bakr, who had been released from prison. When he was being taking to court for his trial, he escaped in 1966.

The Iraqi president (Abd al-Salam Aref) was killed in a helicopter crash in April 1966, and was replaced by his brother. After the Israelis defeated the Arabs in the Six Day War of 1967, the Ba'thists denounced Iraqi ineptitude in strikes and demonstrations. They convinced military leaders to overthrow the government. Saddam promised his fellow Ba'thists that after using the military officers for the revolt, he would then eliminate them personally.

Saddam, always insecure about his schooling and status, wanted a college degree. In 1972, he went to Baghdad University with his pistol to take an examination. He was, of course, granted the degree. He returned to be awarded an M.A. in law in 1976, again without attending classes.

The Ba'thists took over in a bloodless coup in 1968 with President Ahmad Hasan al-Bakr, and Saddam was next highest in authority. He was appointed Deputy Chairman of the Revolutionary Command Council in charge of security. He was a civilian in a military regime, and was again in a position to use force. Because of the small size of the Ba'thist Party, public hangings and a reign of terror were used to coerce the population into cooperation. Saddam personally administered many executions such as firing squads, putting men into baths of acid to dissolve their bodies, or disposing of enemies in a variety of horrible ways.

The Ba'thist government justified executions of their enemies for crimes such as conspiracy to overthrow the government, or spying for other countries such as Iran, Israel or the U.S. Using fear and terrorist methods, enemies were eliminated and criticism was hushed. Some associates who were potential threats were removed by supposedly being given foreign posts and then either assassinated or removed. Saddam carefully culled the men closest to Bakr by discrediting them, and becoming the most powerful man in Iraq even though he was not yet President.

Saddam Hussein and al-Bakr sided with the Palestinians who tried to rout out the Jews in Israel and Palestine. Palestinian guerrilla forces began using Jordan to launch attacks against Israel. Jordan then attacked the Palestinians in "Black September" of 1970, killing 5,000 and wounding 10,000. Iraq sent 20,000 troops to Jordan to protect Palestinians but avoided direct Jordanian warfare. Their avoidance brought on some criticism by Palestinians and Syrians. Many said that direct warfare was avoided because Saddam and Bakr feared losing their position if their own citizens began to die.

Later in 1973 and the Yom Kippur War when Israel was suddenly attacked, Iraq sent troops to aid the Arabs and regained stature in the eyes of their Arab neighbors. However, the Gulf States believed Iraq should not exert pressure on its tiny neighbor, Kuwait. Iraq's threatening posture drew attention by patrolling Kuwaiti borders and withdrawing ambassadors from countries that recognized the Kuwaiti nation.

Saddam blamed Iraq's ills on Jews, Kurds, Iranians and communists. Later when he became the President of Iraq, his prejudices were published in a pamphlet entitled "Three whom God should not have created: Persians, Jews and flies. "

The Kurds, Indo-Europeans of the Muslim faith, made up about one fifth of Iraqis and also occupied several adjoining countries. Most of Iraq's oil comes from the Kurdish area and inhabitants were always trying to get government representation. He nationalized Iraq's oil, which directly impacted the Kurdish area. The Kurds felt used and took U.S. and Iranian aid to fund guerrillas against Saddam's troops.

Saddam's campaign against the Kurds during 1974-75 cost billions and produced thousands of casualties. He finally struck an agreement with the Shah of Iran to withdraw troops and concede some territory. Following the Kurdish campaign, Saddam used chemical weapons and other forms of lethality to reduce their population while giving lip service to wanting them to have representation since they made up part of Iraq. At the same time, he gave 30,000 Kurdish refugee families TVs and allowances to show non-discrimination.

A member of Saddam Hussein's cabinet said that he removed communist party members by inviting them to dinner and shooting them with his pistol over coffee. This story, like so many told by his cronies, was denounced but showed how he generated fear in adversaries by such anecdotes.

Iraq had brought in thousands of scientists and researchers during the late 1970s to develop weaponry. Researchers dealt with the U.S., Britain, Italy, Germany and the Soviet Union to purchase and trade for armaments. After the Soviet Union invaded Afghanistan in 1979, relations cooled with the communists and the Iraqis had to look elsewhere for armaments.

Iraq invaded Iran in 1980 because of supposed conspiracies to overthrow Saddam. Saddam used propaganda saying the invasion was to "liberate" Iran. At the same time, he tried to show his lineage to the prophet Mohammad to decrease support for Iran's Ayatollah Khoumeini. Claiming that he was the best person to fight for Islam and Arabs, he tried to claim linkages to the Babylonian (Iraqi) King Nebuchadnezzar who fought Jews and Persians (Iranians).

Saddam directed his scientists to build up nuclear, chemical and biological weapons to use against Israelis and Iranians. In 1981, Israel bombed a nuclear reactor, acting upon information detected by spies.

Some ten years after becoming the ruler of Iraq, Hussein no longer needed total support as much as the support of men who served in the military and security forces. From February 18, 1990, a man would not be convicted if he killed any woman (wife, sister, mother, niece, aunt) for adultery. It should be added that a defector reported seeing the dead body of a woman with whom Saddam had a sexual liaison, with her throat slit and a blood-soaked shirt on Saddam. Of course, Saddam was married but the marital state of his victim is unknown.

4

Leadership Style

After the Ba'thist coup in July 1968, which put Hussein and al-Bakr in power, rivals were eliminated either directly or by being sent to other countries as "ambassadors." The coup was followed by a purge of all non-Ba'thists from power, which expanded the power of al-Bakr and Hussein.

After Israelis attacked Iraqi forces in Jordan in December 1968, and after turning up Israeli "spies," Bakr and Hussein had Jews hung in public squares for three months. Although the world press brought international condemnation, Saddam showed occasional kindness. He freed a Jewish man who had tipped him well when he sold cigarettes as a youngster.

Hussein and Bakr tolerated communists, sometimes let them publish a newspaper and serve on the cabinet, but also had them arrested, tortured and killed. Saddam had learned the trick of exposing "plots" against the government. He then seemed justified in eliminating his opposition. He also pitted rivals against each other as they competed for high posts, and helped discredit them to Bakr.

Saddam called Bakr the father and leader of Iraq and the champion of Arab nationalism. He allowed Bakr to bask in the glory of leadership but quietly came to control an ever-widening portion of the government. By 1975, all knew that Saddam really ran the country, and he removed two of Bakr's aides for "negligence," leaving the aged leader with little support. He forced Bakr to replace positions with his own family members and friends. He expanded the military after studying books on Nazi Germany about organizing the entire country.

Saddam forced out Bakr, who resigned citing poor health. Saddam became Iraq's president in 1979. On July 16, 1979, 42-year-old Saddam became the leader of Iraq with a speech complimenting Bakr. Within days, he had hundreds of military officers and party officials executed. He put himself in charge of every major group and began a purge of rivals and enemies that made Iraq a totalitarian government.

He changed voting laws so that few could vote and those who did were Ba'thists, with the penalty of death for those who belonged to any other party. In his effort to gain popular support after removing the more charismatic Bakr, he took land from the wealthy and gave it to the poor. He took over the oil industry and used the money for education and improvements.

Saddam instituted literacy education for those who could not read. He upset the view that women were nothing by enacting equal pay for men and women, allowing women to join the military and denouncing polygamy. Unfortunately, his demand that diplomas be granted only to Ba'thist Party members caused schools to lower standards to assure that even those with little ability received awards.

Another of Hussein's tactics was to train children in Ba'thist doctrine from the time they could read. This training resembled Hitler's Germany. Children were taught to distrust foreigners and to report on violations to the Party, including those of their parents.

In an interview with Diane Sawyer of ABC, Saddam said that he believed those who criticized the President should be punished and could not believe that other countries didn't believe likewise.

Hussein used the technique of accusing his victims of indiscretions. He claimed that Kuwait had to be invaded because of a supposed conspiracy against Iraq. Using a "democratic" ploy, he required that all party divisions send an armed delegate to join in firing squads to kill conspirators. Eventually, the Ba'th Party was simply carrying out Saddam's requests.

Saddam made sure that his own family profited during his reign. His half-brothers became wealthy as well as his sons, one of whom owned an ice cream company and a company called SuperChicken. His family members were usually allowed to commit crimes for which others would be penalized.

Hussein had no compunction about violating international standards regarding war and weaponry. He had soldiers string wires at the border of Iran through marshes to electrocute Iranian soldiers. He followed this by creating roadways on top of their dead bodies for tanks and trucks.

He did not permit his generals to make many decisions. He tested and used anthrax, cholera, botulism, as well as a gas that produces gangrene and other chemicals and biological weapons in the Kurdish areas. After a 1985 insurrection, he had some 8,000 Kurds executed, many towns burned and thousands deported and imprisoned. The anti-Kurd campaign included nerve gas, mustard gas, cyanide, and he attempted to develop nuclear weaponry as well. This information was learned through the defection of some of his family members (sons-in-law) and nuclear scientists. When he offered that all would be forgiven to the defectors, his family members returned home and the sons-in-law were immediately killed.

Hussein survived as a leader partly because he viewed the world as hostile and acted aggressively against those around him. He told a guest in 1979, "I know there are scores of people plotting to kill me. I know they are conspiring to kill me long before they actually start planning to do it. This enables me to get them before they have the faintest chance of striking at me."

Saddam used Stalin as the model for eliminating enemies and rivals through purges, fear of torture and death, and secret police spying on everyone. His violence has earned him the nickname "Butcher of Baghdad" and the hatred of many. He increased the number of food testers, clothing testers, and security over time. Even so, numerous attempts to assassinate him and family members have occurred but none have been successful.

Saddam's use of fear to maintain leadership and deter conspiracies is blended with his show of praise. He personally pinned medals on soldiers. Nevertheless, his military leaders are unlikely to challenge his decisions or strategies. For this reason, his wars have often gone on embarrassingly long. In 1986, he lost some 10,000 soldiers in one week during the battle with Iran. His leaders finally defied his orders and turned losses into victories by using their own strategies, which played a large part in the ceasefire of 1988.

To appease his allies, Saddam did not escalate the war using such chemical or biological weapons against Iran. This was despite the fact that the Iranian Khoumeini demanded Saddam's overthrow. Instead, Saddam bombed some Iranian oil terminals and tankers, believing that Iran would try to escalate the war. Other countries urged Iran to sign a ceasefire and by 1988, the war ended. Saddam had created an image of a sane leader against a fanatic leader.

Saddam occasionally tried to put himself into posterity through permanent icons. To celebrate the victory over Iran, Saddam had an arch of triumph made. He used his own arms and fists holding sabers as the model, which dominated the streets of Baghdad. He offered a prize to recreate the hanging gardens of Babylon, one of the original Seven Wonders of the World.

When Iraq attacked Kuwait on August 2, 1990, 100,000 troops and 300 tanks were sent against Kuwait's 16,000 soldiers. The United States rallied immediate international cooperation, moving troops to the Gulf while freezing Iraqi assets in American banks and companies.

Days later, Saddam claimed that it was Kuwait that had been on Iraqi territory.

Hussein could surprise people with his willingness to please at unexpected times. Two months after the invasion of Kuwait, the mother of an American who had been captured wrote him a letter. She had seen that American and British hostages were to be used as human shields against U.S. attacks on Baghdad. She asked that her son be released because her family had always helped Arabs. He was released within days.

Although Saddam smoked cigars supplied by Fidel Castro, he stopped wearing fatigues and replaced them with the appearance of a statesman in suit and tie. He maintained constant publicity and wrote a play that opened in Baghdad in May 2002. According to Johanna McGeary of *Time*, the play was about a king who fell in love with a commoner who was raped on January 17, 1991. That was the day that the U.S. attacked Iraq to repulse them from Kuwait. Foreign infidels caused the murder of the commoner. The king decided he should follow the advice of his martyred love, which was to use strict measures to keep people in line. This apparently fit Saddam's need to continue repressing the populace.

By 2002, he no longer made public appearances for fear of assassination. Instead, he had stand-ins appear but his pictures and statues were seen everywhere. In propaganda efforts, he had dancers and marchers appear with the black facemasks of suicide bomber trainees. He was reported to move from one location to another each night so enemies would not know where he might be sleeping.

5

Stresses

Saddam has tried to protect himself from coups by placing family members in important posts on the principle that family is more loyal than non-family. He also had his family marry within the highest party echelon. Saddam's two sons married important party members, as did his two daughters. Although his relatives and friends have gained financially during his reign, he occasionally yields to complaints of government corruption by removing them from office. He occasionally had to keep his son, Uday, from trying to seduce daughters and wives of important party members. His youngest son married the daughter of one of his main commanders, a man who was prepared to use chemical warfare.

Even though he sent Uday to Switzerland for a while after he killed the man who introduced his father to a lover, Uday often spoke for his father. He claimed that his father was generous with the poor and cared naught for wealth. This was at a time when Hussein's government was asking citizens to do without pay because of the costs of the war with Iran.

In 1978, Hussein established a half-size reconstruction of Babylon to create a sense of history and unity among Arabs and Iraq. As he rose in power, he no longer felt it was important to maintain a humble image. He created a magnificent wardrobe for every occasion, acquired a yacht and indulged in wealthy pastimes. He recently built massive huge mosques and appeared to wish to impress posterity on the basis of the size of structures he authorized.

Saddam was not driven by any particular ideology and can therefore compromise when it serves his purposes. He enjoyed tracing his lineage to the Prophet Muhammad and to Nebuchadnessar, the Babylonian king described in the Bible. As such, he wanted to be seen genealogically as the father of Iraq and a heroic representative of Arabs.

He handled possible rivals by making himself the only visible person in Iraq. His propaganda techniques included having his pictures on stamps, T-shirts, wristwatches, structures such as the Saddam Dam, buildings such as the Saddam International Airport in Baghdad, town sites such as the Saddam Center for Arts, and having songs about him sung by school children. He gave pay increases to the military, and personally visited workplaces, farms, mosques, and hospitals. He supposedly roamed the streets incognito and pretended to listen to people who praised their great leader, supposedly without realizing who they were talking to.

Using his tactic of blaming his victim, he claimed that Israel started the war between Iran and Iraq by supplying Iran with weapons and anti-Iraq propaganda. But at the same time, he supported peace talks between Israel and other Arab states like Egypt.

Before the Gulf War, Saddam told the U.S. ambassador that if the U.S. continued supporting Kuwait against Iraq, there might be Arab terrorist incidents against U.S. citizens. Perhaps misunderstanding the ambassador's reassurance that the U.S. would not declare economic war on Iraq because of neutrality, Saddam attacked Kuwait on August 2, 1990. An interviewer asked Saddam why Iraq attacked the little neighboring nation of Kuwait. He tried to blame Kuwait, the victim. He said, "We took our action because the ruling family in Kuwait is good at blackmail, exploitation, and destruction of their opponents. They had perpetuated a grave U.S. conspiracy against us...stabbing Iraq in the back with a poisoned dagger." This is like a rapist blaming a victim for her attire or a car thief blaming the owner of the car he stole for leaving the keys in the ignition.

He also tried to blame the Jews for his aggression upon Kuwait. He claimed that restoring Kuwait to the "motherland" was the first step in liberating Jerusalem from the Jews. He said that Israelis painted planes to look like U.S. planes, and Jews carried fake U.S. identification papers. His threats to Israel became part of the Kuwait campaign. He argued for a jihad (holy war) against the Saudis who allowed western troops on their land, which supposedly defiled Mecca and the tomb of Mohammad.

These themes were later seen in the al-Qaeda movement of Osama bin Laden. Although Saddam's aggression against Kuwait had little to do with Jews, his continual tirades brought connections to the Arab-Israeli problem in the international press.

Saddam used foreign visitors and residents as hostages similar to Iran during the Carter administration. Bad reactions around the world to a newscast where he visited British hostages caused him to release women and children, and keep only the men. Individual negotiators came and departed with hostages Rev. Jesse Jackson and ex-boxer Muhammad Ali returned to the U.S. with many women, children and ill men.

Saddam's offer to release all hostages did not stop the U.S. and allies from demanding a withdrawal from Kuwait. When allied planes attacked military targets in Iraq, Saddam announced that "the mother of all battles" had begun. He then lied to citizens claiming excessive victories and downed aircraft. He then attacked Israel with ballistic missiles hoping this would stop the allied forces. Israel wanted to retaliate but yielded to allied pressure to wait.

When seven captured pilots were put on Iraqi TV, Hussein threatened to use them as human shields to protect Iraqis. The West threatened to put Iraqis on trial for war crimes and have Hussein removed from office if hostages were mistreated. Hussein retaliated by threatening to put Bush on trial for the invasion of Grenada and the occupation of Saudi Arabia.

During the Gulf War, CNN's Peter Arnett interviewed Hussein. Saddam said that he had mistakenly believed leaders who said that war could be avoided if he released civilian hostages. He also threatened that Iraq could use nuclear, chemical and biological weapons if necessary, a threat that had been successful against Iran. It did not stop the aerial bombardment of his nuclear plants, aircraft and navy. He then told reporters for the London Times that Iraq would use all weapons at their disposal, from kitchen knives to weapons of mass destruction. He brought reporters in to photograph raids on innocent civilians.

Desperate to end the war and appear a victor, he ordered that Kuwaiti oil plants be set on fire. The worst oil slick in history resulted as oil poured into the Persian Gulf and drifted toward Saudi Arabia's supply of drinking water.

When ceasefire was discussed, Saddam tried to save face by having conditions such as Israel's withdrawal from Palestine, and cancellation of Iraq's foreign debts. When these conditions were rejected, he threatened again to unleash weapons of mass destruction. After continued attack, he signed a ceasefire and told Iraqis on TV to remember that on August 2, 1990, Kuwait became part of Iraq. Operation Desert Storm ended after six weeks with the allied forces victorious in expelling Iraq from Kuwait.

Following the Gulf War, Hussein prohibited U.N. weapons inspectors. He lied about the number of missiles (claiming Iraq had only 34 when they had 146), and lied about the amount of stored anthrax (claiming only a few kilograms when they had 8,000 tons). He faced sanctions because he denied access to inspectors, but appeared to prefer the sanctions (even though they have cut off food to a starving population). This may have been because they earned him some sympathy from other nations. Meanwhile, he, his family and his favorites lived lavishly in palaces while many in his country lived poorly.

Saddam became obsessed with looking triumphant after the American attacks against Iraq. McGeary recounts the story of an Egyptian actor who was invited to visit Saddam in 2001. The actor recalled, "Saddam said every Iraqi feels inside him that he is a winner, with his pride intact. Saddam said, 'We did not lose anything. We refuse to be humiliated in front of the Americans'."

Frequently, Hussein got into personal criticisms with the leaders of other countries. Saddam called President Bush a liar who wanted to enslave Iraqis, and Thatcher an old hag with a canine harsh voice who acted selfishly. Earlier he had sent Egypt's President Mubarak a letter reprimanding him for being a nobody from an average family whereas he (Hussein) was descended from Muhammad.

6

Accomplishments

Saddam Hussein improved the literacy rate and the status of women during the early years of his power. He enacted equal pay for men and women, allowing women to join the military, and criticized marriage to more than one woman at a time. During the years until 1990 when he declared that men would not be prosecuted for killing a woman for adultery, these laws had produced profound changes that were not entirely undone. Faced with loss of support by the mullahs, he said what they wanted to hear and reversed his stand about men killing women for adultery.

After the Gulf War, damaged buildings and roads have been repaired and rebuilt. Goods from all over have come in and the salaries have risen to buy them. Flights into Baghdad's Saddam International Airport come in regularly from Jordan, Syria and Lebanon despite embargos.

Medicine, purchased with U.N. money, has been imported. Gigantic building projects such as mosques, palaces, statues of Saddam, and money from oil sales have been spread over Iraq. Baghdad's new palace has columns topped with his own head wearing the helmet of Saladin, who lived in his area of Iraq. The minarets on the new "Mother of All Battles" mosque are shaped like the Scud missiles he fired at Israel during the Gulf War.

Few people are brave enough to plot against Saddam or to leave Iraq, because their departures would expose their family members to torture and/or death. Of his 424,000-man army, some 100,000 are his Republican Guards with an elite group of special security something like Hitler's SS.

Overall, his administration has turned an insignificant country into a mighty force not to be taken lightly. The standard of living has gradually improved in Iraq and Saddam has been largely successful because he tends to lavish rewards upon those who cover up for him and carry out his wishes.

7

Summary

Saddam's life began in the most miserable of circumstances. Survival and physiological needs were of uppermost importance in his earliest years. It was only in later childhood that he could begin to socialize and enjoy the support of others. As he learned that success came from anarchy, his goal for recognition by the Arab world grew. His highest priorities gradually included creating gigantic structures, which would outlive him and leave him a historic legacy.

Saddam's background produced distrust of others because his mother abandoned him to her brother to be raised. Then his uncle "abandoned" him when he was imprisoned and he was sent back to his mother. Her new husband treated him cruelly and built no trust in the little boy. In fact, to survive and win favor with this uncle/father, Saddam was said to have to steal. Therefore, his maturing years included distrust, shame and doubt, guilt and inferiority until he learned how to be an agitator. As an anti-social adolescent, he finally achieved notoriety for trying to kill those in power.

He did not receive unconditional love from his parents. Despite his marriage, his children and his love affairs, he seems never to have achieved the intimacy that requires trust. We are unsure about how romantic he was early in life but his highest level of love appears to have been lust. He has discarded many women soon after he achieved his conquest of them. However, to be accepted by his own people, the appearance of a good husband and father has been important. His family has apparently allowed him to portray that image but he never reached the stage of fidelity and commitment to a female.

He has used interesting stress reduction methods all the way from taking excessive risks, rationalizing his actions with various excuses, to distorting the truth and blaming others for his own errors.

His moral development suggests that he learned early to dodge punishment from his paternal uncle by stealing for him. He learned to seek rewards from his maternal uncle by doing the same things and attacking government leaders. In his group of anti-social adolescents, he received peer approval for bravely trying to upset those in power. He never became a law-abider, however, and only fear of being humiliated or deposed kept him from committing more unethical acts.

In his earlier career, he was the secretive young bad guy in the background. This enabled his older cousin to wield power and be seen favorably. As time passed, he maneuvered his cousin out of power and took over, allowing few to do more than agree with him. After the Gulf War, he became more fearful of assassination and remained behind the scenes while others were visible at public events. McGeary of *Time* reported that at his 65th birthday celebration he was nowhere to be seen but others appeared in his place at public ceremonies. With numerous citizens singing his praises, he seemed to be well liked on public television, but that was part of his propaganda.

Having personally killed those who opposed him, he must be said to show a much higher concern for tasks than for people, and would fall somewhere between tyrant and benevolent autocrat. While trying to run the war against Iran, his orders were countermanded by military leaders, with good results. But his preferred method is to make all decisions and run everything himself with very little input from others.

13

OSAMA BIN LADEN

o o o o o o o o o o o o o o o o o o o o o o o o o o o o o o o
"Everyone sees his own cause as just." Anonymous

1

Upbringing and Early Life

Osama bin Laden was the 17th and youngest son of Mohammed bin Oud bin Laden. Islamic tradition allows four wives and Osama resulted from a marriage to Mohammed's last wife, a petite Syrian beauty called Al-Khalifa ("Alia Ghanem" in Syrian). The other wives called Alia "the slave" and other family members called Osama "son of the slave."

Mohammed maintained three "permanent" wives and kept marrying and shedding the fourth wife according to his wandering eye. So in actuality, Alia was his 11th wife because he had divorced others. He always provided well for his wives, ex-wives and for all of his children who were raised together. In fact, Osama was partially raised by another wife named Hamida who was called his foster- or stepmother.

Mohammed bin Laden emigrated from Yemen to Saudi Arabia in 1932, the year in which the new kingdom of Saudi Arabia was formed. Saudis were a migrant people and Yemenis were settled workers and builders so they had much to offer the new kingdom. Mohammed was unable to read and write, but began work as a laborer and eventually founded a construction empire in Saudi Arabia. He took advantage of his position, bid under his competitors, and used money and illegal means to gain some contracts. He built a palace in Jiddah for the royal family. He financially befriended the royal family, especially when King Faisal was in arrears, which ensured that he received all government contracts.

Mohammed was a religious conservative who financed evenings of theological debate in Saudi Arabia. He brought the 54 children up emphasizing traits of self-confidence and debate in his sons and obeisance in his daughters. With so many children, he had little time for each. In fact, he often forgot information about them, including their names. But they all knew him, and he was greatly respected by all family members.

Mohammed bin Laden founded the Saudi Binladin Group, which built roads, buildings, hotels, and airports and refurbished mosques. The Saudi royal family hired the company for these projects. They also built airstrips and barracks for U.S. troops during and after the Persian Gulf War.

In 1956 Mohammed visited the seaside port of Latakia in Syria. One of his first three wives had been a local woman and he found Alia, his last wife, to be a provocatively beautiful Syrian woman of the working class. She tended to wear pantsuits and smart clothes, which had to be covered by her burka when she went to Saudi Arabia. Latakia is an Alawite Islamic area but Alia's family was Sunni, a conservative arm of the Islamic faith.

When Alia moved to Saudi Arabia with Osama's father, she left behind her two brothers and a sister and the family orange grove. Arabs often called agricultural workers "slaves" even though they were not officially bought and owned by Arabs.

Alia and Mohammed had only one child, Osama, but he was raised in palatial surroundings with his half-brothers and sisters. Every summer, however, Osama accompanied his mother to Latakia until age 17 when he was too busy with school and work. They would go to the beach, swim in the Mediterranean, go camping, ride horses, play football and pick fruit together.

Alia's relatives described Osama as smart, modest, courteous, quiet, and a loner who had trouble relating to other people. He often expressed a desire to grow up and take control of his father's business. Usually he did not flaunt his wealth but one time asked if he could buy an island that he liked on a nearby lake and live on it.

Osama's father had a very authoritarian personality, and believed in discipline, rigid morals, and family closeness. Tragedy struck when Osama was 11. His father died in a 1968 helicopter crash, but the shock may have been offset by an $80 million inheritance. His mother was still married to Mohammed, but she eventually left the bin Laden family compound and remarried.

Osama's oldest brother (half-brother) Salim took over the family business. Salim treated his brothers with some disdain but none more so than Osama, whom he dismissed whenever important family discussions took place. Osama was described as a very quiet, beautiful, intelligent young man who was never pushy. He was clean-shaven, dressed in suits and ties, and stayed meekly in the background of family operations.

When he was 13, Osama and other classmates attending a Westernized school took English lessons. His teacher later described him as "shy, retiring and courteous." He added that Osama stood out because he was "taller, more handsome and fairer than most other boys…and had a good deal of inner confidence."

In 1971, the family went on holiday to a small Swedish town. Osama, or "Sammy" as he sometimes called himself, was photographed wearing western clothing and flared pants, leaning on a Cadillac. He and Salim had visited Sweden the previous year and stayed in a hotel. They drove to Sweden in a Rolls Royce, which had been flown to Copenhagen, Denmark, from Saudi Arabia. They attracted attention at the hotel because the housekeeper found fresh white silk shirts wrapped in cellophane laid out for daily wear in their rooms. They had a big bag of jewelry and wore emeralds, rubies, and diamonds in rings and tiepins.

2

Love Life

In 1973 Osama graduated from secondary school in Jiddah, Saudi Arabia and went frequently to Beirut, Lebanon for drinking, brawling and womanizing during his teen years. Some of Osama's brothers complained about their embarrassment by the "son of the slave" in Beirut. Some were undoubtedly jealous of his good looks and stature since he was taller, some six feet five inches. After two years, Beirut erupted in civil war and Osama stopped his flings and enrolled in a university.

In 1974, when he was almost 18, he sent for 14 year old Najwa, the daughter of his mother's brother, to take as his wife. In Syria, women wore no veils but Najwa was sent to the restrictive world of Saudi Arabia to marry Osama. She was the first of his four wives and their union has produced 11 children.

When Osama was 18, he went to visit his brother Yeslam, who had married Swiss-born Carmen in 1974. He knocked at Yeslam's door in Saudi Arabia and Carmen opened the door. He turned his back because she was not veiled and he didn't want to see the face of his brother's wife, according to orthodox Islam beliefs. This told Carmen that he was very religious. Eventually Carmen and Yeslam divorced and she has had no contact with the bin Laden family since 1990. Carmen told Diane Sawyer of ABC News on October 24, 2001, "I am afraid that Osama or the like of him want to tell people how to live; what is the vision of Islam."

Even though most Muslims no longer took four wives, Osama urged his al Qaeda fighters and leaders to take four wives and did so himself. However one of his older wives became estranged when he married a 17-year old Yemeni girl recently. He also urged his al Qaeda men to take advantage of the practice of "al mutuaa," a short-term (days, weeks or months) sexual relationship for a set fee.

3

Military Experience

In the King Abdul Aziz University in Jiddah, Osama was influenced by Islamic fundamentalists and joined the Muslim Brotherhood in 1975. They preached that the civil war in Beirut was God's retaliation for the sins being committed in the morally lax town. During that year, a deranged relative assassinated King Faisal of Saudi Arabia and many local people blamed American cultural influences for poisoning his mind.

Osama met a fundamentalist Palestinian professor named Abdallah Azzam at university who later became his ally in Afghanistan. Osama worked in the family business while attending college. His brothers paid him $300 million to stay out of the very successful construction business. Osama could see that his brother Salim was his father's successor and he undoubtedly felt ostracized by the family. He graduated from King Abdul Aziz University in Jiddah in 1979 with a degree in civil engineering, his father's field, but could not truly participate in the running of his father's empire.

He was probably seeking a cause or his own niche when the Soviets invaded Afghanistan. In a state of fury over the invasion, Osama went to Afghanistan in 1979. He joined his former professor Azzam to finance the training of Muslim rebels who wanted to fight the Soviets. Although he was only 22, he set up a plan to finance training and weapons and Azzam supplied the troops. Abdallah Azzam, old enough to be his father, had gone to Afghanistan to recruit the mujaheddin, Afghan resistance fighters. The military training camps received support from many countries to oppose the Soviet Union expansion. The U.S. also sent funds to these paramilitary training camps in Afghanistan and Pakistan to oppose the Soviets.

The Reagan administration and the Thatcher government in England provided aircraft, arms and training in covert operations to assist the mujaheddin. Osama spent months flying around the Gulf, extracting donations from various other countries and corporations to fund the Afghans against the Soviets. He also built airstrips, roads, tunnels, hospitals, and telecommunication centers for the mujaheddin.

Although he did not participate in combat early on, by 1986 and 1987 he was involved in fights against the Red Army. He found this action so exhilarating that he claimed to have lost the fear of death. He began to carry an assault rifle that he had confiscated from a dead Russian on the battlefield.

The U.S. was sending weapons into Afghanistan but as the war ended, they urged the Afghans to form a new government of the mujaheddin groups and a general who was earlier a Soviet puppet leader. Bin Laden was against this and said, "We were fighting against the communists and now the United States was pressuring us to cooperate with those very same communists. The United States has no principles. To achieve its own interests, it forgets about every principle."

4

Path to Power

Osama formed the al Qaeda in Afghanistan to support the efforts of Muslims against the Russians. Ultimately, the al Qaeda was to support oppressed Muslims around the world. He revamped the al Qaeda once the war with the Soviets ended, adding a council of advisers and planned to extend it beyond Afghanistan and Pakistan. The council, on which he and his highest associates sat, decided on targets and projects to undermine Americans, Jews, and their allies to remove these "infidels" from Islamic countries.

In 1989, Osama's oldest brother, Salim, was killed in a hang-gliding accident in Texas. His half-brother, Bakr Mohammed, took over the family business. Salim's widow, Englishwoman Anne Carey, remarried

Bakr Mohammed in the Muslim tradition of marrying a brother of the dead husband. This left the door open for another successor for the family business.

With the departure of the Soviets from Afghanistan, Osama returned to Saudi Arabia as a hero. Hundreds of thousands of cassettes of his speeches were produced and sold everywhere in the country. But he saw the impact of Americanization and moral deterioration on Saudi Arabia in the use of alcohol and a lax dress code by women. He denounced these conditions loudly on tapes now banned in Saudi Arabia.

Almost immediately upon his return to work in Jiddah at the family business, Saddam Hussein ordered his Iraqi troops into Kuwait. Americans, British and allied troops arrived in Saudi Arabia to protect against further attacks and liberate Kuwait. Osama was furious and marched into the Saudi government offices with documents to convince them that his Afghan Arabs could train Saudis to defend their own country. Saudi officials tried to mollify him by promising that the American forces would leave once Kuwait was liberated, which turned out not to be true.

He was not mollified and turned against the Saudis for permitting the U.S. forces on their soil. He began to financially support those opposing the Saudis in other countries such as England. When Saudi intelligence caught him smuggling weapons from Yemen in 1991, they withdrew his passport and pressured him to leave the country. His actions alienated the royal family and threatened the bin Laden family business.

He was welcomed by Khartoum in the Sudan. He was greeted by Hassan al-Turabi, the cultured and European-educated leader of the Sudan National Islamic Front party. Al-Turabi had aided Sudan's 1989 Islamic revolution and welcomed a man like bin Laden.

Osama moved his three wives (one Syrian and the other two Saudi) and his 15 children to the Sudan heat. He took a three-story house for himself and his associates. He installed his family in another house that he visited on weekends. His wives taught the Koran to local women in the mosque.

The *New York Times* (9/21/98) reported that Osama flew 480 of his Afghan war veterans to the Sudan but it was hot and there was no opponent to fight. Meanwhile, he developed training camps for terrorists in several areas besides the Sudan. He bought weapons and explosives and set up investments and alliances within Sudan. He built them an airport and a 750-mile road between Khartoum and Port Sudan. He was paid in sesame seeds, which he sold on the world market. He also invested in Gum Arabic Company Limited and developed a monopoly on products used everyday by Americans such as soft drinks, coated medical pills, newspaper ink, etc.

He also set up legitimate businesses in the Sudan such as a tannery, two large farms, a major road construction company, and the Sudanese were happy to have this wealthy Saudi as a guest.

One of Osama's relatives, Abdullah, earned a master's degree in law from Harvard in 1992. Two years later, the law school asked for and received a donation of one million dollars from Osama's brother, Sheik Bakr Mohammed bin Laden, for law students from the Muslim world. The family also gave another million dollars to Harvard's Graduate School of Design. But Osama has never given money to American institutions.

The *New York Times* reported (8/21/98) that on December 29, 1992, al Qaeda agents set off a bomb in a hotel in Yemen where American troops had stopped on their way to Somalia. By the time it exploded, the soldiers had just departed but two Austrian tourists were killed. At almost the same time, al Qaeda terrorists were arrested at Aden airport trying to launch rockets at U.S. planes.

The *Washington Post* reported (8/23/98) that the United States realized that Islamic militants were flocking to terrorist training camps in the Sudan. When they listed Sudan as a country that sponsored terrorism, the loss of trade from other countries hurt the Sudanese economy. Additionally, the U.S. government charged that bin Laden's followers were trying to obtain components of nuclear weapons. Bin Laden was working with the Sudan government to develop chemical weaponry.

On February 26, 1993, the World Trade Center in New York City was bombed. Six were killed and hundreds were wounded. Six Muslims with links to bin Laden were eventually convicted. The F.B.I. investigation revealed that although bin Laden may not have been directly connected with the 1993 World Trade Center bombing, he sheltered its ringleader Ramzi Yousef.

A blind Muslim preacher, Sheik Omar Abdel-Rahman, was also arrested. The Sheikh was charged with "seditious conspiracy" because his rhetoric had inspired some of Yousef's cohorts to violence. However, his own conspiracy attempts were to overthrow Egypt's government, kill Egypt's President Mubarak, and he had ordered the murder of tourists visiting Egypt. He had also plotted to blow up several U.S. landmarks including the United Nations Building, the F.B.I. headquarters, the Holland Tunnel, and possibly other buildings such as the Manhattan Armory. Bin Laden soon began a campaign to free him. In actuality, even though the Sheikh shared ideology with Yousef and bin Laden, he may not have been a conspirator in the World Trade Center bombing even though he is being held in a U.S. federal prison with a life sentence.

As an aside, Yousef had trained men in explosives in bin Laden's terrorist camps. In the 1993 bombing, Yousef did not get the World Trade Center towers to topple into each other or the water to flood into the floor beneath the towers. He escaped to Manila after the bombing.

Since Yousef was in Manila, Bin Laden sent associates to meet with Yousef to ask him to assassinate President Clinton when he visited the Philippines on November 12, 1994. Yousef began to plan the assassination. He considered using explosives along the motorcade route, using ground to air missiles to shoot down the president's plane, or attacking him with phosgene gas, which paralyzes the lungs. However, he decided to postpone the plot because of tight security. He decided instead to assassinate Pope John Paul II, another symbol of the West, who was to visit Manila in January of 1995.

In June 1993, bin Laden began to plan attacks on Middle East leaders who opposed him. He was implicated in a foiled attempt to kill Crown Prince Abdullah of Jordan.

The *New York Times* reported (2/8/99) that on October 3 and 4, 1993, men trained by al Qaeda attacked U.S. forces and shot down a helicopter in Mogadishu, Somalia. Eighteen U.S. servicemen who were part of a humanitarian mission were killed and many more injured. Bin Laden took credit for this when interviewed and called Americans "paper tigers" because they left Somalia after this defeat

Osama said, "Under the cover of the United Nations, the United States tried to establish its bases in Somalia so that it could get control over Sudan and Yemen. My associates killed the Americans in collaboration with Farah Adid. We are not ashamed of our Jihad. In one explosion 100 Americans were killed, then 18 more were killed in fighting. One day our men shot down an American helicopter. The pilot got out. We caught him, tied his legs and dragged him through the streets. After that 28,000 U.S. soldiers fled Somalia. The Americans are cowards." A book and movie about the incident was called *Blackhawk Down.*

Osama exaggerated the fatalities but believed that just as they had caused the Russians to leave Afghanistan, now they had caused the Americans to leave Somalia. This admission and the revelation that Osama was funding Egyptian militants caused Egypt to pressure Saudi Arabia to stop Osama.

The *New York Times* (4/10/94) reported that on April 9, 1994, the Saudis revoked bin Laden's citizenship and froze his Saudi assets because of his support for Muslim fundamentalist movements. He reacted by intensifying his anti-Saudi and anti-American activities. This was at a time when Saudi Arabia was closely allied with America. Bin Laden's family in Saudi Arabia disowned him in 1994. However, some family members still had contact with him and may have contributed to his anti-American offensives.

On December 11, 1994, Ramzi Yousef tested a bomb on a Philippine airplane by carrying it on board in his shoes. He went to the toilet, took off his shoes, assembled the bomb and returned to place it under his seat. It was set to go off two hours later after he had deplaned. Another passenger was blown up but the plane landed safely. After learning of the results, Yousef planned to bomb 12 U.S. airplanes on a single day of terror as they departed from Southeast Asia to America. However, he first tried to carry out the assassination of the Pope who visited Manila in January. When Yousef set himself up in an apartment with access to the Pontiff's apartment, he botched his chemicals, and smoke and acrid odors led police to his room. He fled but was tracked and later arrested in a Pakistani safe house financed by bin Laden.

On March 8, 1995, American diplomats were murdered in Karachi, Pakistan, in retaliation for the arrest of Ramzi Yousef on the charge of masterminding the 1993 World Trade Center bombing. Al Qaeda members murdered the diplomats according to Pakistani intelligence.

Bin Laden backed an attempt to kill President Mubarak of Egypt on June 26, 1995, when Mubarak was visiting Addis Ababa, Ethiopia. This may have been in retaliation to the pressure Egypt had put on Saudi Arabia, which resulted in his homeland and family's renunciation.

The *Washington Post* reported (8/23/98) that on November 13, 1995, bin Laden funded an attack in Riyadh, Saudi Arabia, the homeland that revoked his citizenship. A truck bomb exploded at the National Guard Communications Center and killed five American servicemen and two Indians. The Saudis were so angry that they ordered an attack on bin Laden's home in the Sudan. A car with four men fired at his house and security guards, killing two. Three attackers were killed and the fourth was executed. Bin Laden increased his home security and added more guards.

Also in November 1995, the Egyptian Embassy in Pakistan was bombed. Some 17 people were killed and 60 were wounded. Although the group involved with the blind sheik imprisoned for the 1993 World Trade Center bombing claimed credit for this attack, bin Laden may have partially funded the operation.

In January 1996, America's C.I.A. formed a special bin Laden task force. They found after extensive investigation that bin Laden received money from many other countries including Saudi Arabia. They made many efforts to capture him but he stayed close to home in Khartoum. Two attempts were made on his life without success. Pressure on the Sudan government by America, Saudi Arabia and Egypt to surrender bin Laden or expel him increased.

In April 1996, Sudan asked bin Laden to leave. He considered both Yemen and Afghanistan but chose the latter because he would have the support of his old comrades, many of whom were now involved in the Islamic fundamentalist militia known as the Taliban.

Jane's Intelligence (10/1/98) reported that in May 1996, Osama left Sudan and flew to Afghanistan with his wives, children and supporters.

The *Washington Post* reported (8/23/98) that on June 25, 1996, bin Laden was involved in financing another attack. A large truck bomb exploded near a U.S. military housing complex in Dhahran, Saudi Arabia, killing 19 American servicemen and injuring many more. In interviews, Osama described it as heroic but did not admit sponsorship. However, the C.I.A. found phone call records that leaders of militant groups had called him to congratulate him on the attack.

The U.S. attorney for New York and the F.B.I. initiated a grand jury investigation of bin Laden and al Qaeda's involvement in international terrorism. Bin Laden told reporters, "Only Americans were killed in the explosions.... Unfortunately I did not conduct these explosions personally. But I would like to say to the Saudi people that they should adopt every tactic to throw the Americans out of Saudi territory."

In August 1996, bin Laden wrote an open letter to Saudi Arabia's King Fahd. He pled for guerrilla attacks on U.S. forces to drive them out of the kingdom. It was ignored.

On August 23, 1996, bin Laden signed and issued a "Declaration of Jihad" to drive U.S. forces out of the Arabian Peninsula, overthrow the Saudi government to liberate Muslim holy sites, and support Islamic revolutionary groups around the world. This declaration of holy war against the "Americans Occupying the Land of the Two Holy Mosques" (Saudi Arabia's Mecca and Medina) included a plea to Saudis that they were morally obligated to strike out at the Americans stationed in Saudi Arabia.

Gwynne Roberts reported on an interview with bin Laden in a British documentary program called *Dispatches*. Osama threatened to wage a holy war against the U.S. and its allies if Washington did not remove troops from the Gulf Region. This was also reported in Reuters (2/20/97).

When bin Laden returned to Afghanistan he befriended the leader of the Taliban, Mullah Mohamed Omar. During the war against the Soviets, he had bought Omar a nice house. In 1997 he funded an irrigation canal and bought Omar a new house for his family in Kandahar. He improved utilities for the city of Kandahar and constructed a new mosque. There is some evidence that he married Omar's daughter and Omar married his daughter.

In March of 1997, CNN aired an interview with Peter Arnett speaking to bin Laden in eastern Afghanistan. Bin Laden criticized the U.S. occupation of the land of holy places (Saudi Arabia) with its Mecca and Medina. He also told Arnett that his family was persuaded by the Saudi government to send his mother, uncle, and brothers to visit him in Khartoum about nine times. He said that he refused their request to return to Arabia and to apologize to King Fahd.

The U.S. had been supporting the Taliban because their Islamic beliefs were against drugs. The Taliban argued against drugs but drug production continued as one of the most profitable trades and products on the world market. The Taliban also banned women from work, school, showing any part of their body, or leaving home without a male relative. The Taliban and al Qaeda joined forces with bin Laden's help.

Bin Laden allowed reporters under heavy guard to interview him but he moved constantly to avoid detection. Living quarters for him and for guests included cold caves with poisonous insects, a great difference from the early luxuries he had enjoyed.

In June 1997, C.I.A. officers and diplomats went to the Pakistani border by Afghanistan to offer money for bin Laden's location. The more that news spread about how important bin Laden was to the Americans, the more recruits wanted to join his cause.

In the 1997 trial of Ramzi Yousef for bombing the World Trade Center, testimony revealed that the twin towers could withstand being hit by a Boeing 707. This information may have caused the September 11, 2001 bin Laden conspirators to decide to use two heavier planes and hit the towers between the 40th and 70th floors, calculated to produce the greatest damage.

The *Mideast Mirror* (7/14/97) reported that a U.S. backed multinational 1000-man non-U.S. mercenary force was formed to abduct or kill bin Laden. Witnesses claimed to see cruisers and helicopters going into the Afghan city of Khost.

On February 23, 1998, bin Laden issued an edict, a fatwa, for Muslims to kill American civilians and soldiers wherever they could in accordance with the words of Allah. The C.I.A. sent a memo to Arizona Senator John Kyl, chair of the Senate's committee on foreign terrorism, saying that bin Laden had authorized attacks on American civilians anywhere in the world. Pressure was brought on the Saudis to silence him and the Saudi security chief flew to talk with the head of the Taliban, Mullah Mohamed Omar and bin Laden. He returned with no results even though he told bin Laden that his family business would suffer if he continued his attacks and invective.

The Taliban also realized that they would never be recognized by the United Nations while housing this man who wanted to go to war with the West. But Omar did not ask his guest to leave.

The *Washington Post* (8/12/98) reported that the U.S. participated in a raid in Albania against an Islamic terrorist cell that included bin Laden employees. The C.I.A. took away considerable computer information and documents that led to another raid two weeks later. More bin Laden employees were arrested and since these were Egyptian nationals, they were turned over to anti-terrorist officials in Egypt.

On June 8, 1998, the grand jury investigation of bin Laden, initiated in 1996, issued an indictment charging him with "conspiracy to attack defense utilities of the United States." This caused ABC *Nightline* to broadcast an interview that John Miller had conducted in May 1998 with bin Laden.

Also in June, *The Times of India* reported that police arrested five men for planning to blow up the U.S. Embassy in New Delhi. The conspirators made statements that they worked for bin Laden and had been planning for two years to park a car bomb near the most vulnerable part of the embassy.

The *New York Times* (8/21/98) reported that on August 6, 1998, the Egyptian Jihad group sent the U.S. a message "which we hope they read with care, because we will write it, with God's help, in a language they will understand."

The *Daily Telegraph* (8/12/98) reported that on August 7, 1998, al Qaeda organized two simultaneous attacks on American embassies in East Africa. Two truck bombs exploded outside the U.S. embassies in Nairobi, Kenya, and Dar es Salaam, Tanzania. In Kenya, 213 people including 12 U.S. nationals were killed and more than 4,500 were injured. The blast killed one of the attackers, wrecked a multi-story business college, and severely damaged the embassy and a bank building. Within minutes, in Dar es Salaam, the explosion killed 11 including the suicide-bomber and injured 85 but no Americans died. A computer report by an al Qaeda member was found in Kenya linking the attacks with bin Laden's Afghanistan group. Another African attack was planned at the same time but was delayed and police were able to arrest the terrorists.

The *New York Times* (9/23/98) reported that on August 12, 1998, President Clinton met with a group and discussed evidence that bin Laden was trying to obtain weapons of mass destruction and chemical weapons to use against U.S. installations. Evidence was presented of a mobile phone conversation between two of bin Laden's lieutenants implicating them in the embassy bombings.

The *Washington Post* (8/28/98) reported that August 20, 1998, Clinton ordered cruise missile attacks against terrorist training camps in Afghanistan and a pharmaceutical plant (al Shifa) in Khartoum, Sudan, involved in making chemical weapons. The U.S. added bin Laden's name to a list of terrorists whose funds were targeted for seizure by the U.S. Treasury. Officials realized the cruise missile attacks against bin Laden's base in Afghanistan had been unsuccessful when they heard him on radio in a message to Afghanistan and Pakistan say, "By the grace of Allah, I am alive!"

The *Sunday Times of London* reported that bin Laden was sending Islamic mercenaries to Kashmir to support an Islamic secession campaign in October of 1998.

The *UPI* (10/7/98) reported that an Arabic newspaper claimed (9/7/98) that bin Laden had acquired nuclear weapons from Soviet countries through "influential friends" but others were skeptical.

On November 4, 1998, the U.S. charged bin Laden and Muhammad Atef with bombing two U.S. embassies and conspiring to commit acts of terrorism against Americans abroad, and placed rewards of $5 million for each.

In late November 1998, the C.I.A. began a covert assassination attempt against bin Laden in conjunction with Saudi Arabia. The attack, which bin Laden apparently blamed on the governor of Riyadh in Saudi Arabia, involved a man who was paid $267,000 to poison bin Laden. The attempt was unsuccessful but did result in acute kidney failure and bin Laden walked with a stick afterwards. When he was seen in photos to walk with a cane, some said that he had a diagnosis of Marfan's syndrome, an hereditary degenerative disorder characterized by long fingers, lanky arms, scrawny chest muscles, a tall and skinny frame, which might shorten his life without treatment.

Perhaps to dispel rumors that he was dying as a result of the U.S. attacks on him, bin Laden summoned reporters. On December 23, 1998 a Pakistan reporter (Rahimullah Yusufzai) who also wrote for *Time* Magazine, and John Miller of *ABC News* went to his tent in Afghanistan for interviews. The ABC interview was broadcast on December 24, 1998 and *Time* and *Newsweek* published interviews on January 11, 1999.

The *Time* interview included these lines: "The man the U.S. calls Public Enemy Number One appeared to be in good health, though he admitted to a sore throat and a bad back. He continually sipped water from a cup, and Yusufzai caught him on videotape walking with the aid of a stick. Bodyguards erased that footage."

Yusufzai asked bin Laden, "The U.S. says you are trying to acquire chemical and nuclear weapons. How would you use these?"

Bin Laden replied: "Acquiring weapons for the defense of Muslims is a religious duty. If I have indeed acquired these weapons, then I thank God for enabling me to do so…It would be a sin for Muslims not to try to possess the weapons that would prevent the infidels from inflicting harm on Muslims."

On January 16, 1999, the U.S. Attorney's office filed a complete indictment of bin Laden and 11 other suspected members of the al Qaeda charging them with killing American military and embassy employees, establishing front companies, providing false identities and travel documents and false information to authorities in various countries.

The parents and siblings of Osama's Syrian wife, Najwa, did not see her after they moved to Afghanistan until 1999 when she visited her sister for the summer in Latakia. Not only did Najwa wear a veil but wanted her sister to do so as well. Najwa did not criticize her husband or the crude living arrangements in Afghanistan. She appeared to her family to have taken on her husband's characteristics.

By 1999, bin Laden's assets were being frozen and he lost money in his move from Sudan to Afghanistan but he still had millions. He had trading companies in Kenya, a ceramic firm in Yemen, a construction company, investment firms, a tannery in Khartoum where goat and cattle skins are turned into leather, and he may have been a partner in a lapis lazuli mine in Afghanistan.

In addition, the Taliban ran the Afghan drug trade of heroin from poppies worth some $6.5 to 10 billion dollars annually. Bin Laden helped the Taliban launder money through Russia and other countries, and received a cut of several million a year. Sleeper agents were sent around the world. Cells of Islamic militants trained in Afghan terrorist training camps exist in Pakistan, Yemen, Algeria, Italy, England, Albania, and America. Authorities began to worry that killing bin Laden would result in even more terrorist attacks in retaliation for the martyr.

Bin Laden tried to acquire weapons of mass destruction as early as 1993. These included a suitcase atomic bomb and the al Qaeda is reported to have obtained vials of anthrax and botulism from the Czech Republic. In late 1998, bin Laden and Saddam Hussein had contact through Saddam's son, who was involved in Iraqi intelligence operations. Hussein is said to have offered Osama refuge in Iraq, a packet of valuable blank passports and a list of targets that included organizations that were trying to undermine Iraq. Hussein also invited other terrorists to Iraq and Abu Nidal (responsible for dozens of international bombings and assassinations) did move there in 1998.

At the beginning of 2000, Ahmed Ressam was arrested in connection with a plot to bomb Los Angeles International Airport during the millennium celebrations. He was trained in warfare and explosives at one of bin Laden's Afghanistan terrorist training camps.

In August 2000, Israeli authorities arrested Nabil Oukal, leader of a terrorist ring planning a series of attacks against Israel with suicide bombs and anti-tank missiles. He admitted his links with bin Laden's group after arrest.

On October 12, 2000, a suicide bombing of the USS Cole in the Yemeni port of Aden killed 17 sailors and injured 39 others. The ship with a crew of over 250 had been assisted in mooring by several small boats out in the harbor. After 45 minutes of fueling, a small boat with two men standing up approached the ship and attracted no attention until the attack. The boat carried a torpedo-shaped huge bomb and 48 hours after the initial damage, sailors had to swim below to make repairs to keep the ship from sinking.

The suspects had rented an apartment in Aden some months earlier, and built a fence around it to conceal their bomb making. It was known that American ships moored for re-fueling at the port, usually with 10-12 days notice through the American Embassy. The suspects and their funding were linked to al-Qaeda after F.B.I. investigation.

In January 2001, 15 Islamic fundamentalists with ties to bin Laden were arrested in Jordan after planning to attack Israeli and Western targets in Jordan. A total of 28 suspects were arrested but 12 fled after plotting to attack Mount Nebo, a popular Christian tourist site on the Jordan River where Jesus was supposed to have been baptized.

Also in January 2001, five people with ties to bin Laden were arrested in Milan, Italy. Some of the men were conspiring to attack the U.S. Embassy in Rome in January, and others said that they were involved with a big attack planned for the downtown square of Strasbourg, France. The aborted bomb plans were to attack a city cathedral and American targets in December 2000.

At the marriage of Mohammad, next to oldest of Osama bin Laden's sons in February 2001, Osama wrote a poem called *To Her Doom* about the bombing of the USS Cole. Some of the lines follow:

"Your brothers in the East prepared the mounts and Kabul
Has prepared itself and the battle camels are ready to go.
A destroyer, even the brave fear its might.

It inspires horror in the harbor and in the open sea
She goes into the waves flanked by arrogance,
Haughtiness and fake might.
To her doom she progresses slowly, clothed in a huge illusion.
Awaiting her is a dinghy, bobbing in the waves,
Disappearing and reappearing in view."

Osama's son was married to the daughter of Mohammed Atef; bin Laden's operations commander. Atef was a member of the Egyptian Islamic Jihad, best known for their 1981 assassination of Anwar Sadat. A U.S. bomb later killed Atef in November 2001. At the wedding, in addition to his poem, Osama's ten-year-old son Hamza read a poem warning Americans that they would face "terrible consequences if they chase my father."

Osama bin Laden also read another poem called: *Thoughts in the Light of the Uprising in the Al-Aqsa Mosque: A Greeting Card to the Children of the Intifada.* Here are some of the lines:

"The current hold Intifada of Al-Aqsa created
A big imbalance and an impossible situation...
And it is this Intifada and its leaders, the young children,
Who are the biggest heroes and
What they accomplished with their stones (stone-throwing)...
And the cooperation it received from the Islamic population
That went out denouncing treason and stoning the traitors.
This holy Intifada and its great members were the inspiration of this poem.
Your (the children) eternal blood is a bridge and a passage...
A vision of victory and victory's color is red.
Your blood is the source of determination and power...
It is also the fire that will burn our enemies."

In February 2001, the Director of C.I.A. told Congress that bin Laden and his network were the nation's most immediate and serious threat. The director of the U.S. National Security Agency stated that al Qaeda's sophisticated use of the Internet and encryption techniques had defied Western eavesdropping attempts.

In February and March 2001, the British MI5 discovered ten Muslim men were planning to use London as a base to bomb Western targets and tourist sites. The men were arrested and found to be supporters of bin Laden.

Bin Laden's operations were under particular scrutiny during March, 2001, due to the ongoing trial in New York City of four of his followers charged with bombing U.S. embassies in Tanzania and Kenya in 1998. One was an al Qaeda paymaster who described bin Laden's offices as purchasing clandestine passports, purchasing uranium and elements of chemical weapons.

On April 7, 2001, the U.S. closed three of its South American embassies in Uruguay, Paraguay and Ecuador. They were closed, according to *United Press International*, because bin Laden operatives had been arriving over a period of months to carry out "special missions." One U.S. government official told U.P.I. "There was a certain level of huffing and puffing" between cells of known and suspected bin Laden operatives that gave U.S. security the "feeling we should take certain precautions."

On April 25, 2001, Israeli authorities arrested a man from bin Laden's terrorist training camp who was sent to the Gaza Strip to set up a bin Laden base. Israelis feared that the presence of a bin Laden organization would increase violence at a time when Arafat's P.L.O. and Israel were in peace negotiations.

On May 29, 2001, four bin Laden followers were found guilty of the 1998 U.S. embassy bombings in East Africa. After a nine-week federal trial, the attackers faced the death penalty or life in prison.

Alia, Osama's mother, visited her family in Latakia in the summer of 2001. She was concerned about Osama's safety. She had not spoken to Osama for six years since he went to Afghanistan, because he feared U.S. investigators were monitoring his calls to find him. Alia told her family that she had tried to get her son to return to Saudi Arabia but he wouldn't change his ideology. Eventually, she told people that she could not budge him from his convictions and said, "God protect him."

In June 2001, according to the *Washington Post*, suspects associated with bin Laden were arrested on suspicion of plotting an attack on the U.S. Embassy in Sanaa, capital of Yemen. They were targeting F.B.I. and U.S. Navy personnel investigating the attack of the USS Cole in Yemen the previous October. The U.S. withdrew the investigators over the weeks following what it called a "specific and credible" threat against them. The suspects had grenades and small arms when captured by police.

Also in June, four Islamists were arrested in India while plotting an attack against the U.S. Embassy.

On June 20, 2001, videotape, allegedly used for recruitment of extremists, surfaced in Kuwait and was released to the media. It drew several very graphic references to the bombing of the USS Cole. Clark Staten, who studied bin Laden for several years, told Kuwait Emergency Net News that the videotape in Kuwait was intended to motivate terrorists. Staten said, "With several intended terrorist acts recently thwarted by intelligence law enforcement authorities and a number of his followers now convicted in U.S. courts, we believe bin Laden is feeling 'frustrated' and under some pressure to make his presence felt."

On June 23, 2001, in Pakistan, an Arabic television channel MBC interviewed bin Laden and his staff. Reuters quoted the MBC correspondent saying, "All of them affirm that the next two weeks will witness a big surprise expected against U.S. and Israeli interests worldwide. There is a major state of mobilization among the Osama bin Laden forces. It seems that there is a race of who will strike first. Will it be the United States or Osama bin Laden?" The correspondent was referring to a belief of those close to bin Laden that an air strike on his camp in Afghanistan was imminent, a belief which caused his entourage to flee to the countryside.

On June 29, U.S. Ambassador William Milam delivered a warning to the Taliban at a meeting in Islamabad, Pakistan. Taliban officials were told that they would bear responsibility for any attack on U.S. interests by bin Laden who lived in Afghanistan as a guest of the Taliban.

During the last week of August 2001, a London-based Arab journalist said that bin Laden's followers warned his newspaper by telephone of a major attack. Abdel-Bari Atwan, editor of the Al-Quds al-Arabi newspaper said, "They said it would be a huge and unprecedented attack but they did not specify." Bin Laden had been quoted earlier in that newspaper as saying, "I'm fighting so I can die a martyr and go to heaven to meet God. Our fight now is against the Americans."

On September 8, 2001, three of the hijackers in the September 11th attack wired back $5,000 each to the United Arab Emirates where investigators say bin Laden's financial office collected it shortly before the attacks. They didn't want to die with excess expense money.

September 9, 2001, men who posed as journalists assassinated the leader of the Northern Alliance, which opposed the Taliban. Ahmad Shah Masood died in a suicide bombing. This infuriated the Northern Alliance. They assumed the assassins were the Taliban and/or bin Laden's al Qaeda. They responded by bombing Kabul, the Taliban center two days after the attack on the Pentagon and World Trade Centers.

On September 11, 2001, four passenger airplanes were taken over by terrorists in American airports. Both World Trade Center towers in New York City and the Pentagon in Washington, D.C. were attacked. The fourth plane crashed in Pennsylvania after passengers attempted to overcome their terrorist captors.

On September 12, the Hindustan Times reported that bin Laden's mother, Alia was hospitalized in the American Hospital in Paris for cancer tests amidst great secrecy. They added, however, that she had visited the hospital regularly for similar tests over the past five years.

After the video of Osama talking with a sheik about the September 11, 2001, attack, Alia told reporters, "Osama is too good a Muslim and too good a person to say or do what the script of the video suggests he said and did." She continued, "Osama has always been a good son to me. I love him and care about him. I don't believe he did the terrible deeds they say he did. I believe the evidence against him is not solid...The nightmare began only when he set off for the jihad in Afghanistan more than 20 years ago...Years of war and a tough adult life have also changed him. As a mother, I love him. I don't go along with many of his views and ambitions. I pray that Allah guides him to his true path away from these wrong thoughts, views, ambitions and stands."

Pictures from the frontline after the U.S. attack on Taliban strongholds in Afghanistan showed four of bin Laden's sons: Mohammad, Hamza, Khaled and Laden. Mohammad was holding a rocket launcher. Hamza read a poem hailing the leader of the Taliban, Mullah Omar, calling him a "symbol of manhood and pride." There were reports in December that one of the bin Laden sons was killed during attacks on the Taliban.

Bin Laden was against the U.S. because the U.S. is the largest superpower and controls events by manipulation in many countries around the world. Blinded by his own pride, he believed he was better than American leaders because he had "principles" and would be welcomed by Allah to heaven. He believed his network would strike in his name and was willing to die as a martyr for Allah.

He portrayed himself as a messianic leader. He is so grandiose that he not only believed he was better than superpower leaders but was like Allah. He felt more and more triumphant as recruits continued to join him, and this expanded his grandiosity as time went by. He finally gained significance, which he did not have as the youngest son of bin Laden and as the "son of the slave." A large reward on his head, the toppling of among the tallest buildings in the world meant to him that he was toppling the largest superpower in the world. He may have believed that his father would finally have noticed him and remembered his name.

5

Leadership Style

Bin Laden did not command his disciples so much as he financed and inspired them. Al Qaeda cells have been identified in as many as 50 countries. Bin Laden has trained between 5,000 and 12,000 people in these camps in Afghanistan, said President Clinton's former national security adviser, Sandy Berger.

Bin Laden used the methods of successful fund-raisers. He provided seed money and then looked for other grantors to provide matching funds. He often dealt in cash so that his resources were untraceable. During the Afghanistan war, he raised millions of dollars from wealthy Muslims to fight the Soviets. He received donations from Saudis, including his own family and the royal family who disliked America's presence and domination in their affairs.

In addition to his family fortune, bin Laden also established Islamic charities and took money from relief agencies, mosques, and other groups who shared his goals. His own companies in construction, agriculture, his farms and tanneries offered cover for operatives and sites for training. His followers were helped to set up other income sources such as driving taxis, fishing, and various legitimate small businesses. In fact, Ahmed Ressam said the members of his five-man terror cell planned to support themselves by robbing banks. Ressam was caught at the Canadian border with 200 pounds of explosives while heading to Los Angeles Airport set to explode the night of the millennium celebration.

Bin Laden's concern over money sometimes worked against him. He built roads in the Sudan for the government but when they couldn't pay him, they simply gave him a tannery. Also al Qaeda lost money in a Pakistani-founded bank that was closed for scandalous dealings. One al Qaeda member testified in the embassy bombings trial that bin Laden had told him in 1994 or 1995 that the organization was broke. But when Osama was expelled from the Sudan and moved to Afghanistan, he resorted to more illegal operations.

Bin Laden and the al Qaeda collected funds by protecting Afghanistan's shipments of opium bound for the west. They collected from crime, opium sales, and credit card fraud. They also extorted protection money from wealthy merchants. Afghanistan supplied more than 70% of the world's opium. In this way, he resembled American crime syndicates of the 1930s to 1950s. It was not clear whether the Northern Alliance, who took over after the fall of the Taliban, would continue to trade in opium or whether they would encourage people to grow other crops than poppies.

Vince Cannistraro, former C.I.A. counter-terrorism chief, described al Qaeda as having two parts. One is loosely run with limited help from those closest to bin Laden. The other side offers financing and encouragement for Muslim militants to attack governments around the world but leaves planning to the individual cells. An example is that bin Laden gave Ahmed Ressam $12,000 to bomb Los Angeles International Airport during the millennium celebrations.

Bin Laden operated like a chairman of the board, and oversaw a 30-member board called the "shura" or council. He was consensus-oriented and a team-builder according to former aides who testified during the trial for suspects in the 1998 bombings of U.S. embassies in Africa. One of his aides described stealing $110,000 from al Qaeda. When he admitted it to bin Laden, bin Laden asked him why he stole, told him that he cared more about him than the money, but wanted him to repay all the money. He fled to the U.S. authorities and became a key witness in the embassy bombings trial. Another aide serving a life sentence for the embassy bombings said that bin Laden is known as "the big boss."

A one-hour videotape dated November 9, 2001, showed bin Laden talking to a visiting sheik from Saudi Arabia about the events of September 11, 2001. The sheik could not walk and all sat on the floor on cushions and talked as equals, accompanying almost every phrase with thanks to Allah. No women were involved in these conversations. The sheik was thankful for bin Laden's leadership and both agreed that the people killed in the World Trade Center and Pentagon were "not innocent."

Bin Laden used an allegory ("When people see a strong horse and a weak horse, by nature they will like the strong horse.") He quoted verses from the Koran ("I was ordered to fight the people until they say there is not god but Allah, and his prophet Muhammad.") He praised the suicide bombers ("Those young men said in deeds, in New York and Washington, speeches that overshadowed all other speeches made everywhere else in the world.")

He wanted to impress the visiting sheik with his knowledge of construction ("We calculated in advance the number of casualties from the enemy, who would be killed based on the position of the tower. We calculated that the floors that would be hit would be three or four floors. I was the most optimistic of them all...due to my experience in this field, I was thinking that the fire from the gas in the plane would melt the iron structure of the building and collapse the area where the plane hit and all the floors above it only.") He further tried to impress the sheik with his foreknowledge of the second plane ("When you hear a breaking news announcement on the radio, kneel immediately, and that means they have hit the World Trade Center. They were overjoyed when the first plane hit the building, so I said to them: be patient.")

He even impressed the sheik with his detailed knowledge of the plans, with details of how the men were trained and with the fact that the suicide bombers were ready to die for him ("He did not know about the operation. Not everybody knew...Muhammad Atta from the Egyptian family was in charge of the group...The brothers who

conducted the operation, all they knew was that they have a martyr-
dom operation and we asked each of them to go to America but they
didn't know anything about the operation, not even one letter. But
they were trained and we did not reveal the operation to them until
they are there and just before they boarded the planes. Those who were
trained to fly didn't know the others. One group of people did not
know the other group.")

Both men spoke about visions. The sheik said, "I remember a vision
by Sheik Salih Al-Shuaybi. He said, 'There will be a great hit and people will go out by hundreds to Afghanistan'."

Bin Laden described how another man's dream was a good omen as
if dreaming something would make it come true in a magical sort of
way ("Abu-al-Hasan al-Masri…told me a year ago, 'I saw in a dream,
we were playing a soccer game against the Americans. When our team
showed up in the field, they were all pilots!' He said, 'So I wondered if
that was a soccer game or a pilot game? Our players were pilots. He
didn't know anything about the operation until he heard it on the
radio. He said the game went on and we defeated them. That was a
good omen for us.")

Bin Laden, despite his education, found the thin line of reality
between dreams and reality hard to separate. These ideas about dreams
remind us of those who lived in Biblical times. Osama believed that
dreams were so powerful that he might not want his people to talk
about their dreams. ("He came close and told me that he saw, in a
dream, a tall building in America, and in the same dream he saw
Mukhtar teaching them how to play karate. At that point, I was worried that maybe the secret would be revealed if everyone starts seeing it
in their dream, so I closed the subject. I told him if he sees another
dream, not to tell anybody because people will be upset with him.")

He ended his conversation with the sheik by reciting a poem:

"Our homes are flooded with blood and the tyrant
Is freely wandering in our homes.

And from the battlefield vanished
The brightness of swords and the horses
And over weeping sounds now
We hear the beats of drums and rhythm
They are storming his forts
And shouting: 'We will not stop our raids
Until you have freed our lands.'"

Richard Rosecrance, an expert on terrorism at the University of California at Berkley, described bin Laden's style. He stated that bin Laden had constructed something bigger than a guerrilla group and more complex than a multi-national corporation. He called it a "virtual country" which could be called the Republic of Jihadistan (holy war). Rosecrance said, "It has state-like aspects, but without state borders."

Gideon Rose, deputy director of national security studies at the Council on Foreign Policy in New York said bin Laden's network appeared to represent the coming thing in the age of modern terrorism. The sponsorship of terror groups by Syria and Iraq appeared to be on the decline as al Qaeda took its place with little physical infrastructure to attack.

6

Stresses

The use of dreams played a prominent role in bin Laden's communications with other less educated Muslims and may have played a role in his own philosophy, despite his sophistication. When he described his experience in fighting the Soviets in 1986, he said, "We could hear the enemies' footsteps. Despite the situation, I fell asleep. When I awoke the enemy had disappeared. Perhaps I could not be seen by them. On another occasion a Scud missile exploded very close to me but I remained safe. Such incidents have removed my fear of death."

As a wealthy man, bin Laden was used to having his way. He used his wealth to make himself valuable to various countries. But occasionally, his wealth was not enough. In July 1989, the BBC World Affairs Editor described bin Laden's temper tantrum when his film crew tried to photograph the mujaheddin in Afghanistan firing mortars.

Bin Laden jumped up on a wall, and screamed that the film crew were infidels and shouted to the mujaheddin to kill them at once. They grinned, did nothing, so bin Laden ran over to a truck driver and offered him $500 to drive into the film crew. The truck driver did not take the bait. So the frustrated bin Laden ran off to the sleeping quarters, threw himself on a bed, and beat his fists on the pillow.

When Iraq invaded Kuwait in 1990, American, British, and allied troops landed in Saudi Arabia at their invitation for protection and to launch an attack to liberate Kuwait. Bin Laden was furious that the Saudi government permitted this. He stormed into the Saudi defense ministry offices with maps and documents. He insisted that his small army of Afghan Arabs could train Saudis to defend themselves. He offered his family's bulldozers to dig trenches along the border and lay 'sand traps' against the invading tanks and soldiers.

When asked how his army would deal with Iraq's biological and chemical weapons, he responded that they would defeat them with faith. He was dismissed from the office. His reaction was to become angry at Saudi Arabia and retaliate with attacks against them for refusing to use his suggestions and help.

Bin Laden apparently had trouble getting people to take his movement seriously, according to a videotape in which he discussed the September 11th attack with a sheik. In his attempt to be taken seriously, he issued a "fatwa" or religious ruling as if he was a holy man. In fact, he enjoyed the nickname "sheik" although he is not a cleric. The "fatwa" urging a "jihad" or holy war against Americans was published on February 23, 1998. He argued that the U.S. had occupied areas of Islam, dictated to rulers, humiliated the people, developed bases from which to fight Muslims, and served the aims of Jews and that these were a declaration of war on God and Muslims. He stated, "In compliance with God's order, we issue the following fatwa to all Muslims: the ruling to kill the Americans and their allies—civilians and military—is an individual duty for every Muslim who can do it in any country in which it is possible to do it."

In addition to his pretense of being a holy man, he allied himself with holy men such as the blind sheik Omar Abdel Rahman (held in U.S. prison) and the sheik's son, who was captured by anti-Taliban forces in November 2001. This connection with holy men may have been developed to confer legitimacy upon bin Laden.

The International Policy Institute for Counter-terrorism reported that Russian intelligence found evidence that bin Laden planned to assassinate President George W. Bush when he attended Genoa, Italy for a G-8 summit conference in July 2001. Heavy security measures prevented problems except for minor incidents of anarchist violence.

Bin Laden has often defended himself by making his opponent look bad and himself good. One example was aired by Al-Jazeera news on December 26, 2001. It showed him speaking some ninety days after the September 11th attack even as U.S. forces and the Northern Alliance bombed Afghanistan and continued to search for him. As usual, he appeared with a submachine gun at his side and appeared to plead that his people were mere victims of an unprovoked terrorist attack.

He accused the U.S. of terrorism because they used larger bombs than his "boys" who used smaller bombs in the two African bombings. "It is quite clear now that the West, generally speaking, and in particular America, has an indescribable hatred of Islam. The people who have lived the last months under the continual American air strikes, they know that very well...In Nairobi, when the boys, may God take them as martyrs, used a 4,400 pound bomb, the U.S. said this was terrorism, that this was a weapon of mass destruction. And now the U.S. is using two bombs, each weighing 15,500 pounds. No one is questioning this."

Bin Laden has perhaps drastically affected the American economy, and probably intended to do so. Extremely tall buildings such as the Sears Tower have escalated their rent as much as 25% after the September 11, 2001, attack on the World Trade Center. Financier Warren Buffet has predicted that the closing of such "iconic" buildings will result in a move toward rural and away from urban American building construction.

7

Accomplishments

Osama bin Laden was able to attract many followers throughout the Muslim world. Even those that had not met him knew him from his interviews, radio broadcasts, web site, and tapes. He was thus able to unify various groups of Islamic militants with his ideas. He viewed the Muslim world as a "single nation" with one religion. He unified groups by designating a common enemy: the United States. America's presence in Saudi Arabia, support for Israel and the war against Iraq were reasons to fight the U.S. in bin Laden's mind. The Muslim world had never before bin Laden been unified under a single leader across so many nations.

His influence was so strong that many named their sons and their businesses after him, and pictures and stickers abounded everywhere. It is likely that a martyred bin Laden will still be effective for many years and that others will take up his savvy techniques of funding sleeper terrorist cells across the world.

Many in the F.B.I., C.I.A., Pentagon and the White House believe that Islamic fundamentalism is the greatest threat to the West. Militant Islamic fighters include Iranian groups who fight the Israelis; Afghan/al Qaeda/bin Laden groups, and Islamic groups in a variety of countries (Albania, Algeria, Bosnia, Russia, India, Pakistan, the Philippines, etc.)

In practical achievements, bin Laden funded a much-needed 750-mile highway in the Sudan linking Khartoum to Port Sudan and built the new airport at Port Sudan. When he moved to Afghanistan, he additionally built hospitals and treatment facilities for Afghan veterans, widows, and families.

8

Summary

Osama's family never wanted for anything and with wealth, they also had power. Never very close to his father, raised mainly by his mother, he wanted to be noticed. He eventually wanted to lead Arabs away from the influence of infidels such as America. This prestige would cause him to be the acknowledged leader against the greatest power in the world and might bring him notoriety in this life and rewards in his next life.

He cannot be adequately judged according to American or European standards of maturation. He probably believed that his mother loved him. The rest of the family tried to distance themselves from him when he reached his late teen years. Since he not only re-established the custom of having four wives but also encouraged his subordinates to have paid sexual relations, the issue of intimacy with women is in considerable doubt. Intimacy with men appears strong. Older men who may have substituted for his distant but prestigious father appear to have particularly influenced him.

Information about the stages of his love life is scant but suggests that he had unconditional love by his mother. He was known to have been a handsome and wealthy womanizer in his late teens. Romantic love and lust may have been prominent during his teens and early twenties. He then came to adopt the views of his Muslim heritage in which women occupy an obedient and restricted role. It is doubtful that any woman has ever enjoyed his intimacy, compromise or commitment.

He has employed some unhealthy ways to deal with stress as well as healthy ways, but the European coping techniques may not apply. He has outlets to relieve tension such as writing poetry and numerous sexual outlets. His educational level is such that he can learn, anticipate, and plan well in advance for problems or schemes. He has indulged in a variety of safe versus risky actions and has enjoyed having it publicized that he wreaked violence. His anger outbursts have been seen when he felt blocked or stressed by those who would not carry out his wishes.

Chief among his violent outlets is the unrelenting goal to make his enemy (mainly America) suffer through destruction and fear.

He may indulge in fantasies or dreams that would seem childish in European or American circles but would probably be regarded as profound in his Arab world. His life in the Sudan heat suggested that he could be ascetic despite his wealth. Construction of projects to benefit many suggested a wish to be or to be seen as altruistic. However, there has always been a disturbing tendency to paint others (non-Arabs) as evil infidels suggesting that he coped with criticism by blaming others.

Osama was an obedient boy and young man, trying to behave so that his family would find him acceptable. This ensured that he would continue to be supported by the family wealth. He learned to please others in his culture during his university years. However, the ostracism of his family because he was the "son of the slave" made it harder and harder for him to contribute and be rewarded within his complex family structure. As he sought other avenues for acceptance, his wealth, education and bearing were his greatest assets.

He accepted some rules, such as the basic tenets of his Muslim faith, and became a critic of those who were lax in following these rules. He sought influence using his wealth and this began to produce deviations in his morals. Once he began to put his money and his expertise into violent causes, he lost track of the principles that people have equal worth with him. He started making decisions about who would live or die according to his own beliefs but cloaked them as the beliefs of all Arabs.

His leadership was different than most of the leaders we have described because he did not have a nation at his command. He had vast numbers of people, each of whom had their own agendas and needed only his support, encouragement, training, funding, and guidance. Thus he must be considered a team manager who valued the development of his subordinates as much as he valued the end goals. His goal was the liberation of Arab lands and leadership from outside influences such as capitalist countries. Numerous documents delineate the laissez-faire management style with al-Qaeda, Taliban, employees and others.

About the Author

Diane Holloway, Ph.D. was a Dallas psychologist and was appointed the first Drug "Czar" of Dallas by the Mayor. She has written *Before You Say 'I Quit'*, *The Mind of Oswald, Dallas and the Jack Ruby Trial, American History in Song*, and co-authored *Brushes With Greatness*. She now lives and writes in Arizona with her husband, Bob Cheney.

Bob Cheney, a former college history professor, has written *Interrupted Lives: Hood's Texas Brigade, Tragedy in Black and White* and co-authored *Brushes With Greatness*.

References

Angelo, Bonnie *First Mothers*, William Morrow Publishers, New York, 2000.

Beck, Don and Cowan, Chistopher *Spiral Dynamics*, Blackwell Publishers, United Kingdom, 1996.

Beck, Don "The stages of social development", presented at the *State of the World Forum* in New York in October, 2000.

Beschloss, Michael *Reaching for Glory: The Johnson White House Tapes, 1964-1965*. Simon & Schuster, New York, 2001.

Beyer, Lisa "The Most Wanted Man in the World", *Time Magazine*, September 25, 2001.

Blake, Robert and Mouton, Jane *The Managerial Grid*, Gulf Professional Publishing Co., New York, 1994.

Brill, Steven "Osama's Hidden Tax" *Newsweek*, Jan. 14, 2002.

Carroll, Andrew, Ed. *Letters of a Nation*, Broadway Books, New York, 1997.

Chesen, Eli *President Nixon's Psychiatric Profile*, Peter H. Wyden, New York, 1973.

Chopra, Deepak *The Path to Love*, Random House, New York, 1996.

Clifford, Clark*Counsel to the President*, Random House, New York, 1991.

Cockburn, Andrew and Patrick *Out of the Ashes*, Harper Collins, New York, 1999.

Cohen, Roger and Gatti, Claudio *In the Eye of the Storm*, Farrar, Straus & Giroux, New York, 1991.

Constable, Pamela "African leaders want West to apologize, pay for slavery", *Washington Post*, September 2, 2001.

Cronkite, Walter *A Reporter's Life*, Alfred A. Knopf, New York, 1996.

Davies, Stephen *Margaret Thatcher and the Rebirth of Conservatism*, paper delivered at Ashbrook Center at Ashland University, Ashland, Ohio, Summer, 1993.

Davis, John *The Kennedys*, McGraw-Hill, New York, 1984.

Dole, Bob *Great Presidential Wit*, G. K. Hall & Co., Waterville, Maine, 2001.

Erikson, Erik *Childhood and Society*, Ed. 2, W.W. Norton, New York, 1963.

Freud, Ernst et al, Ed. *Sigmund Freud*, Harcourt Brace Jovanovich, New York, 1978.

Freud, Sigmund *The Ego and Mechanisms of Defense*, International University Press, New York, 1966.

Galbraith, John *The Age of Uncertainty*, Houghton Mifflin Co., Boston, 1977.

Galland, Adolf *The First and the Last*, Henry Holt & Co., New York, 1954.

Gilbert, Robert *The Mortal Presidency*, Basic Books, New York, 1992.

Golden, Daniel et al "Family business 'black sheep'", *Wall Street Journal*, reprinted in the *Arizona Republic*, September 24, 2001.

Graves, Clare "Human nature prepares for a momentous leap", *The Futurist*, April, 1974.

Hanson, Victor *The Soul of Battle*, The Free Press, New York, 1999.

Heymann, C. David *A Woman Named Jackie*, Penguin Books USA, New York, 1989.

Hersey, Paul; Blanchard, Ken et al *Management of Organizational Behavior*, Prentice-Hall, New York, 2000.

Huntington, Samuel *The Soldier and the State*, Belknap Press of Harvard University Press, Cambridge, MA, 1957.

Irving, David *Goring*, Avon Books, New York, 1989.

Kaplan, David and Whitelaw, Kevin "The CEO of terror, inc." *U.S. News & World Report*, October 1, 2001.

Karnow, Stanley *Viet Nam: A History*. The Viking Press, New York, 1983.

Karsh, Ephraim and Rautsi, Inari *Saddam Hussein*, The Free Press, New York, 1991.

Keegan, John *The First World War*, Alfred A. Knopf. New York, 1999.

Kissinger, Henry *For the Record: Selected Statements 1977-1980*, Little, Brown & Co., Boston, 1981.

Kohlberg, Lawrence *The Psychology of Moral Development*, Harper Collins, New York, 1984.

Lewy, Guenter *The Cause That Failed*. Oxford University Press, New York, 1990.

Manchester, William *The Death of a President*. Harper and Row, New York, 1967.

Maslow, Abraham; Stephens, Deborah et al *Maslow on Management*, John Wiley & Sons, New York, 1998.

Matthews, Herbert *Cuba*, Macmillan, New York, 1964.

McCullough, David *Truman*, Simon and Schuster, New York, 1992.

McGeary, Johanna "Inside Saddam's World", *Time.com*, May 4, 2002.

McMillan, Priscilla *Marina and Lee*, Harper and Row, New York, 1977.

Meir, Golda*My Life*, G. P. Putnam's Sons, New York, 1975.

Miller, Judith "Bin Laden relies on wealth", *New York Times*, reprinted in *Arizona Republic* September 16, 2001.

Mosby, Aline *The View from No. 13 People's Street*, Random House, New York, 1962.

Nixon, Richard*Leaders*, Warner Books, New York, 1982.

Payne, Robert *The Life and Death of Adolf Hitler*. Praeger Publishers, New York, 1973.

Reeve, Simon *The New Jackals*, Northeastern University Press, Boston, 1999.

Reeves, Thomas *A Question of Character*, Prima Publishing, Rocklin, CA., 1992.

Regan, Donald *For the Record*, Harcourt Brace Jovanovich, New York, 1988.

Riechmann, Deb "Nixon pondered using nukes", *The Arizona Republic*, March 1, 2002.

Schram, Stuart *Mao Tse-Tung*, Penguin Books Ltd., Middlesex, England, 1966.

Schieffer, Bob and Gates, Gary *The Acting President*, E. P. Dutton, New York, 1989.

Shirer, William *The Rise and Fall of the Third Reich*, Simon and Schuster, New York, 1960.

Short, Philip *Mao: A Life*, Hodder & Stoughton, London, 2000

Smith, Hedrick *The Russians*, Quadrangle: The New York Times Book Co., New York, 1976.

Snow, Anita "Castro still defiant as he turns 75", *Associated Press*, August 13, 2001.

Spence, Jonathan *Mao*, Weidenfeld & Nicolson, London, 2001.

Stephenson, June *Poisonous Power*, Diemer, Smith Publishing Co., Palm Desert, CA 1998.

Terrill, Ross *Madame Mao: The White-Boned Demon*, Stanford University Press, 1999.

Thatcher, Margaret *The Path to Power*, HarperCollins, New York, 1995.

Vaillant, George Editor: *Empirical Studies of Ego Mechanisms and Defense*. American Psychiatric Assoc. Press, Washington, D.C., 1986.

Young, Hugo *The Iron Lady*, Farrar Straus Giroux, New York, 1989.

Zamboanga, Tim McGirk "Perpetually Perilous" *Time Magazine*, January 2, 2002.

Index

0-595-23264-7